Scotland's Heroes

Remembered and Forgotten

The Author

John Lindsey was born on Merseyside but a career, first in public relations and then in sports promotion, took him and his family to Australia – they now have dual citizenship. He was involved with many sports; rugby, show-jumping, polo and particularly golf. The latter brought him to St. Andrews where he now lives in happy retirement with his wife, golf clubs and history books.

Scotland's Heroes

Remembered and Forgotten

by

John Lindsey

Librario

Published by

Librario Publishing Ltd

ISBN 10: 1-904440-87-8
ISBN 13: 1-904440-87-1

Copies can be ordered via the Internet
www.librario.com

or from:

Brough House, Milton Brodie, Kinloss
Moray IV36 2UA
Tel/Fax No 00 44 (0)1343 850 617

Printed and bound by
4edge Ltd., Hockley. www.4edge.co.uk

Typeset by 3btype.com

DAPHNE, DECLAN AND REBECCA

thanks for your tolerance

Acknowledgements

There are many people all over Scotland who deserve heartfelt thanks for their help in producing this book. If I have inadvertently omitted anyone I apologise, they know who they are. I owe a special debt to my long-suffering wife who, like it or not, came to appreciate statues as for two years I dragged her all over Scotland to look at people she rarely knew.

I am also particularly grateful to the following who shared their love and knowledge of Scottish history with me: Dr Jennifer Melville at Aberdeen Art Gallery, David Annand, Roddy Barron, Brian Caster and Kerry Hammond of Powderhall Bronze, Jo Darke of the Public Monuments and Sculpture Association, Robin T. Dettre of the Smithsonian American Art Museum, Ruth at Dumfries Library, John Gray of Dundee City Council, Frances Humphries, Janette Kerr, Dianne King, Alastair Mackay, Colin McAllister, Ray McKenzie, staff at the National Monuments Record of Scotland, Dr Evelyn Gavin of the Rob Roy Preservation Trust, The Scottish Football Museum, St Andrews University Library, Eve Soulsby, Alexander Stoddart, Bob Watt, Sheila West at the Carnegie Library Ayr and lastly Betty Willsher who kept me going through the many dark times and without whose unflagging support and knowledge this book would never have appeared. She led me down roads I had never encountered before and I am sincerely grateful.

Photographing statues is very difficult, I know they don't move but it is very difficult to faithfully reproduce the sculptor's efforts. Asking children to please get off the equestrian statue for a minute, requesting the courting couple to move a few paces, or standing in the middle of a busy road to get the best angle requires patience and skill. All the following displayed that and I am indebted. Especially to one intrepid photographer, Eve Soulsby, who risked having her car blown up and being detained at her Majesty's Pleasure for photographing John Brown's statue in the grounds of Balmoral Castle when The Queen was in residence. Although this made the national press I am pleased it ended with a caution as she also produced the excellent map used in the frontispiece and gave invaluable assistance with many other illustrations. My thanks to all who provided photographs: Margaret Allan, John Anderson, Karen Conway, Archie Ferguson, Neil Foston, Janette Kerr, Daphne Lindsey, Rebecca Lindsey, Judith Livingstone, Robert Livingstone, Margaret Rae, Paul Sinclair, Andrew Soulsby, Eve Soulsby and Betty Willsher.

And finally, book designer Senga Fairgrieve for giving life to inanimate objects.

Contents

Map of Statues

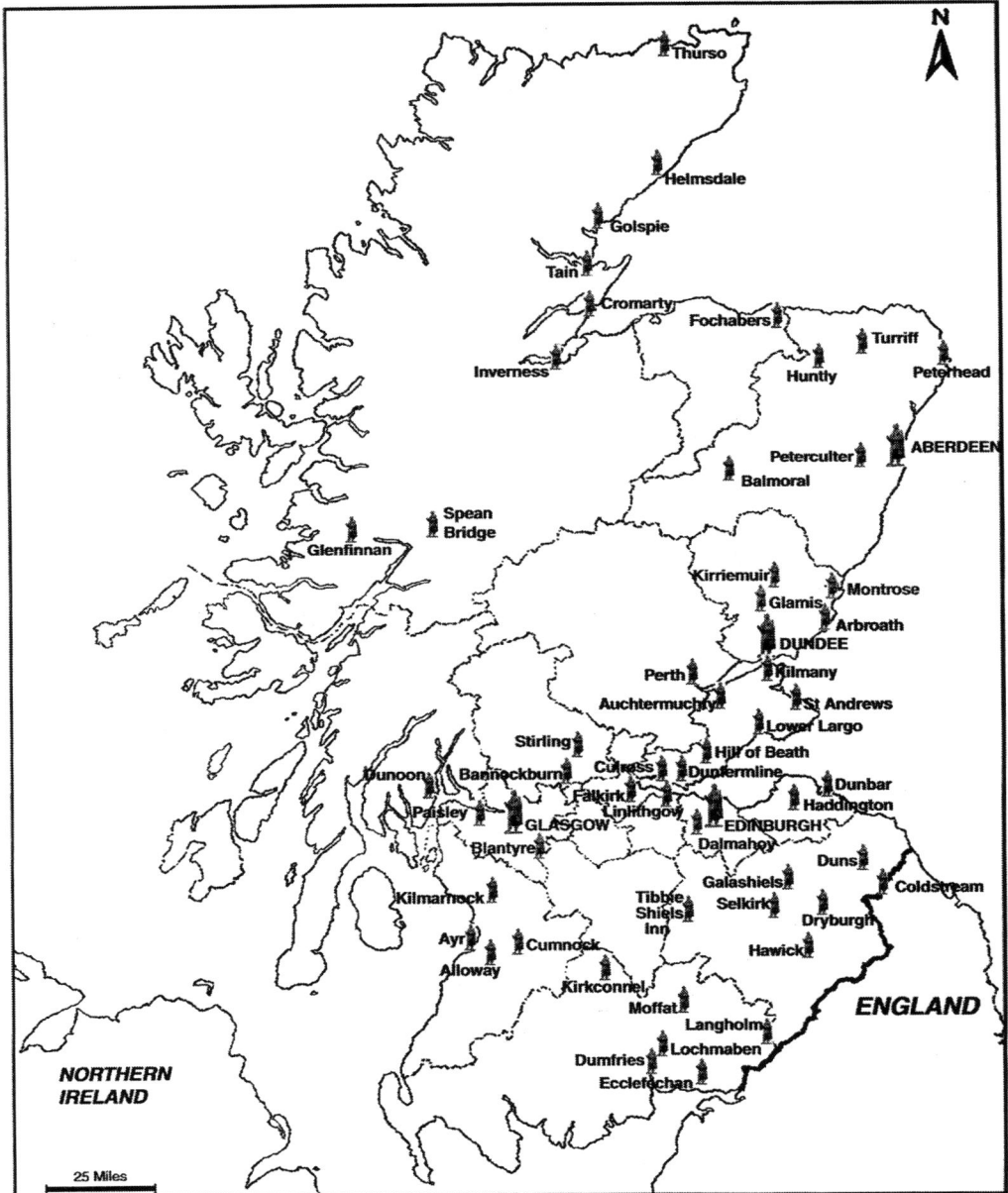

Thurso
Helmsdale
Golspie
Tain
Cromarty
Fochabers
Turriff
Inverness
Huntly
Peterhead
Peterculter
ABERDEEN
Balmoral
Spean Bridge
Glenfinnan
Kirriemuir
Montrose
Glamis
Arbroath
DUNDEE
Perth
Kilmany
Auchtermuchty
St Andrews
Lower Largo
Stirling
Hill of Beath
Dunoon
Bannockburn
Culross
Dunfermline
Dunbar
Falkirk
Haddington
Paisley
Linlithgow
GLASGOW
EDINBURGH
Blantyre
Dalmahoy
Duns
Galashiels
Coldstream
Kilmarnock
Tibbie Shiels Inn
Selkirk
Dryburgh
Ayr
Cumnock
Hawick
Alloway
Kirkconnel
Moffat
Langholm
Dumfries
Lochmaben
Ecclefechan
ENGLAND
NORTHERN IRELAND

N

25 Miles

Introduction

'Unhappy the land that has no heroes'
BERTOLT BRECHT

This book commemorates those heroic Scots remembered with a statue in their own country. Statues around the world enjoy an iconic status. Christ The Redeemer in Rio, The Statue of Liberty in New York and The Little Mermaid in Copenhagen are instantly recognisable. The emotive depiction in the American National Cemetery at Arlington of US Marines raising the Stars and Stripes at Iwo Jima is famous whilst Sadam Hussein's statue being toppled is one of the enduring images of the recent Iraq War.

Scotland remembers its past quite well. In Robert Burns, what the current First Minister describes as 'the best wee country in the world' has a man honoured with more statues worldwide than perhaps any other figure, certainly any other poet.

In Britain the Victorian era was the golden age for statues. In 1840 Thomas Carlyle gave a series of six public lectures on Heroes, Hero Worship And The Heroic in History, talking about famous men from Odin to Burns. The hero was in fact a central element to this great Scottish philosopher and became the leading principle of all his later social writing. The subject was also a major preoccupation for his fellow Victorians who were said to turn admiration from a virtue into a religion – and call it hero worship.

The lectures had an enormous impact, inspiring a nation who immediately campaigned for a statue to be erected in London's Trafalgar Square to one of the country's greatest heroes, Admiral Horatio Nelson. In Scotland men like William Wallace, Robert The Bruce, Robert Burns and Sir Walter Scott were also suddenly commemorated for their sterling deeds in shaping the country.

The Victorians made good statues and made a lot of them too. They were not always to heroes, sometimes just local benefactors, but

they knew all about matters such as the importance of weight distribution. This was illustrated not so long ago when Dundee erected a statue to comic book hero Desperate Dan, and his huge stomach initially caused the statue to topple forwards. Victorian statues were all based around a basic triangular shape and in those days of course there were no welders as we now know them, so any bolts had to be well hidden with the bronze beaten back into the holes. They can be big and they can be heavy as transporting James Watt's statue from the Hunterian Museum in Glasgow to the National Portrait Gallery in Edinburgh showed. It was a huge operation culminating in the front of the Gallery having to be dismantled to enable the statue to be brought in!

Back then the funding usually came from public subscription, a form of raising money so popular that sometimes the amount people were invited to give had to be limited – now it is quite often private commission as was the case with the last statue of Burns to be erected in Scotland, in Ayr in 2006 to promote a new shopping centre. Modern figure statues tend to have little in the way of inscriptions but do study carefully the inscriptions on some old statues; the flowery writing can be a joy to read. Large crowds would attend the unveilings; they were huge public events lovingly covered by the newspapers.

Figure statues in all their glory certainly deserve a closer look to gain a true recognition of the sculptor's work. There is often more to admire than at first sight. How many of the millions of visitors to London have looked at the equestrian statue of King William III in St. James's Square and missed the molehill sculpted in the base of the bronze. His horse tripped on one in Hampton Court and threw the King who died sixteen days later.

The Victorian age was a confident period. From the 1740s onwards Scotland had began to recover from the economic depression it suffered for over fifty years. Within one hundred years a growing industrialization with booming mills and factories had made big and prosperous cities of places like Glasgow, Paisley and Dundee. Philosophers, economists, architects, and poets also all made their mark. Robert Burns had helped put Scotland on the modern map and Walter Scott's writings had launched a new enthusiasm for the country. But it was Queen Victoria's purchase of Balmoral which really opened up the Highlands and the country.

Her Majesty did more for Scottish tourism than anyone else and is rightly commemorated with a statue in every major Scottish city – and some minor ones as well. Her first visit to Scotland was in 1842, describing Edinburgh as 'quite beautiful, totally unlike anything I have ever seen.' By 1866 forty thousand tourists had visited the country and in 1869 the Queen wrote that Scotland was 'the proudest finest country in the world'.

Roads and railways, bridges and canals opened up Scotland, and a number of generous philanthropists contributed to the well-being of their particular home town. Many of the men who made this possible are remembered here although in some cases their names will seem unfamiliar. Three men stand out head and shoulders above all others. Robert Burns is undoubtedly our cultural hero whilst William Wallace and Robert Bruce are clearly our military heroes. There are well over twenty Wallace statues in Scotland and Bruce is similarly well commemorated. For a small country Scotland also has a disproportionate number of heroes whose contribution to the spread of the British Empire is recognized not just at home but abroad.

ROBERT BURNS has more statues to him in Scotland than anyone else.

Burns is eminent not just as the Scot with the most commemorative works in his native Scotland (with more statues planned for the 250th anniversary of his birth in 2009) but also abroad. Burns statues can be found all around the world in diverse places such as London, Toronto, Sydney, New York, Auckland, Dunedin and all across America in cities such as Boston, St Louis, New York, San Francisco, Cheyenne, Chicago, Milwaukee, Detroit, Pittsburgh and Denver where American Burns Clubs keep Scotland's poet before the American public. The model made by George Lawson for his Ayr statue of Burns in 1891 was so popular that copies were made for Montreal, Winnipeg, Belfast and the Sorbonne in Paris, where it was carefully hidden from the occupying German forces during the war to avoid it falling in to Nazi hands.

Sir Walter Scott is also remembered in America. In 1871 on the hundredth anniversary of his birth resident Scotsmen in New York presented a bronze statue to the City of New York. The Borders hero is in Central Park sitting on a rock wrapped in a blanket with a dog at his feet, a copy of the Scott Monument in Edinburgh. 'Braveheart' is not forgotten by the Americans either. A copy of D.W. Stevenson's original of William Wallace on Abbey Craig at Stirling, was presented on St Andrews Day 1893 to the City of Baltimore.

But this book takes a comprehensive look at all the personalities who have shaped Scotland's destiny and been rewarded with their place not just in history but on a plinth in a public place in their homeland as well. Some names are here you might not expect to find. They include a dog, a cow, a woman doctor who spent her whole life convincing everybody she was a man whilst rising to high rank in the Army, and a 'hero' who would now probably be imprisoned for cruelty.

Literature, medicine, inventions, the military services all can claim their numerous heroes and heroines but there are also failures here: men such as Bonnie Prince Charlie. They are almost all dead. It is a fact that living people of note first tend to have a portrait painted, then a bust made and, after they have passed on, a statue if they are lucky to have wealthy or organized friends or a sympathetic council. There are exceptions, Bathgate golfer Bernard Gallacher is certainly alive and well and can in fact admire himself on the first tee at Wentworth Golf Club.

There are sadly only comparatively few women in these pages and just four married couples remembered with full statues. Dumfries has Jean Armour and Robert Burns. The Elders, who contributed so much in so many areas to Glasgow, are thanked there. The Duke and Duchess of Sutherland in Golspie perhaps redefine the word hero with many wanting to tear down the Duke's statue because of his role in the Highland Clearances. Queen Victoria and Albert seem to pop up everywhere.

Scotland's 'forgotten heroes' are not forgotten here, those men and women who have done so much for their native country and deserve lasting recognition. Alexander Graham Bell is one such example. Even in the United States, where he lived for over fifty years, he is only represented with a bust in the Hall of Fame for Great Americans at a community centre in New York alongside ninety-six others. In Scotland he is

ALEXANDER GRAHAM BELL
Inventor of the Telephone
Born here 3rd March 1847

remembered with a plaque on Number 16 South Charlotte Street in Edinburgh where he was born, but surely the inventor of the telephone who has enriched all our lives deserves better, at least a life-size bronze in a major city.

In the last twenty years or so we have seen a resurgence in Scotland of figure statues; maybe the country feels it needs heroes now more than ever. Certainly increased wealth generally has brought increased commissions in public art generally and it is now even written into some planning permissions for major developments. Enlightened cities like Linlithgow and Aberdeen are competing to commemorate 'Scotty' of Star Trek fame who died recently and the progressive Edinburgh authorities want to see more statues of living persons and women on plinths in the city. J.K. Rowling was honoured with a plaque there in October 2006.

There is a resurgence in statues, even figure statues with more interesting positions than the traditional eyes-front-on-a-plinth pose, although the modern art establishment is against 'triumphalism' and the recognition of military men, war heroes, politicians – even missionaries. A full-size figure statue is expensive too and local authorities are naturally cautious with how they spend the taxpayer's money. Cities such as Dundee and Aberdeen have progressive and attractive Public Art Programmes but it is not always easy for the executives in charge; local council budgets are under greater scrutiny than ever before. Hence more 'representative' art: less controversial and requiring lower budgets. Pigeons and vandalism are the enemies of public figures. Donald Dewar in Glasgow has had to be placed on a higher plinth since its original unveiling to avoid vandals.

If you are in the capital look up at Edinburgh Castle from behind the statue to the Royal Scots Greys in Princes Street and on the soldier's busby you will see just one example of the discreet spikes placed on statues to deter our feathered friends.

But we are seeing more famous old Scots remembered now with a statue. This book concentrates, with the well-deserved exception of Mary Queen of Scots, on statues that are readily available on public display for all to see and recognize at no charge. War memorials, of which there are so many, and graveyards are not included. But remember, statues can be altered or moved, especially for road-widening purposes

PIGEONS are the enemy of statues.

etc. Due recognition where appropriate is also given to the sculptors whose work can last for centuries but are often forgotten themselves.

Sculptors put a lot of effort into statues and in the past it must have been dispiriting to see their effort put on a 100ft high column where the work cannot be seen in all its detail. These days it can cost from £30,000 upwards for a life-size bronze and take anything from six months or more for the sculptor and then the foundry to complete their work. But the money has to be raised first and that can take a lot longer, culminating in careful discussions with the local authorities for the best available site, not always an easy task.

I hope reading this book will enable you to look at statues in a fresh light. Usually you will find them in a prominent position in a city centre but just sometimes you have to search down back alleys for them. Montrose and Paisley already produce useful Guides and Sculpture Trails and Aberdeen is planning one. Do look carefully at equestrian statues. Both front legs in the air for the horse means the person commemorated died in battle. One front leg in the air, the person died as a result of wounds received in battle. If the horse has all four legs on the ground, the person died of natural causes.

The Public Monuments and Sculpture Association established in 1991 in London are doing their best with the aid of a good lottery grant to catalogue all the nation's statues. Their National Recording Project is attempting to list every piece of public sculpture in the British Isles and record their condition; many are at risk either from old age or vandalism – in the latter case as Glasgow has suffered with its statues to James Watt and more recently Donald Dewar.

For the Association, Ray McKenzie has produced a magnificent book cataloguing all Glasgow's sculptures and Edinburgh resident Dianne King is doing a similar project for the capital's vast collection, compiling a database hopefully to be

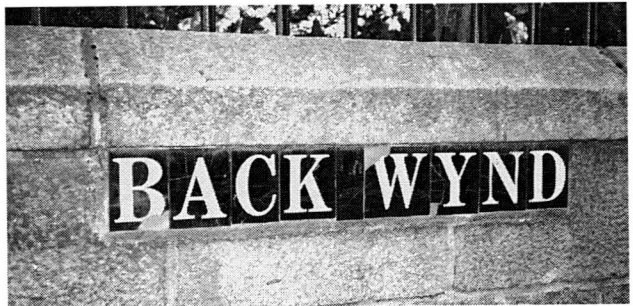

completed in 2007 with an illustrated volume after that.

It is a difficulty task. Councils, who ultimately have the responsibility for the maintenance of statues tend not to list them under one simple 'category' or delegate a single department to be in charge. In Ayr the maintenance of several notable heroes in the city streets is the responsibility of the local cemetery. Only a few towns, such as Paisley and Montrose as noted, produce comprehensive guides to their statues. For readers really wanting to know more, the Royal Incorporation of Architects in Scotland guides are a good source of information and other useful addresses for people who want to know more are in the back of the book.

A few years ago the BBC invited the British public to nominate their hundred greatest-ever Britons living or dead. Ten Scots figured in the list, led by Alexander Fleming, John Logie Baird, William Wallace, Alexander Graham Bell, Tony Blair, Robert the Bruce, James Watt, James Clerk Maxwell, David Livingstone and Marie Stopes. Adopted Scot J.K. Rowling of Harry Potter fame also made the list. You may be surprised at the small number who have qualified for a full statue.

I hope readers will be introduced to Scottish heroes they know, some they don't know and some they won't call heroes at all. If your favourite isn't here, then that is down to me and my choice. Not every Scot with a statue is here, only those who in some way merit a heroic tag. My own Top 100 Scots are selected and nominated. I admit to being fully liable for any omissions or additions that upset or anger. After all, one man's hero is another man's villain.

e.e. Cummings, the eccentric American poet, wrote that a pretty girl naked is worth a million statues. The author doesn't necessarily disagree but this book might help to give another opinion.

John Lindsey
St Andrews 2007

CHAPTER 1

The Borders
Entering Scotland's Past

'The Hero can be Poet, Prophet, King, Priest or what you will according to the kind of world he finds himself born into'

THOMAS CARLYLE

The search for Scotland's heroes starts in the Borders. It is to be expected that an area which separates England and Scotland should have a bloody history. The Borders region of Scotland certainly fits this description, reflecting the lawless past of the country. Some even call it forgotten Scotland; it is certainly wild and remote, no train station anywhere in the region and even now still arguing over a rail link to Edinburgh from the main towns. But at the same time it also has been home to explorers, poets and peaceable sheep farmers.

The M6 Motorway is the most common entrance to Scotland and a few miles over the border is the wonderfully named village of Ecclefechan. This was the birthplace in 1795 of the great thinker **Thomas**

ECCLEFECHAN
The birthplace of Thomas Carlyle who lectured on The Hero in History.

Carlyle. Fittingly, it was he who reawakened the nation's attitudes towards heroism with his lectures on Hero-Worship and the Hero in History. At the end of the village looking down on the small collection of houses sits Carlyle in a replica bronze statue of the one sculpted by J. Edgar Boehm in 1882 in Chelsea. This

SCOTLAND'S HEROES

was cast by McDonald and Creswick in 1929.

Thomas Carlyle, the son of a country stonemason, became known as the Sage of Ecclefechan and the guardian of the nation's morals. He was certainly one of the 19th century's most distinguished men of letters and died at 24 Cheyne Row, Chelsea, in surroundings as different from his birthplace as you could get. This historian, philosopher, biographer and essayist left his native Dumfriesshire village as a fourteen-year-old to walk eighty miles north to the capital Edinburgh. It took three days. He spent four years at Edinburgh University but left without taking his degree in law and abandoned his plans to enter the church. For a while he taught mathematics at Annan Academy in Dumfriesshire and then at Kirkcaldy.

He also started writing and translating a lot of articles. In 1818 he was back in Edinburgh keen on making the law his profession. He loved the city and made money as a private tutor. He met and married Jane Baillie Walsh in 1826 and was now determined to make writing his career. For a while they lived at Craigenputtoch, a farm in Dumfriesshire Jane

inherited on her father's death, but the lure of London was too great and they moved to Chelsea in 1834 to live there for the rest of their lives. A powerful critic, Carlyle wrote on figures such as Oliver Cromwell and Fredrick the Great but after his wife died in 1866 the fire went out of him and he died in 1881. Although much admired in London, Carlyle chose to be buried in Scotland. Towards the end of 2006 there were moves to attract more visitors to his home at Craigenputtoch – his 'wild moorland home' as he described it and where he wrote some of his best works including his famous essay on Robert Burns.

The nearby town of Lockerbie has a sad reputation with its emotive memorial to the victims of the Pan Am plane disaster in December 1988 when two hundred and fifty-nine passengers and crew and eleven residents died as a bomb exploded on the aeroplane. Turn off the motorway to reach the real Border country, an area of gently rolling hills and natural beauty with a bloodstained past. The reiver is unique to the Borders. These cattle rustlers and freebooters came from all walks of life and were really highly skilled guerrilla fighters taking cattle wherever they pleased.

Langholm is where **Rear Admiral Sir Pulteney Malcolm** (1768–1838) became the local minister. In the Navy, he served under Horatio Nelson in the Mediterranean and also commanded St Helena and its celebrated prisoner Napoleon Bonaparte. His statue is in Market Place, by David Dunbar in 1842. Langholm was also the birthplace of noted poet Hugh MacDiarmid – known to some locally by his real Borders name of Christopher Grieve. In 1985 Jake Harvey's bronze memorial to him was unveiled on a site near Whita Yett overlooking the town, cast in the form of an open book with chapters from the poet's life.

Sheep are also big business here and past Moffat you are into the heart of Border country.

It is worth casting an eye over the **Moffat Ram** sculpture on the Colvin Fountain in the centre of town recalling the big part wool and weaving played in this Border town. The economy of the Borders has always relied on agriculture and the woollen industry but

as the textile and knitwear industries have suffered, so tourism has increased in importance and the Borders Tourist body is now one of the best in Scotland.

The Tibbie Shiels Inn is famous. Tibbie (a woman) ran the original inn there and among her customers were Sir Walter Scott and poet **James Hogg,** the Ettrick Shepherd. He was born the

son of a tenant farmer on the banks of the Ettrick Water in Selkirkshire in 1770, and became a shepherd whilst trying to write poetry. He never went to school but was able to write in what was called 'big text' with every letter at least an inch high. He bought an old fiddle on which he learnt to play Scottish tunes. He really only started reading books at age eighteen – his first being *The Life and Adventures of Sir William*

ST MARY'S LOCH
The Ettrick Shepherd enjoys the view that inspired his poetry.

Wallace. His poems were of the countryside he knew so well and he also wrote much prose, his *Confessions of a Justified Sinner* winning much praise for its supernatural content and criticism of Calvinism. He was probably admired more in London than Edinburgh.

Hogg, poet and novelist, was a visitor to his friend's Scott's house in Edinburgh for dinner parties. He and Scott became friends after Hogg's first collection of poems was published and remained close until Scott's death. His shepherding work suffered as his writing grew and he went to Edinburgh convinced he would make his fortune there. It took a while but he succeeded and two years later returned to the Borders. He died there in 1835. On the isthmus straddling St Mary's Loch and the smaller Loch o' the Lowes stands his statue (sculptor Andrew Currie 1860) commanding a great panoramic view.

Statue unveilings used to be big affairs attracting many thousands of people and Hogg's unveiling was no exception. Many of the literary friends and admirers of the poet came from distant parts of the country to this remote spot in numbers never seen before. Some walked for miles, others came by carriage, a total of over two thousand people gathered in rain so torrential that even the local shepherds called it 'a complete wat day.' Donald Bain, the famous 42nd Highlander piper, played some of the airs set to Hogg's songs and led the procession followed by one hundred and fifty shepherds from all over the Borders. The Rev. James Russell of Yarrow invoked the Divine Blessing and as sculptor Andrew Currie uncovered the statue amidst great cheering the sun came out. The monument is eight and a half feet high on a large pedestal. By Hogg's side as he looks out over the loch is his dog Hector, his right hand grasps a stout walking stick and his left holds a scroll with the last line of his *Queen's Wake* – 'Hath Taught the Wandering Wings to Sing.'

In his address Henry Glassford Bell, Sheriff-Substitute of Lanarkshire said – to great applause – that Hogg found his inspiration among these familiar hills and glens. He called him 'a true Scottish poet, not equal to Burns because no national poet was ever equal to him, but fully justified to rank in the second place.'

The Borders has a literary heritage and north-west of here is Tweedsmuir, the home of John Buchan, not remembered with a full statue, but a man who was a prolific writer producing in 1932 a popular biography of Sir Walter Scott. This is Scott territory, particularly Selkirk, originally famous for its shoe-making and strangely not a favourite place of the great Robert Burns. At the ruined church in Kirk Wynd there's a tablet commemorating the occasion in 1297 when William Wallace was declared Guardian of Scotland. But it is the **Sir Walter Scott** connection that probably draws most visitors.

Scott's Courtroom, which also served as Selkirk's Town Hall, was built between 1803 and 1804. From 1799 until his death in 1832 he was Sheriff of the County of Selkirk. The courtroom is now a museum, opened on 20 September 1994 by Mrs Patricia Maxwell-Scott OBE, Honorary Sheriff of Selkirk and great-great-great granddaughter of the novelist. It contains a good bust of Scott with his faithful dog and explores Scott's life, his work and his time in the town. He was a fair and decent sheriff. Outside the courtroom stands his statue (sculptor Alexander Handyside Ritchie). Scott is probably responsible more

SELKIRK
Sir Walter Scott brought the romantic notion of Scotland to a wide audience.

than any other person for the romanticism of Scotland. He was actually born in Edinburgh in August 1771. Not a strong child, he was sent to Bath to take the waters which did little to help his lameness but did introduce him to the delights of Shakespeare and the theatre.

Back in Edinburgh in 1778 he was a pupil at Edinburgh High School and became a great book reader. He started at the age of thirteen at Edinburgh University and studied for the Bar, being called there in 1792. Five years later he married Charlotte Carpentier. In 1804 he took a lease on Ashiestiel overlooking the River Tweed, the great fishing river that is such a feature of Borders life. Within eight years he had earned enough to build his own mansion beside the Tweed at Melrose – Abbotsford, which is open to the public today and contains many great items of Scottish history. It was in the Borders that Scott started to steep himself in Scottish history which was the focal point and attraction of so many of his novels. In 1810 his book *The Lady of the Lake* was highly influential in Europe and he single-handedly kick-started the Scottish tourist industry. This was followed in 1814 by *Waverley* and this new literary form of the novel was a great success.

His was the romantic highlands and for the next thirteen years he produced successful novels using unforgettable real characters and, like Charles Dickens after him, went on to achieve international fame. *Rob Roy* (1817) was a wild and abandoned tale from a man who was pretty respectable and conservative himself. He did a lot to heal the rift between highlanders and lowlanders. His home Abbotsford was a model for Scottish colonial architecture. Victorians loved his novels, the ersatz kilts, bagpipes and shortbread tins of dreams. In August 1822 King George IV visited Scotland, the first visit by a reigning monarch in nearly two hundred years. Scott was the Pageant Master and organized everything. The King came in Royal Stewart Tartan kilt and pink, flesh-coloured tights giving the cartoonists of the day much scope. On the monarch's return to London it was said Scotland had at last a badge of identity. Scott's place in history was cemented. It was much later the industrial age was to bring in more writers and an end of sentimental writing; somehow Brigadoon had disappeared back into the mist.

Scott kept busy in other areas too. He published a pamphlet successfully defending the right of the Scottish banks to issue their own bank notes. In 1818 he rediscovered the Scottish crown jewels lying forgotten in a chest at Edinburgh Castle and collected memorabilia at Abbotsford to his heroes, Mary Queen of Scots, Rob Roy, and the Young Pretender.

He strangely never owned up to the authorship of his novels but they all reflected the stirring history of Scotland's turbulent and romantic past. He kept an Edinburgh town house where he was a great entertainer and giver of noisy dinner parties. In 1826 Scott's world collapsed as he went bankrupt – the publishing firm in which he had a third share went under – and his wife died. He worked prodigiously to wipe out his debts producing a number of novels and biographies. He managed to keep Abbotsford with its great collection of historic relics and weapons including Montrose's sword and Rob Roy's gun but only

a rented place in Edinburgh and died in September 1832 still owing some money. In September 2006 plans were drawn up to manage Abbotsford as a private charitable trust to ensure its financial future as a major tourist attraction following the death in 2004 of the novelist's last direct descendant, Dame Kean Maxwell-Scott.

Near here in Selkirk is a bust of fine Scottish artist Tom Scott on first floor above a shop and the *Southern Reporter* office just before a fine statue of the African explorer **Mungo Park** (1771–1806). The town is very proud of him, he was

SELKIRK
Mungo Park, along with other men of the town, is remembered with a fine statue.

educated at Selkirk Grammar and Edinburgh University, becoming a doctor of medicine at the age of twenty-one. A keen botanist, after voyages to Gambia, and Sumatra as assistant surgeon to Sir Joseph Banks, he returned to Britain and published a book of his travels in 1799. After a few years as a surgeon in Peebles the travel bug bit him again and he returned to Gambia where his anti-slavery views made him many enemies among the slave-traders. Exploring was obviously more fun than medicine; he found backing for his great dream of finding the source of the great River Niger and was off to Africa again. He reached there in July 1796 after great hardships from the hostile conditions and marauding tribes.

Park returned after two years with the first maps of the region but couldn't settle and went back later with tragic consequences. Avoiding an ambush, he drowned at Bousa Falls on the River Niger in early 1806; the body has never been found. The statue, by Andrew Currie, is an impressive one, with figures of African men and women added later around the base. The relief panels are the work of Thomas Clapperton. The inscription commemorates the death of Mungo Park's

companion, Alexander Anderson also of Selkirk, killed on the Niger in 1805 and George Scott, also of Selkirk who died there the same year. Also remembered is Mungo's son Thomas who perished at Aquambo in West Africa in 1827 whilst endeavouring to find traces of his distinguished father.

Nearby is the **Flodden Memorial**. This dramatic sculpture by Galashiels sculptor Thomas Clapperton

bears the simple inscription 'O Flodden Field.' Selkirk men were fans of royalty and the men of the town rallied to support James IV in his ill-conceived fight against his brother-in-law Henry VIII in 1513. Legend says

SELKIRK
Perhaps the most emotive memorial here, the lone survivor of the Flodden Massacre.

eighty men set forth but only one, a weaver named Fletcher, survived.

He captured the flag of Sir Christopher Savage of Macclesfield. Legend is he was so overcome with emotion and perhaps guilt at his own survival he was unable to speak on his return but instead dipped the flag in tribute to his fallen comrades. Some say he then died on the spot. His gesture is commemorated and re-enacted each year in prolonged ceremonies climaxed by a casting of the colours in Selkirk's market place. Flodden turned out to be even more significant for Scotland's future than the great win at Bannockburn over the English. That victory had spearheaded the country's move towards independence; the crushing defeat at Flodden left the political and military worlds bereft of talent and the death of their King heralded a troubled period in the nation's history. It culminated in the union of the Scottish and English crowns and, a century later, the loss of independence through political union.

It truly was a Scottish tragedy fought out by more soldiers than Bannockburn and left twelve thousand dead including one King. The massive defeat was played down in Scotland. James IV's force of maybe thirty thousand men from all over the country with superior in arms and men were defeated by the English army of twenty-seven thousand. Some put the Scottish army estimate even higher and it was the largest Scots army in Scottish history. The opposition army was led by a seventy-year-old cripple Thomas Howard, Earl of Surrey, England's most experienced soldier. It was a bloody battle, no prisoners were taken. The King died with an arrow in his face and his throat slashed. The King's rather inept decision to fight had cost him, his son, and three hundred Scottish nobles – their lives. After his victory Henry VIII was able to repeat his claim of feudal superiority over the Scots.

Hawick also has a statue to commemorate this time in the country's history. The men of the town had similarly been decimated at Flodden but the Callants, the young unmarried men of the town, won a memorable skirmish with the foe at Hornshole near the town. The **Horse Statue** at the east end of the High Street

The Callants, the young unmarried men of the town were also decimated at Flodden but are remembered for a victory at nearby Hornshole.

never looked back, going on to win six times. He was a modest but extremely brave and skilled rider, setting world speed records, riding for Norton and AJS and becoming European Champion in 1935. He died tragically following an accident during a race at Sachsenring in the 1937 German Grand Prix. There are also memorials to him on the Isle of Man and at Sachsenring.

The Jimmy Guthrie Room at Hawick Museum

was given to the town in 1914 by the Hawick Callants Club to remember this fight. Hawick is a great sporting town known for its many rugby internationalists and the yachtsman Chay Blyth who was given freedom of the burgh in 1973. It is popular for its woollen mills and shops.

Wilton Lodge Park is over one hundred acres of beautiful gardens with a municipal art gallery. It also is home to a statue of **Jimmy Guthrie**, Hawick's racing legend. Born in the town in 1897 Guthrie grew up to become a good racer and Hawick Motorcycle Club assisted Guthrie to take part in his first TT at the Isle of Man in 1923. He won his first race there in 1930 and

HAWICK

The lovely Wilton Lodge Park is home to motorcycling ace Jimmy Guthrie.

celebrates this motorcycling hero with his bikes, trophies, medals, photographs etc. The bronze statue of this world motorcycling champion is by Thomas Clapperton and is in mint condition, standing 4ft 6inches high and erected by public subscription.

There is a memorial cairn to another motorcycling ace on an unclassified road after Teviothead off the A7 south west of Hawick and now a statue too. The achievements of **Steve Hislop** include eleven TT wins and two British Superbike Championships. Known as Hizzy to his fans, Hislop died at the age of forty-one whilst piloting a helicopter which crashed near Hawick in July 2003. Friends donated generously for this popular sportsmen and David Annand's sculpture was unveiled in Wilton Lodge Park on 1 October 2005.

Galashiels is not perceived as the loveliest town in the Borders but has one singular claim to fame. During the Second World War the New Gala House was home to an evacuated girls' school from Edinburgh. The school was St Trinians and became Ronald Searle's inspiration for his schoolgirl cartoons. The first woollen factory of the new age was here and the

town became the centre of the Scottish tweed industry. Mill owners did well; their big houses are still seen in the area. But export problems and other factors caused the decline of this side of the town. Thomas Clapperton, a native of the town, is famous in the area with his work all around. On the ground floor of Old Gala House, which dates from 1583, is The Clapperton Room where you can discover all about this

TEVIOTHEAD
Another star with the motorbike, Steve Hislop, is looked over at the foundry prior to being placed here off the A7.

renowned Scottish sculptor. The churchyard in Minto near Denholm has his great memorial of World War One and his talents were also sought in London.

In 1925 he completed the massive frieze on the front facade of Liberty's store in Regent Street. This carving was thirty-six metres long and three metres high and at the time was the largest single piece of sculpture in Britain consisting of over three hundred tons of Portland stone. Some forty figures appear in the work which depicts trade of east and west converging on a Britannia figure in the middle. He was such a well-known sculptor it was strange that when he pitched for the Hawick 1514 Memorial he lost out and even stranger that he lost out to a very similar design by W.F. Beattie.

GALASHIELS

You can't miss Thomas Clapperton's impressive work right in the city centre.

Back in his native town his statue of **The Reivers** is Clapperton's most public work. The son of one of Scotland's pioneering photographers he secured a scholarship to the Glasgow School of Art in 1899, later to the royal Academy in London. His first assignment was the panels on the Selkirk memorial to Mungo Park. After World War One he produced many outstanding war memorials and also created one of the best small bronze statuettes of Robert Louis Stevenson, commissioned in 1909 by the Border Liberals for presentation to Alexander L. Brown, former MP for Border Burghs.

Dryburgh Abbey has a massive statue of **William Wallace,** commissioned in 1814 by the rather eccentric 11th Earl of Buchan. It was the first monument to the great patriot erected in Scotland and can be reached by a one-mile walk through a wood from Dryburgh Abbey. When you get there this rather crude pink sandstone tribute to a great warrior is remarkable for his strange, staring eyes. Carved by John Smith, the great Sir Walter Scott hated it. The signposts around here point to Scott's View, the great man used to

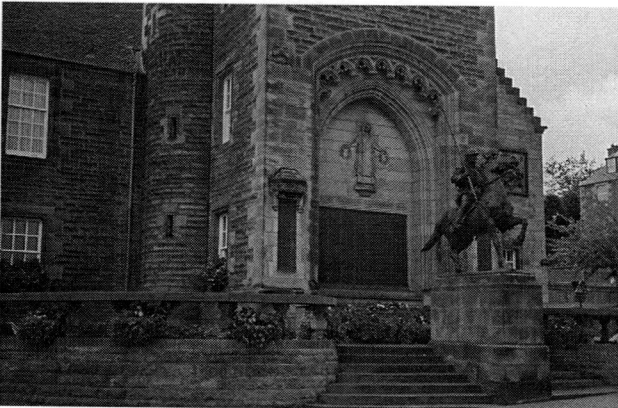

love to sit and see the River Tweed flow by in all its glory. So often did he sit here that it is said some horses in his one-mile-long funeral cortege stopped here without being told to do so.

East of here is Coldstream with its statue to **Charles Marjoribanks,** MP for the area, and a museum telling the story of the Coldstream Guards; it was from here over 350 years ago the regiment set off for London to help restore the monarchy. Next stop is Duns and the **John Duns Scotus** (1265–1308) statue. He was an eminent Franciscan who still ranks as one of the world's greatest theologians. The memorial was erected here in 1966 by the Franciscan Order and he is described on the plaque as a 'Franciscan and Subtle Doctor.' He is probably best remembered by the word 'dunce' and the dunce's cap at school. The word dunce comes from the insult levelled by 16th-century Protestant Reformers at followers of the teachings of Duns Scotus. He was however one of the great mediaeval philosophers, most noted for his defence of the Immaculate Conception which led to him being beatified by the Pope in 1993.

At Eyemouth on the coast, **Willie Spears** is remembered with a 1998 statue by David Annand known as the King Fisher. Spears was leader of the Eyemouth revolt in the mid-1880s against the church tithes on the fishermen. It is also the scene of Black Friday 14 October 1881, when 120 local men lost their lives in a fishing boat disaster caused by a hurricane.

Dunbar sits on the East Lothian coast, said to be the sunniest part of Scotland. It is the birthplace of **John Muir,** the father of world conservation. He was born here on 21 April 1838 and soon developed an abiding love of nature. The John Muir Birthplace Trust has an exhibition of his life and work at 126 High Street, a three-storey first home of the explorer and naturalist who created the United States national park system. East Lothian Council has named its coastal path The John Muir Way, currently being developed to complete a continuous route from Edinburgh to the Borders. The Country Park here is also named after him.

He moved with his family to the United States of America in 1849. A childhood accident left him temporarily blind and when his sight was restored he appreciated nature better. Muir studied at the University of Wisconsin becoming passionately interested in natural history and conservation. He worked at Yosemite as a guide and shepherd. In 1880 he married and settled in San Francisco but Yosemite occupied his mind. He set up the world's first real conservation organization, the Sierra Club, and started a long campaign to get the US authorities to declare the wonderful

DUNBAR

Home to John Muir, the father of world conservation, who made his reputation in America but loved his native land.

Yosemite Valley as a National Park. During his time in the USA he was responsible for many million acres of forest and woodland being turned into national parks and wrote a number of books on the subject. He died in 1914 of pneumonia. There is a John Muir Day in the USA each year in 'honour of the father of American national parks' and in 1976 he was named the Greatest Californian. He was also a great Scot although perhaps only latterly truly recognised in his own country. The statue in Dunbar is by Valentin Znoba.

Haddington is the birthplace of the infamous **John Knox**. His controversial life began here around 1512. Knox started his working life as a teacher. In 1536 he was ordained as a Catholic priest. He first started to show an interest in the Reformation in 1545. The next year he was in St Andrews and witnessed the cruel burning of the Reformer George Wishart at the orders of Cardinal Beaton. In the early hours of 29 May 1546 Beaton was murdered in St Andrews Castle by Protestant assassins who fortified the castle and were joined by sympathisers. John Knox was one of them. Their hopes of an English rescue never came but the

French fleet arrived and Knox with others was taken to France and put to work as a galley slave for nine months which affected his health for ever.

After release he travelled to London where he lived for five years and appreciated the welcome reforming preachers got in the capital. He was soon appointed chaplain at Berwick and married Marjorie Bowes there, a happy marriage and he was a devoted husband. She bore him two sons. When the Catholic Mary Tudor became Queen of England he fled to Frankfurt and Geneva where he met the French reformer John Calvin and was strongly influenced by his doctrines. With the succession to the throne of the Protestant Elizabeth I, the Scottish Reformation gained strength. The Protestant nobility recalled Knox and on 2 May 1559 he landed at Leith to a great reception and began preaching in various towns in Scotland.

When Mary Queen of Scots returned to Scotland in 1561 Knox condemned her vigorously for her religion and behaviour. He is remembered best for this hatred of Mary Queen of Scots and his four meetings with her are recalled in his

HADDINGTON
John Knox was born here and carries the inevitable bible in this statue by D.W. Stevenson.

History of the Reformation of Religion in the Realm of Scotland. The authority of the Pope in Scotland was formally abolished and the celebration of Mass forbidden at the meeting of the newly formed Parliament in Edinburgh. Knox was asked to produce a definition of the new faith and 'in four days of prodigious effort he came up with the twenty-five Articles of Confession of Faith.' The arguments continue as to whether he was a heroic Scot. He did more to Anglicize the country than many others, and his legend lives on. He died on

24 November 1572 having been called from St Andrews to Edinburgh to preach at St Giles Cathedral although so ill he could hardly be heard. The idea for a Knox memorial here in the form of an educational establishment went back as far as 1870.

The Knox Institute in Haddington formally opened for teaching in 1879 but the actual opening ceremony was in January the following year when the life-size statue of the great Scottish Reformer was placed in front of the building. It is by David Watson Stevenson and shows Knox in his Geneva gown with an open bible in his left hand. There are many statues to Knox in Scotland including in the country's capital where he is buried and Edinburgh is also home to many other heroic Scots.

CHAPTER 2

Remembering Sons of Auld Reekie

'What is our task? – to make Britain a fit country for heroes to live in'

DAVID LLOYD GEORGE

Edinburgh, Scotland's Capital, is a city rich in culture and history, a great location for lovers of statues. Edinburgh is a beautiful place to stroll around with magnificent architecture and permanent reminders of the strong literary and military ties the city enjoys. Five million tourists a year do just that.

Princes Street is the obvious spot to begin. This elegant parade under the shadow of Edinburgh Castle has many memorials. There is an unwritten tradition that statues, along with street names, do not honour the living and although some on the current Edinburgh City Council would like to change that, you will mostly see figures from the distant past here.

All of the characters who have contributed to the city's fortunes are well catalogued in the many books on the city but different kinds of heroism are recalled here. Of all the sculptors who have added to the city's culture, Sir John Steell has the most impressive output. He completed ten in all, the first being in the courtyard of the City Chambers. It shows the Emperor Alexander and his horse Bucephalus. The statue is said to represent 'mind over brute force' and the Council themselves admit... 'an encouragement many of those involved in local government will appreciate.' Sadly Steell now lies in an unmarked grave at Old Calton Cemetery, largely forgotten in the city he once graced with impressive statuary.

His, and the city's most famous work, is **The Scott Monument**), a major draw on Princes Street Gardens. Irvine Welsh, modern-day author of *Trainspotting*, a

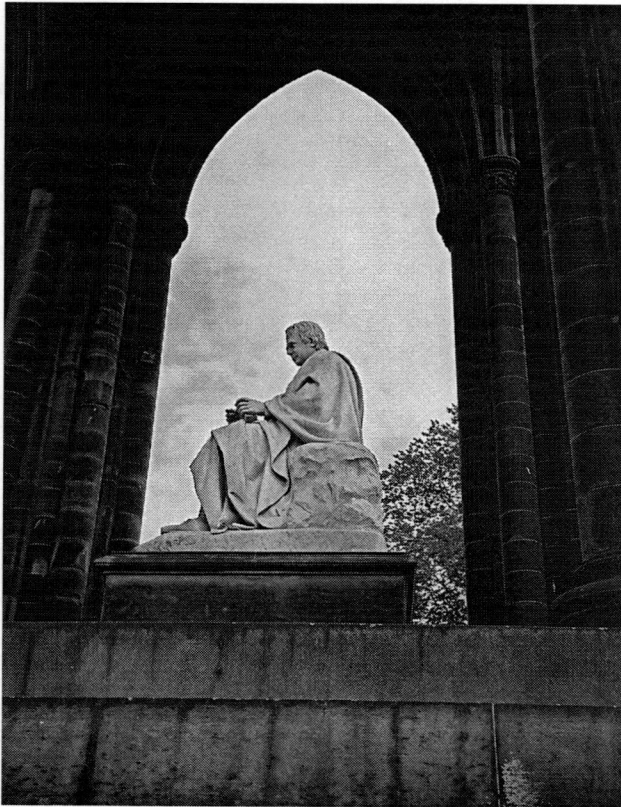

SIR WALTER SCOTT
Built in 1846 his Monument dominates Princes Street and the marble statue by Sir John Steell is seen by millions of tourists.

Bruce, George Heriot, and the Duke of Montrose.

There are many others along Princes Street including **Adam Black** (1784–1874). The sculptor was John Hutchison in 1877. Black was born in Charles Street, Edinburgh and following High School was apprenticed to a bookseller. After work in London he returned to Edinburgh, opened his own premises on South Bridge and bought the rights to the *Encyclopaedia Britannica* and to some of Sir Walter Scott's work. Black was an MP for Edinburgh and twice Lord Provost.

Allan Ramsay (1686–1758) was an 18th-century poet and leading figure in the city's arts scene. This statue, eighteen tons of Carrara marble, is by Sir John Steell. Born in Leadhills, Ramsay was apprenticed to an Edinburgh wig-maker but took to writing poems and music which he sold from a shop in the High Street. He was a keen Jacobite.

Dr Thomas Guthrie (1803–1873) was an Edinburgh cleric who founded the city 'ragged school' during the 1800s and is recalled here in Portland stone by F.W. Pomeroy (1910) in a pose that nowadays would draw

story of drug addiction in Edinburgh, credits Scott as one of his main influences. The marble statue (1846) under the soot-encrusted monument shows the great man with his favourite deerhound Maida at his feet. There are many historical figures on the outside of the monument but annoyingly you can't really get a good look at them. Alongside the many royal figures here are John Knox, Rob Roy, Robert

Sir James Young Simpson (1811–1870) was a pioneer in anaesthesia and introduced chloroform in 1847. His bronze statue is by William Brodie (1876). The man who saved us all a lot of pain was born in Bathgate and went to Edinburgh University. By the time he was twenty-eight he had become Professor of Midwifery and at a party in his home in Queen Street in 1847 experimented with a number of different liquids. When they opened a bottle of chloroform suddenly the party went with a swing, as everyone for a while got very happy and noisy – followed by total silence! They had discovered the anaesthetic although the church and the

THOMAS GUTHRIE

One of the leaders of the Free Church who did so much for the homeless children of Edinburgh.

criticism from the politically correct lobby. From Brechin, Guthrie began medical studies at Edinburgh University before going to Paris. What he experienced there gave him a renewed social conscience. He was a licensed preacher and back in Scotland became a minister in Forfar. He agreed with Dr Thomas Chalmers about State influence over the Church and became a leader of The Free Church. From his church he started the city's Ragged Schools to provide shelter and education for the homeless children of the city. His efforts led to the passing by Parliament in 1866 of a New Industrial School Act.

SIR JAMES YOUNG SIMPSON

This pioneer of anaesthetics probably deserves better treatment, his head disappears into the foliage of Princes Street Gardens.

medical profession objected strongly. But Simpson persisted in his belief and when he was appointed physician to Queen Victoria and she permitted the use of chloroform during the birth of her son Leopold, he was vindicated.

David Livingstone, the famous 19th-century explorer is also here although his home town of Blantyre is a better place to celebrate his life with a great statue. There is also one in Glasgow. This is certainly not the best statue of him but a meeting of the City Chambers in 1874 heard the great explorer described as 'probably the greatest hero of our generation' and that it would be a disgrace not to erect a memorial to so heroic a man. The original design was by Mrs David Hill.

Canongate honours two very different men. **David Hume** (1711–1776), one of the great philosophers of his time, sits on his plinth opposite St Giles. His friend Adam Smith was influenced by Hume and called him 'as approaching as nearly to the idea of a perfectly wise and virtuous man as perhaps the frailty of human nature will admit'. Hume was born in Chirnside in Berwickshire and, able to read Latin and

Greek by the age of twelve, went to the University of Edinburgh to study law. But he spent more time on his writing, producing many publications which took time to be recognized as substantial works. For a period he worked in France as Secretary to the British Embassy in Paris where he was better received. He spent the last years of his life in Edinburgh and is now recalled as a great man.

He lived on the corner of St David Street and St Andrew Square and was a renowned tippler. He was apparently making his way home drunk one night when he toppled into a bog in what is now known as Princes Street Gardens. Unable to get out, the overweight

DAVID HUME

When he appeared in Canongate in 1997 dressed in a toga it certainly brought this 18th century philosopher to a wider audience.

philosopher begged a woman for help. She recognized him immediately as 'Hume the Atheist' and refused to offer her umbrella until he recited both the Lord's Prayer and the Creed. The statue is by Alexander Stoddart and when unveiled drew criticism for showing Hume in a toga but is now a respected Edinburgh landmark. After Hume's death his friends, concerned at the stories that Hume had made a pact with the devil, sat for a week with loaded pistols in Old Calton Graveyard just in case...

One of the most recent statues to be erected in Edinburgh, in October 2004, is that of **Robert Fergusson,** (1750–1774) who in his short life drew many celebrated admirers. Fergusson was born in the Cap and Feather Close in the Royal Mile, the son of an Aberdeenshire clerk. He went to St Andrews University to read Divinity but started to write poetry and on returning to Edinburgh became Clerk to the Commissary Court. However by now his poetry was gaining a wide audience of fans. His first poem was *The Daft Days* about life and squalor in his native city, in his short life publishing over eighty poems. His masterpiece on Edinburgh was *Auld Reekie.* He became a religious maniac and after a bad fall went to the madhouse where he died at the age of twenty-four. He was buried in Canongate Churchyard. When Robert Burns visited Edinburgh in 1786 he was distressed to see Fergusson in a paupers' grave and paid for a headstone to be erected. He wrote: 'No sculptur'd marble here nor pompous lay/ No storied urn or animated bust/ This simple stone directs pale Scotia's way/To pour her sorrows o'er the Poet's dust.' Burns thanked Fergusson 'for making me the poet I am today.' The two poets shared a depressive streak, a sense of humour and a delight in the Scottish language.

ROBERT FERGUSSON

One of the newest Edinburgh statues, outside Canongate Churchyard where his grave has a headstone paid for by Robert Burns.

Robert Louis Stevenson said of Fergusson that 'he died in his acute painful youth.' William Wordsworth said his 'early death was a great loss to the poetry of Scotland'. Stevenson planned to renovate his tombstone but died before he could do so. However the many visitors to this churchyard can now read the inscription. This stone originally erected by Robert Burns has been repaired at the charges of Robert Louis Stevenson and is by him rededicated to the memory of Robert Fergusson as the gift of one Edinburgh lad to another. The Saltire Society on its 50th anniversary, with Edinburgh Council support, commemorated the three Roberts by inscribing Stevenson's words.

These Canongate men are soon to be joined by **Adam Smith** of Kirkcaldy, author of the 18th-century *Wealth of Nations*, inspiration for many an economic theory. He is called the world's greatest economist and is a native of Kirkcaldy like the current Chancellor of the Exchequer Gordon Brown. The book took him five years to write and a further three to revise. He was born in Kirkcaldy on 5 June 1723. His father was a solicitor and at the age of fourteen he went to Glasgow University. The basic theory of the book which is still admired today is that all wealth stems from labour. On completion of the book he went to live in Edinburgh and died there in 1790, being buried with illustrious neighbours in the graveyard at Canongate Church.

The statue commission will please many Scots who have complained for years that this great philosopher and economist has been unrecognized in his own country. The Adam Smith Institute were responsible for finding the money and the project received great support both from America and here; Margaret Thatcher thought it a great idea.

The statue is the work of Paisley sculptor Alexander Stoddart, also responsible for Hume in the Royal Mile. Mr Stoddart's proposal is for a 10ft bronze statue on a 10ft plinth with Smith in 18th-century dress and academic robes. It is certainly going to make an impression in Edinburgh's famous thoroughfare and is worth studying to see the background work and detail a sculptor can put into his work. Smith stands in front of a plough from the latter half of the 1700s as displayed in the National Agricultural Museum of Scotland. This represents the old belief that wealth came from the fat of the land, which Smith superseded with his views. They are represented with the beehive symbol showing the value of 'industry'. There is even a reference to Smith's famous 'invisible hand' – his will be concealed under the gown. The statue unveiling was planned for summer 2007 opposite the City Chambers.

Parliament Square is a lovely spot to spend time. It has **Charles** II, interesting because it is an equestrian statue made of lead, the oldest of its kind in Britain and weighs six tons. The King oddly poses as a Roman General. It was erected in 1685 by an unknown Dutch sculptor. It has regularly needed repairing. Once, in 1767, the City Fathers had it painted white inspiring James Boswell to pen a poem about it.

St Giles Kirk is an important landmark in Scottish history and here you will find John Knox again in a wonderful representation by Pittendrigh Macgillivray. He is actually buried nearby in the parking places outside the Law Courts; in Bay 44 a yellow spot marks the grave.

It is claimed some of his 'monstrous regiment of women' take the opportunity to tread on him as a form of revenge.

Anther Knox statue, by John Hutchison, is in the Church of Scotland Assembly Hall grounds on The Mound.

The Law Courts, as you would expect, celebrate some of the great legal minds of the city.

Robert Blair (1741–1811) is here, the work of Sir Frances Chantrey. Blair was born in East Lothian, became an advocate and went on to hold most of the top legal positions.

CHARLES II
He has the distinction of being the oldest lead equestrian statue in Britain and weighs in at six tons.

David Boyle (1772–1853), a lawyer who became MP for East Ayrshire in 1807 until he was made Lord Justice Clerk in 1811, a position he held for 30 years. (A John Steell statue again.) **Henry Cockburn** (1779–1854) is remembered with a statue by William Brodie. Cockburn was a lawyer, very popular in the city, who defended Mrs. Burke in the Burke and Hare case of 1828. He wrote for the *Edinburgh Review* and between 1830 and 1934 was Solicitor General for Scotland.

Duncan Forbes (c.1644–1704) is commemorated with a magnificent marble statue (sculptor Roubiliac). Forbes was born near Inverness, studied law in Edinburgh and became Sheriff of Midlothian. He went on to become MP for Inverness Burghs and took over the family estate at Culloden. In 1737 he became Lord President of the Court of Session and revitalized the Scottish legal system. His power over Scottish legal matters was such he was nicknamed King Duncan and the majesty of the statue and its pose shows that. **Francis Jeffrey** (1773–1850) is sculpted by John Steell. Another lawyer, his great love was literature and with friends founded the Edinburgh Review. He became Lord Advocate in 1830.

There is one, at first sight, less imposing statue you may initially miss but is certainly worth stopping to admire. John Greenshields, a self-taught Lanarkshire sculptor, carved **Sir Walter Scott** out of freestone and was said by friends of Scott to have captured the best likeness anywhere of the great hero of Scotland.

Outside in Parliament Square is an imposing memorial to Walter Francis, 5th **Duke of Buccleuch** (1806–1884) with the Duke standing in the robes of the Order of the Garter over a base with six panels showing the family history.

Dr. Thomas Chalmers (1780–1847) by sculptor Sir John Steell can be seen at the Castle Street and George Street intersection. Chalmers was born in Anstruther, Fife and studied for the ministry becoming an eminent member of the Church of Scotland in the 19th century and a superb orator. In 1843 a ruling of the Court of Session ruled that a lay patron could choose a minister even against the wishes of the congregation. Chalmers disagreed, stating that the Church and State must be separate. With four hundred and seventy other ministers he marched out of the General Assembly in what was known as The Disruption and created the Free Church of Scotland.

George IV, a dissolute unpopular monarch who ruled from 1820 to 1830 is in a prominent position at the junction of Hanover Street and George Street looking down to Princes Street. Many overseas tourists stop here for a photograph as the base says George IV Visited Scotland – and they like sending the photo home with a caption saying 'So Did I...' The statue is by Sir Francis Chantrey in 1831. The King's visit to the city in 1822 was the first by a reigning monarch and, as described, the events were stage-managed by Sir Walter Scott. It was the first visit from a reigning monarch since 1650 and he did his best to look the part – his plump limbs draped in what he had been told was the Royal Stuart tartan, finished off with pink tights. But it was his niece, Queen Victoria, who paid most attention to Scotland.

Earl Haig (1861–1928) is shown on horseback on the esplanade of Edinburgh Castle (sculptor G.E. Wade).

This controversial figure led the British Army during World War I. He was born at No. 24 Charlotte Square, on the south side of a lovely square restored by The National Trust, now with its headquarters at No. 28. Educated at Oxford and Sandhurst he served in India with the 7th Hussars and rose to become a Brigade-Major during the Boer War. His rise continued and he became Major-General and Commander-in-Chief in

EARL HAIG
On the esplanade of Edinburgh Castle this controversial solider has his critics but is admired for starting the tradition of red poppies on Remembrance Sunday.

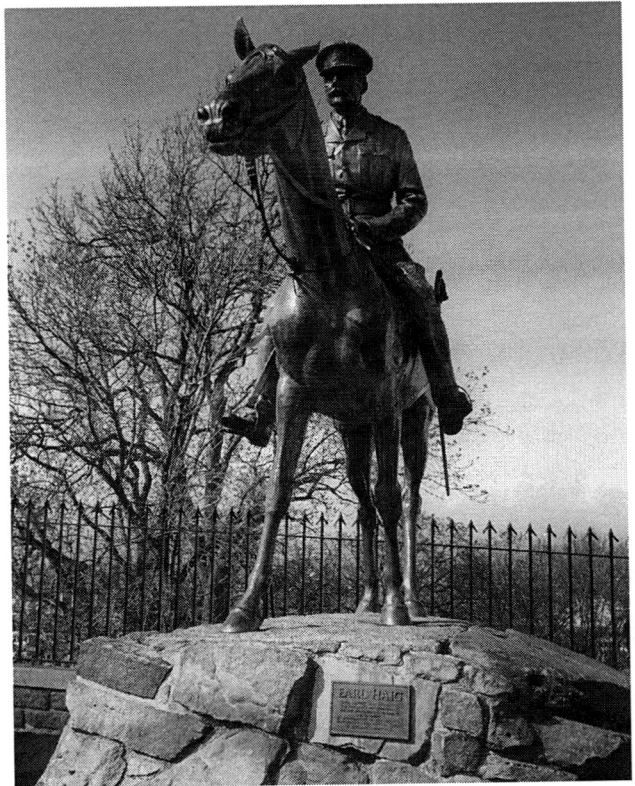

France during the War. Haig received heavy criticism for apparent unconcern about heavy loss of life in achieving his objectives. After the War he worked for the British Legion and started the tradition of red poppies on Remembrance Sunday.

As you pass the Royal Bank of Scotland building in St Andrew Square it is worth stopping to see the statue of **Sir John Hope 4th Earl of Hopetoun.** This statue to the Governor of the bank was put there in 1834 and it is noteworthy because of his dress. Sir John (1765–1823), a soldier who fought under Wellington in the Peninsula War, was once asked how he would like to be portrayed and chose to stand as a Roman general in front of his horse. The sculptor is Thomas Campbell.

William Ewart Gladstone

(1809–1898) came to be at Coates Crescent Gardens from its original site at St Andrew Square where it had become a traffic hazard. It certainly is very large (sculptor Pittendrigh Macgillivray) with eight bronze works around the base reflecting his politics. Gladstone's father's family was from Leith and he was connected with Thomas Gledstane who bought Gladstone's Land in the Lawnmarket in 1617. He was Prime Minister three times over a twenty-six-year period.

Prince Albert (1819–1861) is seen on horseback in Charlotte Square by John Steell and unveiled by Queen Victoria on 17 August 1876. Queen Victoria liked this work so much that the sculptor was later knighted by the Queen at Holyrood Palace. The bronze statue

Left

EARL OF HOPETOUN

He chose to be remembered as a Roman General with his horse – strange for a bank official!

Right

PRINCE ALBERT

His place in Charlotte Square Gardens is well maintained but sadly not open to the public to admire the detailed work around the statue.

SCOTLAND'S HEROES

shows him dressed in a Field Marshall's uniform. The work around the base was done by D.W. Stevenson and Clark Stanton.

Ist Viscount Melville (1742–1811) is in St Andrew Square but unless you have wings you won't see what he looks like – the Melville Monument is modelled on Trajan's Column in Rome and stands 150 feet high. It was designed by William Burn and erected in 1820–23. A 14ft high statue of the Viscount by Robert Forrest was placed at the top of the column. Henry Dundas, the first Viscount Melville, was born and bred in Edinburgh. He trained as a lawyer and in his early twenties was made Solicitor-General for Scotland. In 1774 he was made MP for Midlothian and in following years William Pitt the Younger gave him a number of top cabinet posts. In time Dundas gained complete control over the electoral system in Scotland and was known as 'the absolute dictator of Scotland' or 'Harry the Ninth, uncrowned King of Scotland.' In 1805 his fortunes changed dramatically when he was charged with embezzling funds whilst Treasurer of the Navy. However, he was acquitted. The 2nd Viscount is in Melville Crescent (Sir John Steell 1857). Like his father he was a staunch Tory and MP for a number of constituencies in England and in 1800 for Midlothian. He had a number of top posts including 'Manager for Scotland' which involved organization of the electoral system for Parliament.

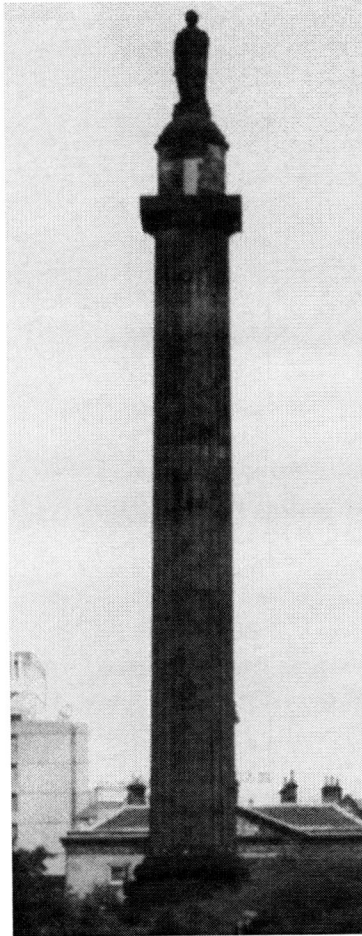

VISCOUNT MELVILLE

At 150 feet up in the air over St Andrew Square you have to wonder what detail the sculptor Robert Forrest put into his work which is 14 feet high itself!

Edinburgh Castle is visited by millions from all over the world and at its entrance are the ubiquitous Robert The Bruce and William Wallace although we learn more about these two great figures in their more historic setting of Stirling. Other figures remembered in Edinburgh but also with statues all over the country include Queen Victoria, Robert Burns and William Pitt – which is an unusual tribute as this 18th-century Whig Prime Minister is the man who introduced income tax!

Greyfriars Bobby is in Candlemaker Row, a life-size bronze of the faithful dog which from 1858 for fourteen years kept watch over his master's grave. It is the work of William Brodie in 1872. Bobby was a Skye terrier and there are two stories about him. One says that he was the companion of Auld Jock Gray, a Pentland Hills farmer who ate each day in a restaurant in Greyfriars Place in the Grassmarket. After his death Bobby is supposed to have lain on his master's nearby grave for fourteen years going into the restaurant every day to be fed. However, as this story was spread by the restaurant owner some doubt its

veracity. The other view is that Bobby was a police watchdog belonging to John Gray, who also ate in the restaurant, and who died of tuberculosis in 1858. Whatever the truth, the dog died in 1872 and his likeness now sits upon a granite drinking fountain here.

William Chambers (1800–1883) in nearby Chambers Street is another renowned Scot with a street named after him. The statue was made by John Rhind in 1891. Born in Peebles, Chambers made his name in Edinburgh where he became a bookseller and printer along with brother Robert. He became Lord Provost of Edinburgh in 1865 and made great civic improvements,

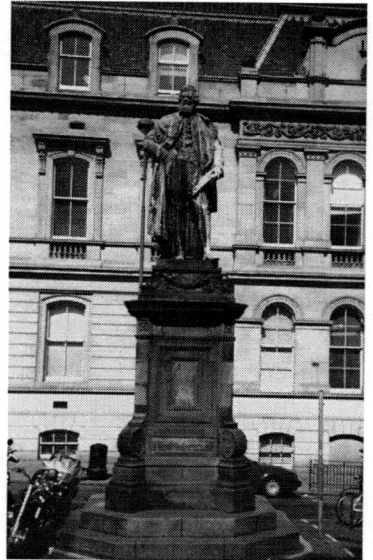

WILLIAM CHAMBERS
This popular Lord Provost of Edinburgh enjoys the distinction of having a street named after him.

clearing slums, widening the High Street and building new avenues. He acquired much wealth and helped pay for much of the restoration of St Giles Cathedral as well as endowing a fine museum, library and art gallery in Peebles.

One of the city's literary giants Sir Arthur Conan Doyle is remembered with a statue of **Sherlock Holmes** in Picardy Place. The most famous amateur detective in the world was the creation of Conan Doyle who was born in May 1859 in a flat overlooking Picardy Place, now a busy roundabout junction of York Place and Leith Walk. His father was a good artist but a drunk and his mother sent the nine-year-old Arthur to boarding school. After returning to Edinburgh in 1876 he began a five-year medical studies course. He had started to write short stories and based Sherlock Holmes on a professor who had taught him at university. After graduation he became a GP at Southsea in Hampshire where he wrote *A Study in Scarlet* in 1887 and introduced Holmes to the world.

He returned to Edinburgh again in 1900 to stand unsuccessfully as a Liberal Unionist for a Central Edinburgh seat at Westminster. Back in London and Sussex again he gave up medicine and enjoyed the good life from writing. The sleuth's pipe and deerstalker hat trademarks soon became famous the world over. The books made him very rich and were translated into sixty-six languages. But, stifled by their success, he said it cramped his style and grew to hate Holmes. He killed him off but the public demanded he be brought back and the author had to oblige. The statue, by Gerald Laing, was put up in 1991.

Leith has the inevitable Queen Victoria, and Robert Burns whose statue, instigated by the Leith Burns Club and designed by D.W.

SHERLOCK HOLMES
This creation of Sir Arthur Conan Doyle looks out over Picardy Place where the writer was born.

Stevenson, was last year moved three feet across Bernard Street to allow for road widening!

Another famous literary son – some say the greatest – and one who asked that no statue be erected to him in his native city is **Robert Louis Stevenson** who was born in Howard Place in November 1850 but eventually settled at Heriot Row. He was sick as a young boy with bronchial trouble. He was from a family of engineers but didn't follow their profession. His schooling was interrupted because of ill-health and he was sent abroad to find a cure giving him his first taste of travel. Stevenson had a love-hate relationship with Edinburgh where he went to university. His mind was too active for the course as a civil engineer and he changed to law and although it bored him, he passed his bar examinations in 1875. Stevenson had already done some freelance writing and determined to make this his living. He produced a couple of travel books and that was that – goodbye to the law.

As a young boy Stevenson loved to visit his maternal grandfather, Rev. Lewis Balfour, who was Minister of the parish of Colinton before he died in 1860. Stevenson appreciated the contrast there with the smoky city, writing of the lovely sound of the water and the birds. He called the climate of Edinburgh 'one of the vilest under heaven.' In 1880 he married divorcee Fanny Osbourne, ten years older

ROBERT LOUIS STEVENSON

Not an admirer of statues, he wouldn't be disappointed with this memorial in Princes Street Gardens.

KIDNAPPED

The great writer would no doubt approve of this new work by Alexander Stoddart showing David Balfour and Alan Breck from the famous novel.

than himself. His great literary years followed with *Kidnapped, Treasure Island, Jekyll & Hyde* etc. Still unwell, he moved to the South Coast in 1884 but even Bournemouth's sea air didn't help and he left Britain in 1888 for the South Seas, settling in Samoa. He was popular with the natives who called him Tusitala (weaver of tales). He died there of a cerebral haemorrhage in 1894. He is remembered outside the Scottish & Newcastle headquarters in Corstorphine Road, Murrayfield with a 20 ft statue of two figures from Kidnapped. By Alexander Stoddart, it shows David Balfour and Alan Breck as fugitives fleeing the 1745 Rebellion in the Highlands with a depiction of the writer's profile on the base.

Edinburgh's military connection is apparent throughout the city with, among others, striking memorials to The Royal Scots Greys and King's Own Scottish Borderers. On Princes Street is a **The Royal Scots Greys** figure, a magnificent trooper on horseback commemorating the men who fell in the Boer War (sculptor W. Birnie Rhind).There is also a carving by Pilkington

Jackson to the Royal Scots near here.

Just below in the gardens is an impressive work unveiled in 1927 and gifted to the people of Scotland by Scots who had emigrated to America. The statue entitled **The Call** shows a young soldier sitting with his rifle over his knee and cements the relationship between the two countries. The King's Own

Scottish Borderers is actually on North Bridge; people often rush past it on their way to work or the station.

In Old Calton Cemetery is another military memorial showing the link between the two countries and you may be forgiven at first glance for wondering what **Abraham Lincoln** is doing here. The 15ft high granite sculpture

THE CALL
Edinburgh has many fine military statues and this one is in Princes Street Gardens.

ABRAHAM LINCOLN

What is he doing in Edinburgh's Old Calton Cemetery? – this work commemorates the Scots who fell in the American Civil War and was the first of Abe outside America.

is the burial place of five Scottish soldiers killed in the American Civil War. Lincoln is shown 'emancipating the slave' and, in 1893, was the first statue of Abe seen outside America.

On 7 November 2004 a commemorative stone cairn was unveiled in France in memory of the Scots soldiers who fought in the 1916 battle of the Somme. The memorial at Contalmaison honours the men of the 16th

Royal Scots, including the entire Heart of Midlothian first team in Edinburgh who were football league leaders when they enlisted in November 1914, prompting others to follow suit. More than half the team were killed (a stone plaque was unveiled in Edinburgh's Haymarket in 1922). The Hearts Great War Memorial Appeal raised the money with help from both Edinburgh City Council and the Scottish Executive.

Readers wanting to know more of Scottish history could do no worse than visit the National Portrait Gallery. The gallery was founded in 1882 and since 1889 has been housed in this remarkable red sandstone building on Queen Street modelled on the Doges Palace in Venice. Around the outside of the building are statues of notable Scots including many Royal figures. Also there on the South-East Tower are poets John Barbour, William Dunbar, Gavin Douglas and Sir David Lindsay. The North-East Tower shows James Hutton (geologist), John Hunter (surgeon), Sir Henry Raeburn (portrait painter), Viscount Stair (statesman) and John Napier (inventor). On the western facade can be seen Sir James Douglas (soldier), John Knox (reformer), George Buchanan (humanist), Cardinal Beaton (Archbishop of St Andrews) and the 2nd Duke of Argyll (statesman and soldier).

The main foyer display changes but usually houses a number of busts and statues to famous Scots including Thomas Carlyle, James Watt and Robert Burns and architect William Adams responsible for much of the city's fine architecture including the original design of Hopetoun House.

But it is the frieze above the Central Hall by William Hole whose work gives a unique visual history of Scotland through the paintings of those who shaped it. His paintings of one hundred and fifty two persons from history start with the 19th-century historian Thomas Carlyle and include such diverse characters as Julius Agricola, Roman General and Governor of Scotland.

The film *Chariots of Fire* brought **Eric Liddell** to a wider audience. A statue of the Olympic athlete and Edinburgh University graduate can be seen in the reception area of the University's Old College. In the 1924 Paris Olympics Liddell famously refused to run in the heats of the 100 metres because they were being held on a Sunday. He went on to win the bronze medal in the 200 metres and set a new world record in the 400 metres winning the gold medal. The statue is by Lesley Power and shows Liddell's exaggerated running style with head thrown back. At his graduation ceremony the University Principal Sir Alfred Ewing crowned him with the traditional Olympic victor's crown of wild olive and said: "Mr Liddell, you have shown that no one can pass you but your examiners."

Liddell, the son of two Scottish Missionaries, was born at Tientsin in China in 1902. He became known as The Flying Scotsman but after

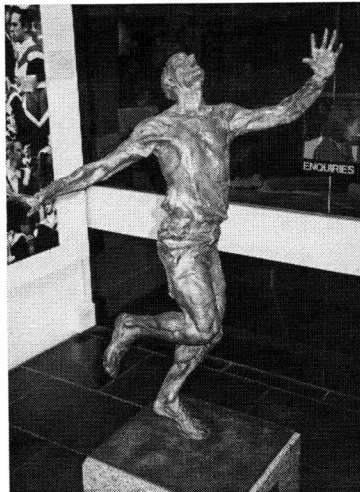

ERIC LIDDELL
Just inside the reception area of the Edinburgh University Old College is this distinctive memory of the Chariots of Fire hero.

his Olympic success, in 1925 he returned to China to work as a missionary for the Scottish Congregational Church. He was interned by the Japanese in World War II and died in internment in 1945 at Weifeng. Another statue to this committed Christian is erected to him there.

Liddell remains a true hero to Scots, displaying all the virtues they admire. When votes were cast for the Scottish Sport Hall of Fame he easily came in first with twice as many votes as anyone else. A Community Centre in Edinburgh bearing his name remembers his work.

At the King's Buildings of Edinburgh University stands **Sir David Brewster** (1781–1868) one of the top scientists and writers of 19th-century Scotland. Born in Jedburgh, he made his name at St Andrews University where he was responsible with friends for the first photographs in Scotland. He was also a great inventor: the lens for lighthouses was his work and the popular toy kaleidoscope. He was also a founder member of The British Association for the Advancement of Science. In 1859, at the age of seventy-nine he became Principal of Edinburgh University.

Outside Edinburgh is

James Braid at Dalmahoy Golf Course. By the first tee of the East championship golf course, it is noteworthy because it is that very rare breed – a wooden statue. It was made by a local company for just £1,500 in 1997 with a chainsaw and is lovingly looked after by the greenkeeping staff. James Braid is one of the Great Triumvirate of Golf – Taylor, Vardon and Braid. He was one of the greatest golfers of all time, winning five Open Championships, and became a celebrated golf course architect, leaving a legacy of wonderful golf courses. Braid was born in Elie, Fife in 1870 and played golf nearly every day until his death in 1950. He designed, reconstructed or advised on an amazing two hundred and fifty golf courses

James Braid, who designed this course, is a statue carved out of wood for a fraction of the cost of a bronze memorial!

throughout the British Isles with his courses at Dalmahoy, Carnoustie and Gleneagles perhaps his best achievements.

As 2006 drew to a close discussions were still continuing on where to commemorate **James Braidwood,** the founding father of firefighting, more than 160 years after his death. He created the first municipal fire service in 1824 at the age of 24 and wrote a book on firefighting that is still used today for training. He also became the first superintendent of London's fire brigade when set up in 1833. The newly formed James Braidwood Memorial Fund was set up at the initiative of 91-year-old former Lothian and Borders fireman Frank Rushbrook CBE who kicked it off with a generous donation. Glasgow sculptor Kenny McKay worked on the statue and fundraising was well advanced. The Fund wanted to see the statue placed near where Braidwood set up the first fire station in the city. The Council favoured a site near the Lothian and Borders HQ in Lauriston Place.

Surely another new statue that would grace the capital's collection is to another of its most renowned literary figures who helped project Edinburgh to a wider audience and died in early 2006. Another statue to a famous *woman* would also find favour with many.

Dame Muriel Spark was born in Edinburgh in 1918; her father was an engineer and her mother a suffragette. She married at age twenty and went to live in Africa but the marriage didn't work and she returned to London in the 1940s to work for the Foreign Office. Her writing skills were first apparent at her Edinburgh school, James Gillespie's High School for Girls and her most successful novel, *The Prime of Miss Jean Brodie* (1962) was based on her experiences there and the teacher Miss Kay. This catapulted her to fame capturing well the atmosphere of the city leading up to the Second World War. The film was so successful that Spark told an Edinburgh Book Festival audience: 'many people thought Maggie Smith wrote the book...'

But she has also written a number of biographies and other novels. She was awarded an OBE in 1967 and became a Dame in 1993. She lived most of her later life in Italy but said she felt very Scottish and was a great Ambassadress for the country. Her career spanned six decades and she has the claim to be one of Scotland's greatest modern writers. Spark always said she considered Edinburgh her home although she left there in 1937. She died in Tuscany in early 2006.

The Muriel Spark Society was founded in Edinburgh in 2001 with her personal blessing and the purpose of spreading enjoyment and appreciation of her work. The Women Writers Committee consider her a real heroine of our times and produced a poster of 'One Hundred Scottish Women Writers – a Scottish Inheritance.' with Spark in pole position. They wrote: 'Death does not level writers. In Scotland gender, more than worth determines memorial tribute. Education, anthology and critical works reveal only half the cannon. This poster reveals the buried half, those great writers diminished because they were women, listed here because they are writers of stature of whom Scotland should be vocally and gloriously proud.'

CHAPTER 3

Moving North to a Land Fit for Heroes

'It is never difficult to distinguish between a Scotsman with a grievance and a ray of sunshine'

P.G. WODEHOUSE

Central Scotland is home to many men and women who have helped shape Scottish history. But towns and cities here do not live in the distant past. Recent years have seen many statues erected to recently-deceased personalities and more are planned. Linlithgow is a good example to the rest of Scotland as to the value of statues and modern thinking. In July 2005, the Council moved very quickly after the well-publicised death of Scottish-Canadian actor John Doohan. He was famous for portraying Scotty of 'Beam Me Up Scotty' fame in the popular TV series *Star Trek*. His fictional character came from Linlithgow and the council saw his potential for tourism, a great example of a council erecting statues for a different reason to the past. Aberdeen is also considering using the character in a similar way.

But perhaps the figure most associated with Linlithgow is the figure most associated with Scotland in the eyes of many people all over the world, **Mary Queen of Scots**. Surprisingly this famous, or infamous lady depending on your opinion, had not been remembered in Scotland with a public statue until 2004. Even then it is in the garden of a museum with a small entrance fee but it certainly worth paying to see the work of sculptor Alan Herriot who also created the striking Black Watch statue at Perth. The statue is in the grounds of Annet House in the High Street and came about through the efforts of certain local individuals who wanted to remember this critical figure from Scotland's past. Local MP Tam Dalyell and his wife, Johnston Press, and Friends of Linlithgow Heritage Trust supported the

LINLITHGOW

Mary Queen of Scots was finally rewarded with a statue in Scotland as late as 2004 with this work of Alan Herriot in the gardens of Annet House.

initiative of the late Tom McGowran OBE, a considerable figure in the town who thought more should be done for Mary Queen of Scots, who was born here. The statue was unveiled by McGowran's widow.

Is she Scotland's greatest-ever heroine or a rather weak and loose-moraled woman? Which ever view you subscribe to, ask any non-Scot the figure they most associate with the country

and they are likely to reply 'Mary Queen of Scots'. With religion being such a divisive issue it is perhaps understandable why more statues are not erected to her in Scotland. Mary Stuart was the daughter of James V and his second wife Marie de Guise-Lorraine and great-grand-daughter of the infamous Henry VIII of England. She was born on 8 December 1542 at Linlithgow Palace just as her father lay dying at Falkland Palace. The infant Queen was promised in marriage to Prince Edward of England in 1543 but the Scots wouldn't allow it to go ahead. She was then offered in marriage by treaty to the Dauphin of France whom she eventually married as a teenager in 1558 and her time in France was to influence her early life. After her husband died in 1561 she returned to Scotland, a country now troubled by the Reformation.

Although she stayed devoutly Roman Catholic she permitted freedom of worship amongst her people and allowed Protestant noblemen a hand in leadership. This caused her to run up against her greatest opponent, John Knox. Wooed by many all over Europe, she chose for her second husband her rather foppish cousin Lord Darnley. He became a drunk and a nuisance and was murdered in 1567. Three months later she was married again, this time to James Hepburn, Earl of Bothwell, who had conspired in the murder of Darnley and 'abducted' the Queen. This cost her support of the nobles of the land and after she was defeated at the Battle of Carberry Hill in 1567 she was imprisoned in Loch Leven Castle by the Earl of Moray. There she was forced to abdicate in favour of her son James VI.

She managed to escape but her followers were defeated again at the Battle of Langside and she crossed into England where she thought she would find favour and protection from her cousin Elizabeth I. She didn't and became a prisoner. The English Queen agonized over what to do with Mary as her advisers kept warning of the threat the Scottish Queen posed. These advisers eventually falsely implicated Mary in a plot by Catholics against Elizabeth who finally signed the death warrant. Mary was executed for treason at Fotheringay Castle on 8 February 1587. At first she was buried at Peterborough Castle but

when her son became James I of England he had his mother's body transferred to Westminster Abbey

'Remember Bannockburn' is the cry every time Scots want to put one over on the English – mostly heard at sporting contests now. The Battle of Bannockburn is one of the defining moments in Scottish history and although the site is now rather run-down, it is rightly described as part of the very fabric of the nation. In 1314 in this battlefield near Stirling, King **Robert the Bruce** routed the English forces of King Edward II and

BANNOCKBURN
Perhaps the most iconic statue in all Scotland, sculptor Pilkington Jackson has created a masterpiece fit for this Scottish hero, King Robert The Bruce.

won Scotland's freedom. The immortal words recounted here echo with every Scottish schoolchild: 'We fight not for glory, nor for wealth, nor honour, but only and alone we fight for freedom which no good man surrenders but with his life.' The iconic statue by Pilkington Jackson stands commanding great views over the battlefield although the surrounding displays suffer from a lack of money and maintenance.

After the battle of Falkirk in 1298, William Wallace, depressed at losing so many comrades, resigned as Guardian of Scotland and two new guardians were appointed. They were Robert Bruce and John Comyn the Red from the two main families of Scotland. Bruce's father died in 1304 and in 1306 the feud between the two families exploded with Bruce stabbing Comyn to death in the Greyfriars monastery in the centre of Dumfries. Bruce's coronation was on Friday 25 March 1306 at Scone Palace. His wife Elizabeth was Queen, but the shadow of Edward of England was across the land. England and Scotland's relationship was at its lowest point. Soon after, his wife, sister and daughter were captured and kept in awful

conditions. His brother Nigel was hung, drawn and beheaded. The Pope considered Bruce's killing of Comyn in a religious building to be sacrilege and excommunicated him. But still Bruce vowed to regain his kingdom, revenge for family treatment, and freedom for all Scots.

Bannockburn happened because Robert's brother, Edward, struck a deal with the English governor of Stirling Castle that he had one year for the English to save him or the castle would fall to the Scots. The English came, led by Edward Longshanks but in what numbers is a matter for conjecture: maybe twenty thousand foot soldiers and archers and two thousand five hundred heavy cavalry plus hangers-on. Bruce had around six thousand spearmen and five hundred horsemen but no heavy cavalry. He was outnumbered three-to-one but had plenty of time to organize provisions and drill the troops. The English massed at Berwick, reinforced with bowmen from Wales and foot soldiers from Ireland. Bruce had his men near Stirling where the Bannockburn Heritage Centre now stands. It was the second day of 24 June 1314. Bruce split his men into four divisions, led by himself, his brother Edward, Randolph Earl of Moray and James Douglas whose father had been saved by Bruce. He was nicknamed Black Douglas and had a fearsome reputation. The whole army dropped on one knee to pray to God for victory – King Edward thinking they were praying for mercy.

The Scots advanced, clerics displaying the *breacbannoch*, a casket shaped like a house said to contain the bones of either St Andrew or St Columba. The Bruce statue faces where the English advanced. Bruce struck the first fatal blow at an English knight, Sir Henry de Bohun, who burst out of trees to surprise him. The Scottish spearman fought hard, bringing horses and heavily armoured men crashing down and the burn ran red with blood. Scots cleverly fought in tight areas so that not all the superior numbered English could join the battle and with a Scots victory in sight, Edward fled toward Stirling Castle They said they wouldn't admit him for the safety of all and he kept fleeing only managing to avoid the pursuing Scots by taking a boat at Dunbar over

to Northumberland. It was said by the end of the slaughter the Bannock Burn was so full of dead you could walk over it dryshod.

Some of the top English military commanders were captured and ransomed in return for Bruce's wife Queen Elizabeth, his daughter and sister and Bishop Wishart who had been held hostage. Edward Bruce and Black Douglas continued to spread mayhem for the English. Englishwomen would sing their children to sleep with 'Hush ye, hush ye, little pet ye/Hush ye, hush ye, do not fret ye/The Black Douglas shall not get ye'.

Bruce's legend grew after Bannockburn. On 6 April 1320 The Declaration of Arbroath was signed by eight earls and thirty one barons. This was a memorable year for Bruce, his wife produced a girl named Maud, thought unlikely after a long imprisonment. Other children followed including a son. The Pope received the Declaration of Arbroath and wanted peace between the two warring countries but the latest Edward of England wanted war again like his father and marched north with another big army. It was a disaster; he was chased back into England where he narrowly escaped. Bruce's Queen Elizabeth died on 26 October 1327 just three days before peace negotiations were held at Newcastle.

Bruce eventually got the sovereignty of Scotland he had fought so long and hard for. The Treaty of Edinburgh was signed on 17 March 1328 but Bruce was now ill and died a year later on 7 June 1329 one month before his fifty-fifth birthday. On his deathbed he said he wanted his heart removed on death and taken on a crusade to the Holy Land, presented at the Holy Sepulchre in Jerusalem and returned for burial within Melrose Abbey. Bruce asked his friends to choose a man to carry this out and they wanted Douglas who, in tears, agreed to his king's request. Bruce was buried in Dunfermline Abbey next to his wife. Douglas carried the heart in a silver casket around his neck as he fought the Moors in Spain, only to lose his life there. The heart was found and taken back to Scotland according to the king's wishes.

Stirling certainly remembers its local heroes well. On the castle esplanade is another statue of Bruce, a Victorian memory designed by George Cruikshank and sculptor Andrew Currie. He stands 11ft tall looking toward Bannockburn and sheathing his sword. This castle is well worth a leisurely visit; it is certainly one of the most stunning in Scotland and has the Chapel Royal where Mary Queen of Scots was crowned in September 1543. Stirling council offices have statues of Bruce and Wallace as you go in one door. The castle esplanade also has a memorial to members of the **Argyll and Sutherland** regiment who fell in the South African War of 1902, a kilted soldier in bronze by W. Hubert Paton.

In Dumbarton Road there are several monuments in the gardens worth seeing. They include a bronze statue to Robert Burns by sculptor Albert H. Hodge of London and the gift of David Bayne, Provost of Stirling in 1914. There are inscribed plaques with scenes on them and the lines 'Then Gently Can/Your Brother Man/ Still Gather/ That Ling'ring Star'. Liberal Party Prime Minister **Sir Henry Campbell Bannerman** is also remembered here, in robes of the Order of The Bath, by Paul R. Montford of London.

Also famous in these parts was outlaw **Rob Roy** and there is a striking statue of

Top Left

STIRLING

Robert The Bruce looks out over old battlegrounds from Stirling Castle.

Top Right

STIRLING

MPS were probably more popular in the old days. Sir Henry Campbell Bannerman did become Prime Minister and resides in Dumbarton Road.

Bottom Left

STIRLING

The Castle Esplanade is where you will find W. Hubert Paton's bronze to the old Argyll & Sutherland Regiment.

Bottom Right

STIRLING

The outlaw Rob Roy was used as a threat to misbehaving children by parents warning 'behave or Rob Roy McGregor will come and get you...'

SCOTLAND'S HEROES

63

him by Benno Schotz. He stands on a rocky cairn brandishing a sword. Rob Roy or Robert MacGregor (1671–1734) was the second son of Donald Macgregor of Glengyle. Until 1661 the Wicked Clan Gregor had for a century been in trouble but Rob Roy was living quietly as a grazier at Balquidder. However, as his lands were plundered he had to employ a band of armed followers for defence. In 1691 he espoused the Jacobite cause, purchased land from his nephew and proclaimed himself chief. His lands were then seized in turn, his cattle taken. He borrowed money from the Duke of Montrose but couldn't repay the debt, his houses were plundered and so he declared war on the Duke of Montrose and in 1715 fought at the Battle of Sheriffmuir.

He got into a number of scrapes and the Duke of Argyll gave him protection. In 1717 he was arrested and sentenced to transportation but then pardoned. He received the King's Pardon and died on 31 January 1734 at Inverlocharig Beag at the head of the Glen of Balquhidder. When he lay dying he was visited by his old enemy John Maclaren and is supposed to have said:

STIRLING

John Cowane over the doorway of his hospital.

'I forgive my enemies, especially John Maclaren,' quietly whispering to his son Robin, 'but you see to him.' The visit exhausted him and when the visitor left he said to Mary: 'The piper, bring him in to play *I Return No More*.' He died, aged sixty-four, as the song was being played. Robin shot Maclaren dead a few months later.

Sir Walter Scott's Rob Roy was published in 1818. The Rob Roy Visitor Centre at Callander tells the story of this Scottish equivalent of Robin Hood who may certainly have robbed from the rich but only to help the poor.

Over the handsome doorway of Cowane's Hospital in Stirling is a

SCOTLAND'S HEROES

painted statue of **John Cowane** with the inscription 'This hospital was erected and largely provided by John Cowane, Deane of Gild for the entertainment of decayed Gild Bretheren 1639. Also Matthew 25 verse 35. For I was an ahungered, and ye gave me meat: I was thirsty and ye gave me drink; I was a stranger and ye took me in.' The legend is that just after the bells have tolled midnight on New Year's Eve the statue of Cowane, known as Auld Staney Breeks, comes down to dance in the courtyard. If children want to know why he didn't appear parents say he was obviously deafened over the years by the constant noise of the bells!

The Valley Cemetery Stirling is full of interesting statues including a strange one near the Holy Rude Church to **Margaret Wilson and Margaret McLaughlin.** Within a glass octagonal dome are the figures of these two seated Presbyterian sisters. When Elizabeth 1 of England determined to stamp out extremist Covenanters there were many martyrs and these two ladies were tied to stakes and drowned by the incoming sea. Also recognized on the memorial is the younger Wilson sister Agnes who was saved when her

father paid a considerable sum to spare her because of her teenage years. In the cemetery are many other interesting statues by Andrew Handyside Ritchie, including badly vandalised ones of John Knox and James Renwick, the last Covenant martyr.

But most people come to this area for one remarkable memorial to Scotland's national hero and its greatest

STIRLING

In the Valley Cemetery sisters Margaret Wilson and Margaret McLaughlin are covered by a glass dome.

historical figure, **William Wallace.** There are in fact over twenty statues of Wallace around the country. The National Wallace monument is just outside Stirling on Abbey Craig. It was from a vantage point at the summit of this hill that Wallace watched the English army cross the Stirling Bridge. He then rallied his troops and fought a famous victory. The monument, built between 1861 and 1869 is two hundred and twenty feet high and has two hundred and forty-six steps, taking eight years to complete and costing over £10,000. A mood of nationalism was sweeping Europe at this time and the money was raised by expatriate Scots with many international figures contributing towards the construction.

Above the main entrance is the impressive Wallace Statue sculpted by D.W. Stevenson and everything you want to know about Braveheart is there including the Wallace Sword.

Wallace was born at Elderslie in 1270. His father had refused to pay homage to Edward. At the age of twenty-six William murdered the English Sheriff of Lanark which sparked off his campaign to rid Scotland of the English. He raised an army which carried out guerrilla warfare in the forests of Scotland at first before spreading into a national rebellion against the hated enemy.

After his devastating defeat of Edward Longshanks in 1297 at the Battle of Stirling Bridge and taking of Stirling Castle, he was made Guardian of

Braveheart by Tom Church is a recent addition to the Wallace Monument and very popular with tourists for photographs.

Scotland. But peace did not last for long as Edward wanted revenge. Making York his headquarters, and with an army of twelve thousand five hundred soldiers, he marched into Scotland and defeated Wallace and his men at the Battle of Falkirk. But Wallace survived and the war continued and with several Scottish nobles submitting to Edward, Wallace was hunted down and betrayed. Put on trial at Westminster Great Hall in London he was accused of betraying a King whom he had never acknowledged. He was sentenced to the most barbaric of deaths, dragged through the streets to Smithfield to be hung, drawn and quartered. His severed limbs were sent to Newcastle, Berwick, Perth and Aberdeen as a deterrent to troublesome Scots. But he paved the way for freedom finally won by Robert the Bruce and his memory received a fillip with the Mel Gibson film *Braveheart* which, although not historically totally accurate, attracted great audiences.

Many myths have grown up around Scotland's greatest patriotic hero. The main source for tales of this nationalist is Blind Harry who wrote about Wallace almost two hundred years after his death using references never proved. However such was the impact of Wallace's fight for freedom that the work, one of the very first to be published in Scotland, was reprinted time and time again over the centuries. In 1722 an edition became the most commonly owned book in Scotland after the Bible.

Wallace was a big man as anyone seeing the sword he wielded will agree. He was also clearly someone with a big personality, a born leader and a man of the people who fell out with the nobles of the period. It is no wonder Scots still adore him. The Hollywood movie inspired triple-heart-bypass survivor Tommy Church from Brechin to create his Freedom Statue by the entrance to the monument. This thirteen-ton sandstone structure was carved in his spare time and unveiled by author Nigel Tranter on 11 September 1997, the 700th anniversary of the Battle of Stirling Bridge. Receiving much criticism, but popular for tourist photographs, it is now for sale.

On Level Two of the Monument is the Hall of Heroes created following a worldwide appeal by the custodians of the monument in 1885 for 'marble statues of very notable Scotsmen.' This led to an original sixteen busts being installed representing prominent Scottish figures from military, scientific and literary backgrounds. An audio-visual presentation pays tribute to heroes and heroines of the 20th century.

There are many famous Fifers and Dunfermline has its fair share of them. However one man and one name stands out more than any other. **Andrew Carnegie** (1835–1919) is the world's best-known philanthropist and for a time the world's richest man. By the time of his death he had given away the equivalent of $US350 million to provide free libraries, church organs, schools and colleges. The Trusts and Foundations he set up in Britain and America still distribute over $150 every minute. His is an extraordinary rags-to-riches story, from very humble beginnings to the richest man in the world.

The son of a jacquard loom weaver, Carnegie was largely self-educated and to escape a life of poverty following his emigration to America in 1848 started work at a steel mill in Pittsburgh. He went on to make millions in the steel industry, controlling most of the American iron and steel production. He never forgot his home town and in 1903 founded the Carnegie Dunfermline Trust 'to bring into the monotonous lives of the toiling masses of Dunfermline more of sweetness and light'. He made funds available for workers' pensions, schools, church organs and building of libraries. He must have had a sense of mischief and delight when he bought Pittencrieff Estate because he had been refused admittance there when a child – he gave it to the town. Carnegie once said that to die rich is to die disgraced. His statue by Richard Goulden stands

DUNFERMLINE

Andrew Carnegie looks down over the town he endowed with such riches.

there and his generosity is remembered all over this attractive and historic town.

The Hill of Beath is near Cowdenbeath and here is footballing legend **Jim Baxter.** This charismatic character figures in many World XI of All Time selections. Certainly he is revered amongst Scottish followers of the game for one act in particular: playing 'keepy-uppy' at Wembley the year after England had won the World Cup in 1966. Scotland became the first team to beat the reigning World Champions.

Baxter was born in 1939 and went on to be capped thirty-four times by Scotland. His slim figure was worshipped in Glasgow where he was seen to burn the candle at both ends but still play like a god every Saturday. He stood 5ft 11ins but only weighed 9st 12lbs and cynics say they never saw him make a tackle in his life. He didn't head the ball, couldn't use his right foot and people right at the touchline swear they could still smell the drink off him as he passed them. But he became an iconic figure in the game, a game he left at the age of thirty. He died tragically young in 2001. Appropriately his statue, by Andy Scott, stands in front of Hill of Beath Hawthorn Junior FC and was unveiled by local MP, the Chancellor Gordon Brown in 2003. The £80,000 money required was raised within two years which shows the affection for Baxter, coming from sportsmen's nights, suppers and donations from Rangers Supporters Clubs.

This is old coal-mining country and at Kelty there is a memorial to the Kelty Miners commemorating all those who lost their lives in the pits. The statue is by David Annand.

Not far away is a man who was known as Fife's own 'Master and Commander' and grew up in the small seaside village of

Culross. **Admiral Lord Thomas Cochrane** was the inspiration for C.S. Forester's fictional hero Horatio Hornblower. Born in Hamilton, he moved to Culross at the age of three and at the age of fifteen learned seamanship aboard his uncle's ship, *The Hind*. His glittering naval career lasted over sixty years and he served with such distinction in the Napoleonic Wars that the French Emperor dubbed him 'The Sea Wolf'. He served all over the world, helped command the Chilean, Brazilian and Greek navies in their fight for independence and is still revered in Latin America. A tall figure by any standards, 6ft 5in with bright red hair, he certainly stood out in the 18th century.

He was also a noted inventor with gas lights, barbed wire and the torpedo amongst his creations. He introduced street lighting to a part of London and also introduced the use of sulphur gas in warfare. In 1805 he entered parliament as an independent MP standing against corruption which was ironic because he was wrongly convicted of fraud in 1814 when he was imprisoned, struck off the Navy and stripped of all honours. He had fallen out with the establishment. He eventually received a full pardon from Queen Victoria in 1832. He lived until the age of eighty-five when he was accorded a burial place in Westminster Abbey. In the summer of 2004 a large bust of Cochrane sculpted by Scott Sutherland in 1968 was placed in front of the village's town house. Founder of the unique fighting force the SAS, **Sir David Stirling** (1915–1990) is recognised near his family home of Doune with a 9ft bronze statue unveiled in June 2002. He joined the Scots Guards in 1939 but seeking more excitement became a commando and went on to great feats of bravery in North Africa seeing the need for a small mobile unit and created the Special Air Service before being imprisoned in Colditz. Field Marshal Montgomery who led the Allied forces in the desert said: "The boy Stirling is quite mad, quite, quite mad. However, in war there is often a place for mad people." The unit was disbanded at the end of the war but reformed with the Malaya crisis and living up to its reputation as Who Dares Wins. He was awarded the OBE and DSO and knighted the year he died.

Round the coast a little is the small fishing village of Lower Largo, forever associated with **Robinson Crusoe.** Daniel Defoe's famous book was inspired by a sailor from the village, Alexander Selkirk. It is also probably unique in the world of figure sculpture because recently you could have bought the statue – it is on the wall of a small house which was for sale in the summer of 2005 with offers over £50,000. Selkirk was born in 1676 and at the age of nineteen went to sea to try legalized piracy against Spanish ships on the high seas. He was a very skilful sailor and became Sailing Master on the Cinque Ports.

Lower Largo is now officially twinned with the South American tropical island seven hundred miles off Chile where Selkirk was put ashore in September 1704 after falling out with the ship's captain. It was originally named Juan Fernandez Island but the Chilean government changed the name to realize the tourism potential. He lived as a castaway there for four years and four months before being rescued by two British ships who dropped anchor nearby. In 1713 he published an account of his adventures

LOWER LARGO
Daniel Defoe's classic Robinson Crusoe was inspired by a sailor from this Fife village.

and his story inspired Daniel Defoe to write the classic story in 1719. Robinson Crusoe Island only has five hundred inhabitants now.

The figure of Crusoe on the statue is six feet high and is dressed in a rough coat of goat skins and short ragged breeches and sandals with leather thongs. He carries a long lock pistol and an axe in his belt with an old Scottish claymore to hand. A goatskin cap is on his head. The inscription is 'Erected by David Gillies, fishing net manufacturer to Andrew Selkirk who died 1723 aged forty-seven years on the site of this cottage where Selkirk was born.' The statue is by T. Stuart Burnett and it was unveiled in 1885 by the Earl and Countess of Aberdeen. A good crowd gathered and a procession through the town was led by figures dressed as Robinson Crusoe and Man Friday on horseback led by the Lower Largo brass band.

St Andrews, seat of learning and Home of Golf has a long and fascinating history recounted in the town's Kinburn Museum. As well as religious pilgrims, golfers have their pilgrimage here for years and the two memorials worth seeing recognize both these groups. In the grounds of the Botanic Gardens stands an 8ft high statue of **Saint Andrew** in front of his saltire. It is a copy of one by Francois Duquesnoy (1594–1643) which stands in a niche on a pilaster in the Cupola of St Peter in Rome.

Duquesnoy was born in Brussels but studied and worked as a sculptor in Italy. He was a contemporary of the more famous Lorenzo Bernini who created the great colonade in front of St Peters – commissioned by Pope Urban VIII.

This statue, now going slightly green from its verdant surroundings, is believed to have been sculpted by Alexander Handyside Ritchie (1804–70) who was born in Musselburgh, went to school in Edinburgh, and studied art and sculpture in Rome. It was commissioned by the North British Mercantile and Insurance Company (now defunct) for above the main doorway of their offices at 64 Princes Street in Edinburgh in 1850. When

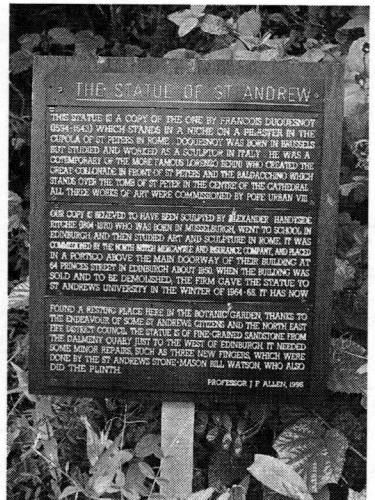

ST ANDREWS

Where else would you expect to find the Patron Saint of Scotland?

the building was demolished at the beginning of 1965 they gave the statue to St Andrews University. There it lay unnoticed for many years until discovered by local teacher Callum McLeod who arranged for it to be repaired (it is made of local sandstone from an Edinburgh quarry) and erected. Some say it should be placed in a more prominent position at the beginning of the main entrance to the town. Another suggestion as a site is in the grounds of the ruined cathedral where there are the graves of **Tom Morris,** and Young Tom who also has a relief statue above his burial place. Father and son helped make this town synonymous with golf and their memorials are often adorned with golfing items placed there by visitors, particularly Americans.

Old Tom Morris (1821–1908) was born in St Andrews and apprenticed to the famous golf ball- maker Allan Robertson. After marriage he moved to Prestwick on the West Coast and laid out their links which hosted the first ever Open Championship. The Royal & Ancient brought him back to the Old Grey Toon in 1865 and appointed him Keeper of the Green on a salary of £50

ST ANDREWS
Tom Morris was appointed Keeper of the Green here in 1865 at £50 a year salary.

a year. Morris won The British Championship belt four times and also laid out many other courses. His son, the better golfer with a better record, died tragically before him, and also won four times in succession. He won in 1868, 1869, 1870 and 1872; there was no contest in 1871. Old Tom died falling into the cellar on the New Club alongside the links, mistaking it for the toilet. There is a full-size statue of him in the Golf Museum behind the R & A clubhouse. It was commissioned by the Golf Course Superintendents' Association of America to commemorate their seventy-fifth anniversary and donated to the museum in 2002. The sculpture is by American

Home to racing ace
Jim Clark who
strides along the
pavement
purposefully here.

Brad Pearson who manages
to balance a full-time job as
greenkeeper at Holdrege
Country Club in Nebraska
with part-time sculpting.

As you would expect in
the Home of Golf there
is another renowned figure
from the game remembered
with a statue. In the
restaurant of the luxurious
St Andrews Bay Resort and
Spa just outside town is a
statue to the great American
Gene Sarazen.

Scots are in the first rank
of speed merchants and one
of the most famous and
heroic is **Jim Clark.** He was
Scotland's first Formula One
world champion and one of
the very greatest Grand Prix
drivers of all time. Clark was
born on 4 March 1936 in

Kilmany, a small village in
Fife. When he was six the
family moved to Berwickshire
where his father became a
farmer outside the village of
Chirnside. He helped his
father on the farm but his
love of motors and speed –
and ownership of a Sunbeam
Talbot Mk 3 Saloon – led
him to local rallies.

His talent was obvious
for all to see and with fellow
farmer Ian Scott-Wilson he
started the Border Reivers
Motor Racing Club. He
progressed to a D-Type
Jaguar and competed in the
1958 Spa Grand Prix. The
following year Clark. made
his debut at Le Mans and his
career was underway. In
1960 he joined Team Lotus
under the renowned Colin
Chapman driving a Lotus 18
and in 1962 took second
place in the Formula One
World Championships. That
was the start and he went on
to win two World
Championships in 1963 and
1965 as well as becoming the
first Briton to win the
gruelling Indianapolis 500, in
1965. Clark won twenty-five
Grand Prix events beating the
great Fangio's record of
twenty-four. On a wet
morning in April 1968 he
was killed whilst racing at
Hockenheim in Germany in a
minor event where his car

went off the track at 150 mph and into trees; a death that brought about the modern safety requirements in motor racing.

After his death his parents gifted the majority of his trophies to Duns Town Council where the Jim Clark Room attracts many visitors. This museum of memories to a great driver was opened in 1993 by Jackie Stewart, another Scottish motor racing star who shared a flat with Clark for a while in London and called the older man his inspiration. However it is Kilmany that gives the most emotive memory of the racing hero. As you drive into the village and turn a corner there you will see a life-size figure of Clark striding along the grass verge, a good example of how statues can blend with the landscape. The sculptor, David Annand, lives in the village.

Two statues with 'royal' connections are in this area. Falkland Palace was built in 1539 for James V and has the oldest Royal Tennis Court in the country where Mary Queen of Scots shocked her courtiers by wearing breeches to play. By the church in the square is another life-size bronze of **Oneispherus Tyndall-Bruce** who was one of the Keepers of The Palace.

This man with the splendid name was a barrister from England. When the Falkland Estate was in serious decline in 1876 he poured money into the estate rebuilding the parish church and building the House of Falkland and the Bruce Fountain. His statue is by Sir John Steell and there are two others here, to Dr John Bruce and Colonel Bruce.

Auchtermuchty became known to readers of John Junor's column in the *Sunday Express* as the barometer of political opinion in the country. It was also home to **Jimmy Shand** (1908–2000) the world renowned master of the Scottish accordion who delighted dance goers for so many years. This miner's son from Fife sold millions of records and became a true music legend in his lifetime; he lived until he was ninety-two. After

AUCHTERMUCHTY
Home to the legendary Jimmy Shand whose statue was unveiled by his son (left) and sculptor David Annand.

Sir Jimmy Shand MBE died on 23 December 2000 some of his closest friends obtained approval from the Shand family to raise the £40,000 necessary for Fife sculptor David Annand to create a life-sized bronze sculpture of the musical maestro.

The sculpture depicts him in the Fifties and Sixties when the band was touring the world playing to huge and appreciative audiences. Tremendous generosity was shown in the fund-raising by Scottish and Irish Dance Bands, well-known entertainers, accordion and fiddle clubs, branches of the Royal Scottish Country Dance Society, Masonic Lodges, Burns Clubs, Probus, Scottish societies everywhere and just friends of Sir Jimmy. The money was raised quickly and shows how energy and hard work can still produce results for recently departed heroes.

It stands on Upper Greens, Auchtermuchty and was unveiled on 12 September 2003 by his son.

The inscription reads Happy to Meet – Sorry to Part – Happy to Meet Again – and shows him playing his Hahner Special accordion in a pose chosen as a family favourite. A large crowd gathered at the ceremony swapping tales of his feet-tapping music and remembering many of his concerts including Royal Variety Performances and his advice, 'keep it simple, son'.

CHAPTER 4

Across The Tay for Soldiers, Traitors and Children

'My Lady, there are few more impressive sights in the world than a Scotsman on the make'

J.M. BARRIE

Perth sits in a lovely setting alongside the River Tay and Sir Walter Scott called it "the most varied and beautiful city in Scotland". In November 2004 a nationwide Campaign for Courtesy decided after two years of research that the city should be known as Polite Perth, one of the most courteous cities in Scotland. Perthshire is also known for magnificent trees and is a favourite spot for tourists. But it has also been an angry city. In 2005 the future of the Black Watch was in doubt along with other famous Scottish regiments. A decision was made to form a new Royal Regiment of Scotland from six existing regiments. The Royal Scots, The King's Own Scottish Borderers, The Royal Highland Fusiliers, The Argyll & Sutherland Highlanders, The

Highlanders, and the Black Watch would merge and lose their proud history. At first it was said each battalion would keep their individual caps and badges but later this was changed. The Black Watch were to lose their distinctive red hackle for public parade. A commentator at the time said 'this whole episode has been a depressing litany of half-truths, cover-ups, broken promises and an enormous amount of bad faith'.

The Black Watch were sent at the end of October 2004 to the dangerous Babil province south of Baghdad. The Iraq War to depose Sadam Hussein had effectively ended so the decision caused much resentment. Their commanding officer Lt. Col James Cowan, trying to calm the situation at the time said: "There has been much

The Black Watch
were incorporated
into the new Royal
Regiment of
Scotland in 2006
much to the fury of
it's veteran soldiers.

sensationalist talk about the threat we will face. Frankly this regiment beat Napoleon, beat the Kaiser and beat Hitler. For the Jocks of the Black Watch this is just the latest chapter in our history and another job to be done." Sadly the chapter closed with the loss of lives. Within a week of their arrival three members of the Black Watch were killed in a suicide bombing.

There are a number of statues around Scotland to the **Black Watch** but the

Perth memorial one formed the focal point of a campaign to save the regiment. The regiment is commemorated with a striking statue unveiled in May 1995, a day of tears and celebration and marking the 50th anniversary of VE Day. The tribute to the men of the 51st Highland Division takes the form of a little Dutch girl presenting a posy to a Highland piper during the liberation of her village. Over two thousand veterans and ten thousand spectators gathered at the North Inch to see the distinctive statue unveiled after a moving ceremony at the Wellshill Cemetery where two hundred Polish and sixty-five British war dead are buried. Pipe Major Peter Snaddon, 3 Black Watch, played the haunting *The Flowers of the Forest*.

The statue, by Alan Herriot and unveiled by Provost Jean McCormack, is an exact replica of the original erected in Holland to commemorate their liberation by the Scottish soldiers. As one veteran commented: "Perth has done us proud. We will never forget it." There is another Black Watch Memorial on the banks of the River Tay at Aberfeldy not too far away, erected in 1887 to mark the rising of the regiment, the 42nd

Regiment of the Line. The Watch was originally created in 1667 by several of the clan chiefs to help secure peace in the Highlands and has an illustrious history. Their fighting men so impressed the German soldiers in World War Two they were known as 'the ladies from hell'.

In Perth there are also statues to Sir Walter Scott and Prince Albert. Nearby is Scone Palace, the crowning place of many Scottish Kings, and birthplace of David Douglas, botanist and explorer, who gave his name to the Douglas fir and is remembered here with a permanent exhibition. Douglas died young, only aged 35, in Hawaii when he fell into a wild cattle trap and was gored to death by a bull.

Sculptor Alan Herriot is also responsible for one of the newest statues in Scotland. In October 2006 at The House of Bruar off the A9 near Blair Atholl there is another military memorial. The Veterans of the 51st Highlanders were instrumental in organizing this soldier in full dress with pipes to commemorate these proud fighters.

Dundee is the City of Discovery and is certainly discovering itself as it undergoes a facelift to try and rid itself of its declining fortune as the City of Jute, Jam and Journalism. It is also a major centre for cancer research in the UK. Dundee's central waterfront has been described by the local newspaper as ... 'for the best part of 30 years standing seemingly as a monument to the ugliest aspects of modern architecture. Dundee's central waterfront area is a collection of widely despised buildings and badly laid-out roads, managing to create dirty coal from what should be a diamond of a setting on the banks of the Tay Estuary'.

Now the City Council has come up with ambitious and costly plans to renovate the whole area over the next twelve years in a £270 million project. Regeneration is the key word for Dundee now. It also has an inspirational public arts programme led by the energetic John Gray, the Town Planning Officer and the driving force behind the innovative resurgence of public art in the city. Many interesting new sculptures have gone up alongside the old faithfuls, the most striking of which are two comic characters to be found in the main shopping street.

Desperate Dan is the work of Tony Morrow and the

Desperate Dan
and Minnie the Minx
are landmarks in the
centre of town.

accompanying **Minnie the Minx** was made by his partner Susie Morrow, working as a team on the striking sculpture. Tony was also responsible for the nearby dragon figure which makes this a popular area for children. The statue of Dan dates from July 2001 and when presented with the work, the Powderhall Foundry said the eight feet high statue would topple over forwards as Dan's stomach was too large from eating too many cow heel pies. Therefore a dog, not originally a character in the comic stories, was added to the statue for balance.

Dan first appeared in the *Dandy* comic on 4 December 1937. There have been plans to retire Dan, notably a few years ago when he sailed off with the Spice Girls but a storm of protest brought him back. In 2004 D.C. Thomson, the Dundee-based publishers of the world's longest-running comic, announced an update of characters including its first black family. But Dan remained unscathed although he lost his gun and some of his portly stomach. Sales of two million a week in the 1950s have declined to around fifty thousand but there are said to be still over four hundred thousand loyal readers.

The Dragon close by is famous from local folklore as having killed nine daughters of a local farmer before being put to flight. It was designed by Alistair Smart who died before completion and was finished by Tony Morrow who had been a pupil of his and worked from the original maquette.

The controversial bronze of **Admiral Adam Duncan** nearby was made by Janet Scrymegour Wedderburn and, it has to be said, is not universally loved. The commissioners who moved this project forward had not been involved in such an operation before and selected the artist because she was related to the Duncan family.

The City's Public Art Programme, on hearing of the project when it was over halfway to completion offered help and the advice of a professional sculptor. This was declined and Janet, self-trained and with a good reputation for figurines, finished the work to her design. Critics say Duncan was a man of impressive stature even by today's standards, never mind in the period he lived, and that the statue does not reflect this. There is also conjecture as to what he is actually doing with his telescope.

Doubts were also expressed over the eventual site of the work, rather dwarfed by the Cathedral behind it. However, the statue stands in the High Street near the Admiral's birthplace in Seagate. It was unveiled on 11 October 1997, the 200th anniversary of the Battle of Camperdown, the Admiral's finest achievement. At over seven foot high on a five foot plinth and weighing between four and five tons it is certainly imposing. Admiral Lord Horatio Nelson credits Duncan with teaching him his craft and helping him win the Battle of Trafalgar. Duncan's finest hour was destroying the Dutch fleet at the Battle of Camperdown off the coast of Holland in 1797, thereby preventing a Napoleonic invasion of Britain.

Duncan was born in 1731 and joined the navy aged fifteen. He commanded *The Valiant* in the sack of Havana in 1762. He then commanded the *Monarch* at Cape St Vincent in 1780. In 1795 when Holland and France were at war with Britain, he took command as Admiral of the North Sea Squadron to watch for the Dutch fleet. A mutiny over pay spread to his ships but he went on to win a famous battle over Dutch Admiral De Winter. He was commanding a British fleet which engaged a much bigger Dutch enemy but the Dutch

DUNDEE

Controversial in design and location, Admiral Adam Duncan stands in front of the Cathedral although other sites were suggested.

admiral admitted defeat after losing 2000 men. The French troops poised to invade England were left stranded. His victory earned him the title Viscount Duncan of Camperdown and areas of his home town changed their name in his honour. He was Scotland's greatest admiral.

There is a fine memorial to Queen Victoria's Consort, Albert, in the shape of a magnificent building in the centre of Albert Square, originally the Albert Institute and now the McManus Galleries (currently closed for refurbishment). It was built in 1865–67 to designs by Sir George Gilbert Scott. Dundee was bankrupt at the time so the project was financed by private sources and largely bankrolled by the Baxter family. This is where you will find the main statues in the city. On one corner is an imposing statue of **Robert Burns** by Sir John Steell, the same as one in Dunedin, New Zealand and New York showing Burns seated holding a quill pen. It is set on a polished Peterhead granite pedestal with base course and cornice, and a grey granite plinth. Even although there is fencing around the statue it often suffers from graffiti or advertising posters stuck on it. In fact there used to be a number of plaques in Dundee commemorating past citizens but vandalism means many have been removed.

The Burns statue is a little worn but understandably perhaps – it was erected in October 1880. The inscription below is from one of Burns' *Thou Lingering Star*, a melancholy song composed around 1789 on the third anniversary of the death of his great love Mary Campbell (Highland Mary.).

DUNDEE

This pose of Robert Burns by Sir John Steell holding a quill pen is repeated in Dunedin and New York statues.

It reads: 'Thou ling'ring star with less'ning ray/ that lov'st to greet the early morn /again thou usher'st in the day /my Mary from my soul was torn'.

Also here is a bronze of **James Carmichael**, a noted engineer (1776–1853) and erected twenty-three years after his death. This was sculpted by John Hutchison with appropriate cylinder and fan blower. Another Sir John Steell creation is **George Kinloch**. The pedestal is inscribed: 'George Kinloch of Kinloch, outlawed for the advocacy of popular rights 22 December 1819. Proclaimed member for Dundee in the first reformed Parliament in 1832. Born Dundee 1775, died London 1833. Erected by public subscription to commemorate a signal triumph of political justice, 3 February 1872.' Wherever Albert is then Queen Victoria is bound to be also and this is no exception. There is a massive statue of Her Majesty here by the sculptor Harry Bates who sadly died just after finishing the work and before it was put on site and unveiled.

Lovers of more contemporary art will also see many examples around the streets and buildings of this Angus city but budget restrictions mean we will

DUNDEE
Also by Steell, George Kinloch MP campaigned vigorously for public rights.

have to wait a while to see a suggested statue to the jute women, those hardy souls who suffered for their work but did so much for the reputation and early wealth of the city.

Glamis Castle, twelve miles north-west of Dundee, is the family home of the Earls of Strathmore and Kinghorne and has been a royal residence since 1372. It was the childhood home of Her Majesty Queen Elizabeth the Queen Mother and the birthplace of Her Royal Highness the Princess Margaret. It is the legendary setting for Shakespeare's Macbeth and is surrounded by magnificent gardens. The castle is open to the public from March to December.

There were four statues originally in the gardens here and two remain – King Charles I and one of **King James** VI which manages to make him look rather a simpleton. It is the work of 17th-century sculptor Arnold Quellin who was commissioned by the Earl of Strathmore and they are now the oldest surviving lead statues in Scotland. Lead statues became fashionable in the reign of Charles I. James VI was born in 1567, the son of the troubled Mary Queen of Scots and crowned according to Protestant rites a year later. He was taught to hate his Catholic mother and for a while kept captive in 1582 by the Earl of Gowrie. He escaped and tried to make friends with his mother's captor Elizabeth I. However he did not try to secure his mother's release and only reacted to the news of her execution with a formal note of protest. In 1603 Elizabeth died and James became King of England as well. The man once called 'the wisest fool in Christendom' now controlled Great Britain. He died, still a popular monarch to Scots, in 1625.

The coastal town of Arbroath in Angus, is known to gourmets for its 'smokies' and to historians for the famous **Declaration of Arbroath.** On the road into town from Dundee by the football stadium is a large statue by Fife sculptor David Annand to the men who in 1320 scripted this beautiful and stirring piece of prose, sometimes known as the Declaration of Independence. In 1305 King Edward I, after completing the conquest of Scotland and the death of

Left
GLAMIS

The oldest surviving lead statue in Scotland, King James VI and friends.

Right
ARBROATH

The Declaration contains some of the most inspiring writing about Scotland's struggle for independence.

William Wallace, was prepared to destroy any hope the smaller nation had of reasserting its right to rule. The following year Robert the Bruce killed his nearest rival in Scotland, John Comyn, and was excommunicated by the Pope. He had himself proclaimed King at Scone in the strangest coronation Scotland has seen and his followers, including the leading Scottish churchmen, gathered at Scone ready to defy not just Edward but the Pope.

They were successful. Bruce conquered the English at the Battle of Bannockburn in 1314 and the tide turned. King Edward II succeeded his father but with none of the same spirit for battle. Bruce was still *persona non grata* with the Pope for the slaying of Comyn and not recognized in Europe as an independent monarch. It was therefore decided to send letters to the Pope in 1320 to have him accepted and to petition the Pope to write to Edward II telling him to leave Scotland in peace. This Declaration of Independence was written in florid language and Robert the Bruce presided over its signing. It ends with the memorable words: 'For so long as a hundred of us remain alive, we will never in any degree be subject to the dominion of the English, since it is not for glory, riches or honour we fight, but for liberty alone which no good man loses but with his life.' It worked, Europe was won over.

Fans of **Robert Burns** won't be disappointed in Arbroath – although some say the statue outside the library makes him look like a young David Beckham.

Children will love to stop at Kirriemuir and the **Peter Pan** statue. The author of this children's classic, J.M. Barrie, was born at Kirriemuir in 1860, the son of a simple weaver. He went to Dumfries

The author of the classic Peter Pan, J.M. Barrie, was born into humble surroundings here.

Academy and on to Edinburgh University at age eighteen. He enjoyed life there; English literature was his main subject and he always wanted to be a writer which probably suited his rather reserved and withdrawn nature. Shy and depressed at times, he graduated in 1882 and returned home to this quiet spot keen to become an author, the solitary life appealing to him.

Freelance writing for newspapers encouraged him to move to London which he did in 1885. In Kensington Gardens (where there is another statue of Peter Pan) he met two little boys, George and Jack Davies, and their nurse. Five-year-old

George straightaway decided that Barrie, who talked to him about what he wanted to hear, was not a real grown-up and could be trusted. A true friendship evolved and the seeds of Peter Pan were born. He said he wrote *Peter Pan* for the brothers' enjoyment. It is claimed the Peter Pan character was an amalgam of all five Davies brothers.

It is also said he invented the name Wendy after Margaret Henley, the daughter of an Edinburgh poet and journalist. She couldn't pronounce her 'r' properly and called him 'my fwendy'. She died aged six so Barrie in his grief decided to give the copyright and royalties to The Great Ormond Street Hospital for Children in London. They have never admitted how much this brings into the hospital but it is a considerable amount. In 2005 the hospital realized their agreement and monies would run out in 2007 so decided to commission a sequel to the literary classic and chose children's writer Geraldine McCaughrean as author. The book, called *Peter Pan in Scarlet* and published in October 2006, contains all Barrie's principal characters such as Captain

Hook, Tinker Bell etc. The author said: "It is an astonishing, daunting privilege to be let loose in Neverland, armed with nothing but a pen and knowing I'm walking in Barrie's revered footprints."

James Matthew Barrie wrote other books but will always be remembered for his tale of the boy who never grew up. Barrie was only just over 5ft tall with black hair all his life. James Matthew Barrie died in 1937 and is buried alongside his mother in the town where he had enjoyed the rural life himself with an almost feminine innocence. He had been an enormously popular dramatist and one hundred years ago was considered by some to be the Andrew Lloyd Webber of his day.

Although Barrie died in 1937 interest in him hasn't ceased. In December 2004 Sotheby's in London held the auction of the world's largest privately owned collection of letters, photographs, manuscripts etc. relating to Barrie and the boys from whom he got the idea for the book. The auction coincided with the hundredth anniversary of the first performance of Peter Pan at the Duke of York's Theatre in London and the release of a major new film called *Finding Neverland* and starring Johnny Depp, Kate Winslett and Dustin Hoffman.

The original statue was commissioned by the Angus Milling Company in 1968 and erected in Glengate, Kirriemuir, but following damage to the original a cold cast replacement was provided by public subscription. The sculptor was Alistair Smart who had created the original figure. This statue was recast in bronze and unveiled by the Countess of Airlie on 27 August 1983.

Montrose doesn't figure too largely in some tourist brochures which is a pity. For sculpture lovers it certainly should, it has a wide array of statues. But Montrose is probably best known for the Basin, a wildlife centre par excellence with each September the migrating geese as they return making a wonderful sight.

Montrose has a Sculpture Trail leaflet which tells the history of sculpture in the town. At the start of the 20th century Montrose had a modest selection of typically Victorian works, nothing exceptional. But one man was to change that. William Lamb RSA (1893–1951) was a native of Montrose, born in a small cottage in Mill Street. At the age of thirteen he was apprenticed to his older brother James as a stone mason and monumental sculptor. His talent was immediately recognized but the outbreak of World War One saw him fighting in Belgium and France with the Queen's Own Cameron Highlanders. He was wounded twice and his right hand so damaged he had to relearn his art with his left hand. After periods in Edinburgh and Paris he returned to Montrose and set up his first studio in the town in 1924.

Later, after some Royal commissions, he started a studio in Market Street from where he produced a prolific output in clay, plaster, wood, stone and bronze. Many of these works are still displayed in the studio or around the town, figures including a **Seafarer**, a **Minesweeper**, and a **Blacksmith**. William Lamb, a major figure in 20th-century Scottish figurative art, died in 1951, and it was

MONTROSE

Noted sculptor William Lamb has his studio here and his work is all around town, the Seafarer or Trawlhand was erected by Montrose Harbour Trustees in 1978.

THE SEAFARER
A memorial to the seamen and fishermen of Montrose and Ferryden
A contribution to the environment and a tribute to
WILLIAM LAMB A.R.S.A.
A native of the town and renowned sculptor
Erected by Montrose Harbour Trustees
SEPTEMBER 1978.

his wish that the studio be left as his memorial gift to the town. It is well worth a visit to see his sensitive portrayal of the working people of north-east Scotland.

Some of the great names in Scottish sculpture also have works on show in Montrose. Alexander Handyside Ritchie created **Sir Robert Peel** in the High Street, D.W. Stevenson has a bust of Episcopal Minister Dr Robert Brown in the Library and William Calder Marshall has a statue to **Joseph Hume** MP. It was erected in Montrose High Street in September 1859 to this younger son of a shipmaster from Ferry Street

who went on to become an popular campaigning MP for the town. Also of interest in Mid Links is a statue to **Robert Burns** by Birnie Rhind, unveiled in July 1912 by the great Andrew Carnegie who had an uncle and a cousin living in the town.

But the hero or villain – whichever way you look at it – most associated with this Angus coastal resort is one of Scotland's most colourful and controversial historical characters – James Graham, the 1st **Marquis of Montrose** (1612–1650). His statue, by Michael Snowden, was unveiled in 2000 by the current Duke of Montrose, commissioned by the local Marquis of Montrose Society with funds donated by members of the Graham family and supporters from

MONTROSE
Joseph Hume was the local MP who stood up for Montrose at Westminster.

MONTROSE
Hero or villain? The 1st Marquis of Montrose excites opinion either way.

all over the world. It marked the 350th anniversary of the execution of the Marquis at the Mercat Cross in Edinburgh. He is one of the most misunderstood figures in Scottish history, considered a traitor or loyal friend for his role in the struggle between King Charles I and the Covenanters and after winning Scotland for Charles I was hanged by Charles II.

After finishing at St Andrews University in 1627 Graham travelled abroad and on his return in 1637 became one of the noblemen who put their name to the National Covenant in 1638 which argued against royalist religious innovations in Scotland's Presbyterian Church. He was a leader of the Covenanters but after meeting Charles I at Berwick, became disenchanted with the new constitution proposed and distrusted the motives of Archibald Campbell, another prominent Covenanter and a staunch Calvinist who appeared eager to exploit the troubles for his own personal benefit. Montrose joined with other nobles in switching sides and helping the King.

The King was no match for the English Parliament Army led by Oliver Cromwell south of the border but in Scotland it was different. As Lieutenant-General of the King's forces in Scotland Montrose fought one of the most remarkable campaigns in Scottish military history. Between 1644 and 1645 he achieved notable victories against the odds, in places such as Dumfries, Perth, Dundee and Aberdeen and on to Edinburgh.

Charles was tried by the Parliament of England and executed in January 1649. Montrose was said to have fainted when told of the King's death but vowed to fight on. But, largely deserted by the Highlanders and the Irish who had fought with him, he was facing a rampant Covenanters Army who showed no mercy. In April 1650 he was captured at Ardvreck Castle, declared a traitor and hanged.

The Government has recently expressed increasing fears of anti-social behaviour amongst the young and there was a move by some stores to ban youngsters wearing hoods. Angus Council immediately took umbrage at the maligning of this form of dress and said it would commission a bronze statue of a 'hoodie' from Dundee University artist Des Smith to be placed in Montrose. He said his sculpture would

depict a 'young woman in a hooded top and baggy trousers standing in a languid pose, hands in pockets'. Called Nike it won an Angus Council art prize and was unveiled to controversy and cries of "Neo-Nazism" in October 2006.

The latest statue to add to the town's collection further cements Montrose's position as a statue hot-spot. Angus Council upgraded the quayside area of Wharf Street overlooking the new bridge and the harbour estuary and on 17 October 2006, in the presence of The Duke of York and other dignitaries, a statue there to Bamse was unveiled. Who is he you might ask?

Bamse was a legendary Norwegian dog. Sculptor Alan Herriot was commissioned to recreate the St Bernard that was part of the crew of the Norwegian minesweepers which sailed out of Montrose and Dundee

during the Second World War. Bamse was a registered member of the crew of the Thorodd vessel and went on to become a symbol of his country's freedom from Nazi oppression. The dog was said to be fearless under fire and helped with sentry and other duties, saving the life of two men. He was awarded a posthumous Gold Medal for gallantry.

When Bamse died in 1944 his coffin was carried through the streets of the town by crew members. He is buried in Montrose and his grave along the estuary is lovingly tended by both locals and the Norwegian Navy on visits. The target of £50,000 for the project, part of the Montrose Sculpture Trail, was quickly reached through dog shows and other events with generous support coming from Norway. The story doesn't end there; there is talk of a book and a film.

CHAPTER 5

Highland Tales

'Seeing Scotland Madam is only seeing a worse England!'

DR SAMUEL JOHNSON

From Montrose the A92 coast road heads north, passing Stonehaven on a fast stretch of road, where Lord Reith, the first chairman of the BBC, was born. But Aberdeen is the major city in this region, noted as far back as the 16th century as a seat of learning. The 17th century was a time of huge urban growth in Scotland – Glasgow, Edinburgh, Aberdeen and Dundee were the four main cities. In 18th century the town grew considerably and Union Street was created; this Oxford Street of Aberdeen is now always busy with shoppers.

Granite is largely responsible for the city's wealth; in the late 19th century it was exported widely to America and Scandinavia until the latter part of the last century when the last working quarry closed. Other wealth came from farming and latterly oil.

Behind the city is a fertile hinterland with two great rivers, the Dee and Don, alive with salmon. The discovery of oil in the 1970s has changed the city popularly known as the Silver or Granite City because it can sparkle in the sunshine. Aberdeen's motto is Bon Accord (meaning good luck). Visitors comment on both the striking architecture and the popular two-mile beach.

Aberdonians are known as a careful people, perhaps as a result of living for much of the time in a cold and grey environment. The obscure language of Doric is still spoken here and they have their own festival each year. This north-east dialect of Scots has a beauty all its own and survives thanks mainly to some hardened folk singers. The 1970s oil boom saw American accents mingling with the Doric and huge property price rises.

Towards the end of 2006 ambitious plans were announced for a £200 million city centre refurbishment scheme with some unsightly old buildings to go and new cafes, shops, restaurants etc. to take their place. St Nicholas Kirk will remain the 'green heart of the city.'

It is home to only around two hundred and thirty thousand people and Union Street is the heart of the city. The first Union Bridge collapsed and Thomas Telford was called in for the reconstruction, a structure that was seen as a great wonder when completed. Many notable architects have operated from here. They include William Thornton, responsible for the impressive Capitol Building in Washington DC, and John Smith & Son who helped design Balmoral Castle with Prince Albert. John Smith, son of a local builder, was Aberdeen's first ever city architect responsible for many of the city's finest buildings and is buried in St Nicholas' Kirkyard. Gordon is a popular local name – the Gordon Highlanders' Regimental Museum is here. The regiment was given the freedom of the city in 1949 and the museum shows most of the twenty-five Victoria crosses won by them.

The city has links with Rob Roy, William Wallace, Lord Byron, and in modern times Denis Law and Annie Lennox. Queen Victoria is well remembered here. The Town House has an entrance hall with a statue of Queen Victoria moved from its original site in St Nicholas Place to protect it from the weather. Another Queen Victoria on the move went from Union Street onto a traffic island in front of Queen's Cross Church – a bronze statue done in 1893 by G.B. Birch. In the Assembly Rooms saloon on Union Street facade is yet another statue of the young Queen.

Aberdeen's famous architectural trio is known as Education, Salvation and Damnation. These are the Central library (1891), St Mark's Church (1892) and His Majesty's Theatre (1904). Opposite the theatre and pre-dating it is a 16ft high statue of **William Wallace** sculpted by W. Grant Stevenson. Blind Harry wrote of Wallace's exploits in Aberdeen and of the twenty or more Wallace monuments in Scotland the Aberdeen memorial is one of the earliest, unveiled here in June 1888. No fewer than

of his life and the patriot is shown in armour but without helmet, and a large cloak hanging from his shoulders. The statue was erected from funds bequeathed in 1888 by John Steill of 38 Grange Road, Edinburgh, son of James Steill, sometime of Easter Baldowrie in Angus. Behind Wallace is **Prince Albert**, seated on a large chair, the work of Italian Baron Marochetti. Further along Union Terrace is **Robert Burns** (H. Bain Smith 1892), often festooned with garlands. In his hand is a daisy. Burns was known for his love of a dram and in 1954 during Rag Week Aberdeen University students painted footsteps with whitewash coming down off

twenty-five designs from various sculptors were submitted and Duthie Park was originally earmarked for the statue. On the edifice, a most imposing structure at 23ft high, is the whole story

ABERDEEN

One of the first of Scotland's memorials to its great patriot William Wallace and one of the largest.

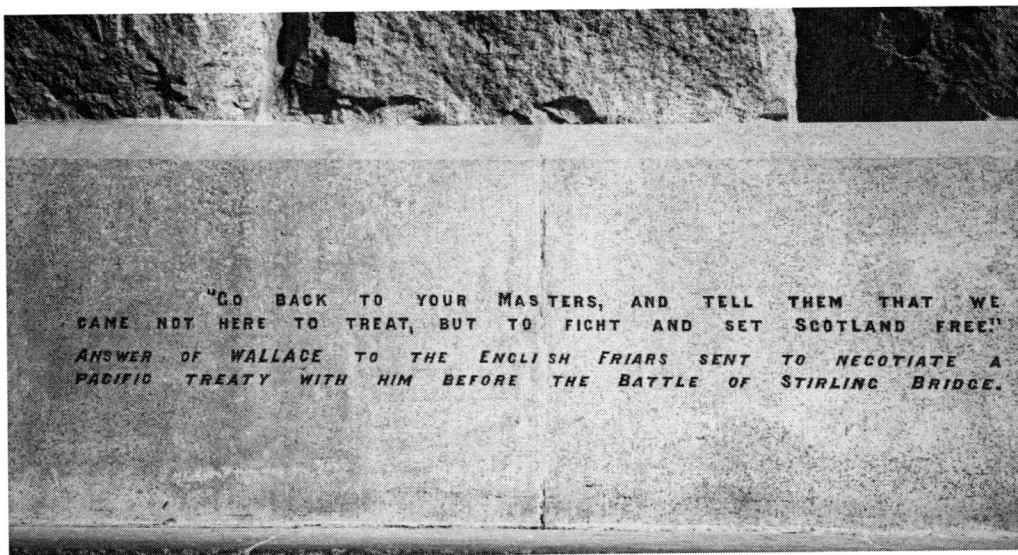

"GO BACK TO YOUR MASTERS, AND TELL THEM THAT WE CAME NOT HERE TO TREAT, BUT TO FICHT AND SET SCOTLAND FREE." ANSWER OF WALLACE TO THE ENGLISH FRIARS SENT TO NEGOTIATE A PACIFIC TREATY WITH HIM BEFORE THE BATTLE OF STIRLING BRIDGE.

Robert Burns in
Union Terrace.

ABERDEEN

Robert Burns was
known for liking a
drink and in 1954
students painted his
footsteps coming off
the statue in as
straight line into a
pub – and back
again in a wavy line.

the statue in a straight line to
the Caledonian Bar opposite
and footsteps back to the
statue – but in a wavy line

this time! The town
councillors were said to be
incensed with rage.

In Union Terrace Gardens
there is a restored and gilded
statue of Edward VIII
(sculptor Alfred Drury.) This
statue replaced the memorial
to Prince Albert moved to a
poor spot in the shadow of
huge Wallace statue.

In Golden Square is the
first granite statue in the
world. George, the fifth and
last **Duke of Gordon**
(1770–1836) is another
monument that has been on
the move, transferred from
Castlegate where it was
erected in 1844. The Duke

ABERDEEN

The first granite statue in the world – to the Duke of Gordon.

stands on a cannon with sword in hand. He actually wasn't long in Castlegate; the council asked the War Office to take over the statue, they refused, so he went to Golden Square, a smarter area of town.

Aberdeen Grammar School has a statue of **Lord Byron** (1788–1824) by James Pittendrigh Macgillivray. The school's most famous pupil was Byron. His mother was Catherine Gordon of Gight, the only child of Sir George Gordon after whom her son was named. Byron was actually born in London in 1788 to a runaway father and a mother who was mentally unstable, passing some of her characteristics onto the son who was capable of great affection and great bouts of temper. His father spent what was left of the Gight fortune and fled to France; a despairing mother made her way to Aberdeen. Little George, the future poet, went to school in the city. He also had a nurse who read him the Bible but treated him badly. Byron also had a club foot which caused him grief when young. In 1798 he fell heir to the title and things began to look up, when he left Aberdeen Grammar School for Harrow.

However it is said Scotland shaped his attitudes to life. Pittendrigh Macgillivray was an early Scots Nationalist and a leading sculptor. He died before completing the statue and it was finished by Alexander J. Leslie in 1920. The sculptor produced a

ABERDEEN

Lord Byron said Scotland shaped his life and, as an Old Boy of Aberdeen Grammar School, present pupils can admire this work by James Pittendrigh Macgillivray.

Gordon of Khartoum's statue is seen by some as "rejoicing in war" and maybe why he is hard to see among the trees outside Robert Gordon's College.

detailed report on exactly where he thought the statue should be placed. He dismissed Broad Street, Union Terrace, Golden Square, the old and new Grammar School sites recommending the quadrangle in front of Gordon's College with Duthie Park a second best. Even although he went into great detail on how the statue, a 'dark object' will

look best in sunlight, silhouette etc. he did not get his way and the notorious womaniser is now passed by impressionable schoolboys every day.

Close to Aberdeen Art Gallery is **Gordon of Khartoum**. Gordon is a true hero who gave his life fighting for Kitchener against the Mahdi 'the expected one' who dominated Sudan in the 1880s. The Mahdi declared holy war on the West and is now considered as the Osama Bin Laden of the nineteenth century. After wiping out an Egyptian army of ten thousand men he besieged Khartoum in 1884. Eventually on 26 Jan 1885 his followers destroyed the capital killing most of its thirty-five thousand people including General Charles Gordon. Prime Minister Gladstone had sent Gordon to Khartoum as a rather pointless gesture and refused to send a relieving force until too late. The statue was created by T. Stuart Burnett in granite. The *Aberdeen Journal* of the day (16 Sept 1886) reported... 'the likeness of the hero of Khartoum is regarded by Sir Henry Gordon, the general's brother, as being eminently successful'. The statue depicts the great soldier in the costume of an Egyptian officer. In his right hand he carries the little stick with which he entered battle and which in China was called 'The Magic Wand.' On his military cloak are the many honours and decorations he won.

On the wall of Robert Gordon's College can be seen a statue of **Robert Gordon** – it was quite normal practice in earlier days to reward a 'donor' with his likeness on important buildings. In Hazlehead Park is the **North Sea Memorial** Garden with a moving statue of three North Sea Oil workers,

a tribute to the one hundred and sixty-seven men who died on the Piper Alpha platform in July 1988.

If you started a school in the old days you were quite likely rewarded with your statue there, certainly Robert Gordon was at his college.

ROBERT GORDON'S COLLEGE

Aberdeen might be seen as dour by some but probably not if another suggestion comes to fruition. The city wants to erect a statue to Scotty, the fictional first engineer of the Starship Enterprise from the popular TV series *Star Trek*. Edinburgh, Elgin and Linlithgow have all claimed Montogomery 'Scotty' Scott as their own but the show's archivist confirmed the character, played by Canadian actor James Doohan, was in fact an Aberdonian. On a more serious front, statues are under consideration for Robert the Bruce (who established the Common Good Fund in Aberdeen) and the Gordon Highlanders, budgets permitting.

Another famous Aberdonian recalled with a plaque and (early in 2007) with an 'encircling container' memorial, but not with a figure statue – is missionary **Mary Slessor**.

The story of the latest memorial is told more fully in Chapter 8. However in Belmont Street – high up above a cashpoint so you might miss it – is a plaque to her memory. It reads: 'To The Glory of God and In Sacred Memory of Mary Slessor of Calabar who as a girl worshipped in this building when Belmont United Presbyterian Church of Scotland. Born Aberdeen December 2nd 1884. Died Use Nigeria January 13th 1915. Erected by the Rotary Cub of Aberdeen November 1957.'

Just west of Aberdeen, at Peterculter is another **Rob Roy.** He was visiting his uncle, James Gregory, in Aberdeen to persuade his cousin (Gregory's son) to join the Jacobite cause. The father said 'no' and on leaving Rob Roy ran into some redcoat soldiers and fled. The redcoats chased him all the way to the Leucher Burn at Coulter where he jumped. You can just see the statue here, stop at the bridge over the Leucher Burn and you can spot it in the distant trees. In fact since the 1830s there have been four statues here, all of wood which is very rare in Scotland. The first was originally the figurehead of an old Peterhead whaling ship and

Mary Slessor's plaque was erected high up on a wall above a cash point to the annoyance of her supporters.

TO THE GLORY OF GOD
AND IN SACRED MEMORY OF
MARY SLESSOR OF CALABAR
WHO AS A GIRL WORSHIPPED IN THIS BUILDING
THEN BELMONT UNITED PRESBYTERIAN CHURCH OF SCOTLAND
BORN ABERDEEN, 2ND DECEMBER 1848
DIED USE, NIGERIA, 13TH JANUARY 1915
ERECTED BY THE ROTARY CLUB OF ABERDEEN, NOVEMBER 1957

PETERCULTER

Look carefully over the Leucher Burn and you can see Rob Roy in the trees, there have been a number of statues here over the years to the famous outlaw going back to the 1830s.

responsible for painting the popular sixty-five-year-old statue for forty years. The old weather-beaten figure was much loved. The current statue, by Arnold Smith, has a laminate finish for protection but isn't universally admired. This latest Rob Roy looks less wild and more refined but a huge postbag to the Aberdeen *Evening Express* in 1991 showed strong views against the changes. He was variously described as a 'a wimp', 'like Frank Spencer with that beret' and: 'it should be removed to some Charlie Chaplin or Laurel and Hardy museum.' George Shaw, Chairman of the Trust, defended the statue saying it was more authentic and realistic than its predecessor.

had two logs added for legs and a piece of canvas tied around it to represent a kilt. A Culter resident had a brother among the crew of the ship and in 1850 took it to the village when it was removed from the ship. A few years later it was replaced with a carved wooden statue which remained amongst the trees until 1926 until the wood rotted. The next one, wood again, remained among the trees for sixty-five years until replacement at a cost of £12,000. The Rob Roy Preservation Trust helped restore it and the statue, by John and David Graham, can now be viewed in the Peterculter Heritage Centre.

Local Culter decorator, George Shaw, was

ROYAL DEESIDE

Not many get to see this statue to John Brown in the grounds of Balmoral Castle – certainly when the Queen is in residence.

Queen Victoria's purchase of Balmoral Castle opened up the Highlands. At nearby Braemar is the cottage where Robert Louis Stevenson wrote *Treasure Island*. He came here on holiday in 1881 and to amuse his stepson one day brought out his paint box and between them they painted a map of an imaginary island. Suddenly, according to Stevenson, the characters came alive and he started on the famous story. His friend John Silver lived in Chapel Brae, Braemar.

Balmoral is the Scottish home of the Royal Family and a significant part of Scottish history. It was originally a sixteenth-century tower house visited by Victoria and Albert in 1848. They loved the area; in June 1852 the Castle was purchased by Prince Albert and the pair had many happy times here. In the grounds is a statue to **John Brown** (1826–1883) the favoured ghillie of Queen Victoria. Some say he was more than a servant but there is no proof their friendship was anything other than platonic. The inscription on the monument reads: 'Friend More Than Servant – Loyal – Truthful – Brave – Self less than duty, even to the grave'. The statue is by Sir Edgar Boehm who was appointed the Queen's Sculptor in 1881. Many people comment that rather eerily in some lights a ghostly figure of the Queen can be seen in the trees behind the statue. It is half a mile from the Lochnagar Distillery up the side road of the grounds of Balmoral Castle which is only open to the public between April and July each year.

At Peterhead, once a busy whaling and then herring port, is a statue to **Field Marshall Keith**. James Keith was born at Inverugie in

PETERHEAD
Field Marshall Keith was a noted soldier of fortune.

1696 and turned soldier of fortune in Europe after the failed Jacobite Rising of 1719. He became a close adviser of Frederick the Great of Prussia and a Field Marshal in the Prussian Army but was killed at the Battle of Hochkirchen in 1758. A marble statue was erected in his honour in Berlin in 1786, a bronze replica later being erected in its place when the original was moved to the Military Academy. Peterhead Town Council asked King William I of Prussia for the marble statue. The King declined but generously agreed to gift a replica. It was unveiled in front of the Town House on 16 August 1869.

Huntly took its name from the Gordons of Huntly who laid it out, and has a statue in the main square of **Charles Gordon Lennox** (5th Duke of Richmond) sculpted in 1862 by Alexander Brodie.

Turriff lies in farming country north of Aberdeen and has one of the stranger memorials to a Scottish 'hero', the **Turra Coo**. The story behind the monument to this heroic freedom fighter is of a riot in 1913 after a cow was poinded for public sale following the refusal of farmer Robert Paterson to pay National Insurance for

his men. There was a widespread strong rural response to central legislation. Paterson, an active Union man, was fined for his refusal to pay stamps for his workers. The case again came to court on 15 September 1913 but he still refused to pay. The court determined that goods of the appropriate value should be taken from the farm and sold to cover the arrears. When the Government officials came to collect the cow – an Aberdeen shorthorn cross – a riot ensued and the officials were pelted with eggs, leeks, cabbages and lumps of soil. The cow had to be sold back to the local community three days later and the cow returned to Robert Patterson. A crowd of approaching four thousand people welcomed her back as a band played *See The Conquering Hero Comes*. This was on 20 January in 1914. On 31 October 1971 a memorial was erected at the entrance to Paterson's farm at Lendrum, made of stone collected from the seven farms owned by Mr Paterson and from the site of one of his sawmills. The cow became a national hero – souvenir plates, mugs, ashtrays, glasses etc. are held at the National Museum of

The Osprey is making a return to Scotland.

collecting by Victorians and the destruction of their habitat contributed to their decline. However in 1954 a migrant pair successfully nested in the Highlands and since then this symbol of Scottish power and beauty has increased in numbers and spread throughout the country.

Ahead is Inverness, home to a true heroine. This attractive gateway to the Highlands was the birthplace of **Flora Macdonald** and outside the castle is her statue. Born in 1722, she was to be one of the most famous of many Highlanders who risked their lives to protect the Young Pretender. They first met on 20 June 1746 at Ormaclete on the Isle of South Uist. Prince Charles was on the run in the Highlands and Islands for five months after his defeat at Culloden with a price on his head of £30,000, a huge sum in those days. Flora sheltered the Prince for eleven days and then accompanied him in his escape. He was disguised as a maid with the name Betty Burke. They sailed from Benbecula to Skye and on 1 July he returned to the mainland. Flora was arrested and taken to London but there she was treated by

Scotland. After another six peaceful years at Lendrum the cow sadly died of bovine tuberculosis and is buried there. In the spring of 2005 Kate Ferguson of the Turriff Tourism Action Group announced that they were fundraising to erect a proper statue of the cow itself.

We are in Moray country now and onto Fochabers and **The Osprey**. There is a striking statue of the bird in flight by David Annand. Ospreys are an integral part of Scottish wildlife. These magnificent fish-eating birds of prey were once a common sight over Scottish lochs but disappeared from Scottish skies around one hundred years ago. Shooting, egg-

Flora Macdonald is loved by everyone who knows the story of Bonnie Prince Charlie and her role in his escape.

many as a heroine. In July a general amnesty was declared and within three years she was free to return to Skye. In 1774 she and her husband and two sons emigrated to America where the family were involved in the American Revolution. Her husband Allan and son Alexander took part in the first, and brief, battle of Moore's Creek and were taken prisoner. A year later Flora was stripped of the family plantation because she refused to take the oath of allegiance to the North Carolina Congress. The family moved to Nova Scotia and from there returned to Skye. Flora died on 4 March 1790 and her funeral procession consisted of thousands of followers and was over a mile long. The sculptor of this imposing work, unveiled in 1899, was Andrew Davidson of Inverness.

Travellers arriving or leaving Inverness by air will be confronted with a statue at the airport terminal. It remembers a true aviation pioneer who opened up the Highlands to air traffic, Captain Ernest Edmund (Ted) Fresson. He was born in 1891 and actually brought up in Surrey and Essex but fell in love with Scotland when a pilot returning from the First World War. He started the first scheduled air services in the Highlands between Inverness, Wick and Kirkwall in May 1933 and went on to form Highland Airways Limited which expanded throughout the region and became the first UK airline to be given a Post Office contract to deliver domestic mail. He died in Inverness on 25 September 1963 and is remembered at the site he had once suggested to the Air Ministry as a wartime airfield.

Cromarty is known for **Hugh Miller.** He was born here on 10 October 1802 and died in Edinburgh on Christmas Eve 1856. This geologist and lay theologian was considered one of the finest geological writers of the 19th century. After early literary ventures and a six-year period as a bank accountant in Cromarty, Miller went to Edinburgh in 1840 as Editor of the newly founded newspaper *The Witness*. The newspaper, which opposed patronage in the Church of Scotland, gained a wide reputation through Miller's leading articles. He wrote a brilliant geological series for it, also published in book form as *The Old Red Sandstone* (1841). He described his discoveries in Cromarty of fossils from between 408 to 160 million years ago and aroused the public to a new understanding. He was a tall (nearly 6ft) man with flaming red hair and very blue eyes possessing immense physical strength. He wrote about the history of the earth in an eloquent and imaginative way that no one had done before. Miller was a shy, introverted man prone to melancholy who committed suicide fearing approaching insanity with a single shot in the chest at his home in Portobello outside Edinburgh.

At Hugh Miller's Cottage in Cromarty is a statue on a column funded by public subscription and sculpted in 1859 by Handyside Ritchie, from Musselburgh. It is visible for many hundreds of yards. The memorial to this great but troubled man is so high you can't see the detail but he is wearing shepherd's plaid and below his right hand is a pile of books. His left hand is upraised. Immediately below his feet on top of the column is carved the Devonian fossil fish he is famous for discovering. The Hugh Miller Museum now comprises two buildings open to the public, the cottage of his birthplace and next door a Georgian three-storey sandstone villa in Church Street built by his father in 1797.

In Tain High Street is a memorial statue to **Kenneth Murray,** a member of a successful merchant and banking family and a noted agriculturist. It is worth seeing just to see if you agree with the statement that it looks like a 'mini Scott Monument'. Tain is probably more famous for being headquarters of Glenmorangie, one of the last independent Scottish whisky makers, and sold to the French in October 2004 for £300million. Moet Hennessy bought this little bit of Scotland. They began operating in 1893 and produce 1.6million cases of whisky a year and boast the most popular malt in the domestic market. The particular taste of this malt was entrusted to the care of the Sixteen Men of Tain, craftsmen producing whisky in the old-fashioned way.

Glenmorangie means Valley of Tranquility in Gaelic but this area wasn't always so tranquil. The Highland Clearances are one of the darker episodes in Scottish history as anyone visiting Dunrobin Castle by Golspie and the home of the Duke and Duchess of Sutherland knows. The Duchess can be admired in the grounds of Dunrobin Castle but the monument that excites most interest is to her husband.

The Sutherland Monument is at Ben Bhragaidh just over a mile north-west of Golspie in Sutherland, erected by his tenants in 1836–8 as a memorial to the first **Duke of Sutherland.** The monument stands at thirty-three metres high overall and dominates the surrounding area. It is an octagonal pedestal on a tall square base both with sloped tops and built of local red sandstone. They support a colossal statue of the Duke in white Brora stone. The pedestal and base were designed by William Burn with advice from Sir Francis Legatt Chantrey and the statue was executed by Joseph

GOLSPIE
You had better be quick if you want to see this statue (!), those still bitter about the Highland Clearances would like to destroy this memorial to the Duke of Sutherland for his part in the tragedy.

Theakston from a model made by Chantrey. The inscription says that in 1834 it was erected by a grateful tenantry to a judicious, kind and liberal landlord who would open his hands to the distress of the widow, the sick and the traveller. However there is another side to the story. Known as the Scottish Jo Stalin, he evicted fifteen thousand crofters from his estate of one million acres. Many have wanted to smash the structure to the ground and replace it with a statue to the victims of the Highland Clearances instead.

At the former herring port of Helmsdale founded to house evicted tenants from Strath Kildonan, they have announced plans to erect just such a statue. In September 2002 plans were announced to raise £5 million to recognize the Highland Diaspora and place a statue of four bronze figures on Creag Bun Ullidh by the town.

At the far north of Scotland stands Thurso, the most northerly town on the Scottish mainland given a population boost 50 years ago with the nearby Dounreay Nuclear Power Station. In mediaeval times it was a big trading port with Scandinavia. The most northerly figurative

statue on the mainland is to **Sir John Sinclair** (1754–1835) who laid out most of the town on a grid system and made a number of improvements, particularly to the fishing port. He was born in Thurso Castle, became a barrister and MP and was the first President of the Board of Agriculture, appointed by William Pitt the Younger. He was also responsible for compiling the first Scottish 'census.'

Coming South again, Loch Ness is a great attraction for tourists and bounty hunters alike. Children will be captivated by the giant sculpture of Nessie at Drumnadrochit. At Spean Bridge, thirty-one miles north-east of Fort William and a mile out of town on the A82 Inverness road is one of the most evocative statues in the country, largely because of its remote location. The bronze **Commando War Memorial,** in a dramatic moorland setting, comprises a group of three commandos on a stone pedestal done by Scott Sutherland 1949–52. The accompanying plaque reads: 'In Memory of the officers and men of the Commandos who died in the Second World War 1939–1945. Their country

was their training ground. United, We Conquer.'

Hero or not? The debate continues. The Glenfinnan Monument to the clansmen who fought with **Bonnie Prince Charlie** is a battlemented 18.3 metre high round tower built by Alexander MacDonald of Glenandale in 1815 to commemorate the start of the Jacobite Rising seventy years earlier. It is on the A830 three miles from Kinlocheil, the most stunning location for any statue in Scotland. On 22 June 1745 the Young Pretender sailed from France with only seven companions. On 25 July he reached Loch Nam Uamh, twelve miles west of where the monument now stands. He initially failed to rouse any great enthusiasm, being criticised for arriving without French backing. However he gained Macdonald support and got the influential Donald Cameron of Lochiel to join him. He fixed 19 August as the time for his followers to gather at Glenfinnan. After a slow start, men and promises began to pour in and by afternoon his standard was raised. The Old Pretender was formally claimed King James VIII and the Prince his Regent.

The Visitor Centre here tells the subsequent story of the Rising with initial and widespread success but culminating in awful loss and flight from Culloden for the Bonnie Prince. In 1834 Angus MacDonald of Glenandale removed ancillary buildings from round the foot of the tower and placed on its top a stone statue of a Highlander by John Greenshields showing Prince Charles Edward looking east to the pass along which Lochiel and the Camerons came to join the cause.

To many this romantic figure is a loser who ended his days in Italy a depressed drunk. To others he is the very symbol of Scotland's heroic fight to assert its right to manage her own affairs. Charles Edward Stuart (1720–1788), the Young Pretender, certainly became a

SPEAN BRIDGE
One of the most dramatic sites for a statue in Scotland, to the Commandos who trained in this area prior to the Second World War.

GLENFINNAN

Arguably the most spectacular setting for a statue in Scotland, at the head of Loch Shiel, is the memorial to Bonnie Prince Charlie.

legendary figure the moment he sailed into exile. The memorial is certainly imposing but not everyone

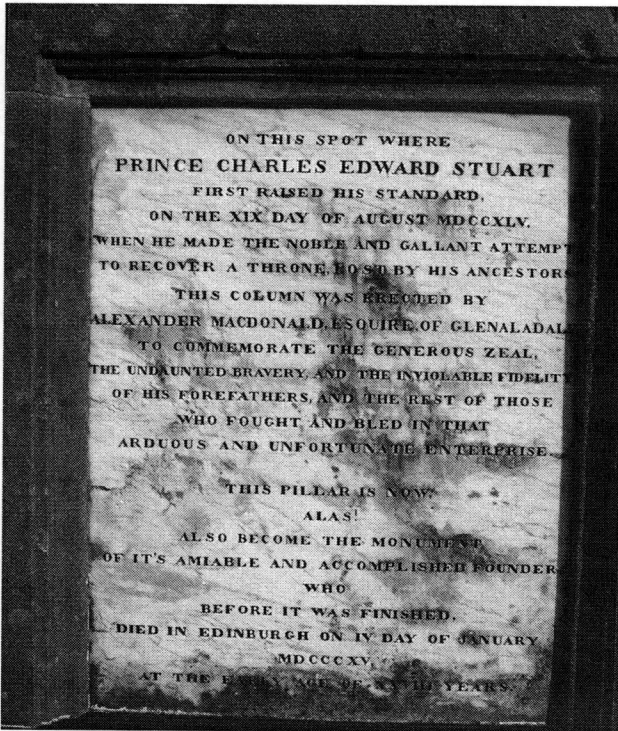

ON THIS SPOT WHERE
PRINCE CHARLES EDWARD STUART
FIRST RAISED HIS STANDARD,
ON THE XIX DAY OF AUGUST MDCCXLV.
WHEN HE MADE THE NOBLE AND GALLANT ATTEMPT
TO RECOVER A THRONE LOST BY HIS ANCESTORS
THIS COLUMN WAS ERECTED BY
ALEXANDER MACDONALD, ESQUIRE, OF GLENALADALE
TO COMMEMORATE THE GENEROUS ZEAL,
THE UNDAUNTED BRAVERY, AND THE INVIOLABLE FIDELITY
OF HIS FOREFATHERS, AND THE REST OF THOSE
WHO FOUGHT AND BLED IN THAT
ARDUOUS AND UNFORTUNATE ENTERPRISE.

THIS PILLAR IS NOW,
ALAS!
ALSO BECOME THE MONUMENT
OF IT'S AMIABLE AND ACCOMPLISHED FOUNDER
WHO
BEFORE IT WAS FINISHED.
DIED IN EDINBURGH ON IV DAY OF JANUARY
MDCCCXV,
AT THE EARLY AGE OF XXVIII YEARS.

likes it – Queen Victoria described it as 'very ugly, looking like a lighthouse with a statue on top.'

The islands off the West Coast of Scotland are dramatic and wild. But they are not great hunting grounds for statue fans. The 'Wee Frees' are not lovers of statues. If you see a monument it is likely to be a war memorial or a religious statue. One of the most notable is at Glenelg on the shores of Glenelg Bay overlooking the Isle of Skye. This particular war memorial is a startling Parisian apparition in this remote West Highland setting. Designed by Robert S. Lorimer in the 1920s the sculptor was Louis Deuchars. It shows a colossal bronze group consisting of a scantily clad kneeling lady (Stricken

Humanity) appealing to a similarly half-clad figure of Peace across a moustachioed Cameron Highlander (Victory) looking totally bemused at proceedings.

Lorimer's son, Hew, is the sculptor of the 28ft high Our Lady of The Isles on the Island of South Uist. It was erected in 1957.

Hew Lorimer (1907–1993) was the second son of Sir Robert (1864–1929) and was educated at Loretto School in Musselburgh before going to Magdalen College, Oxford. He left there to study design and sculpture at Edinburgh College of Art from where he graduated in 1934. His deep

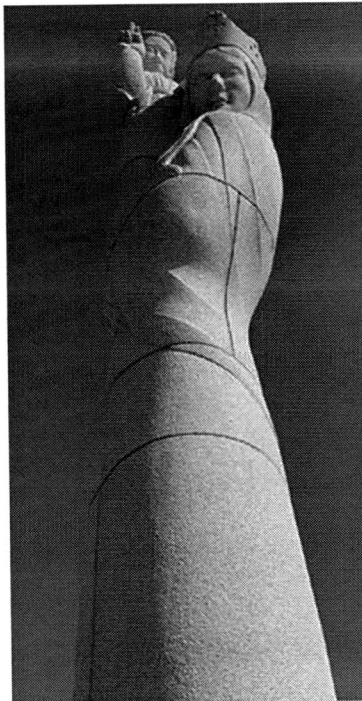

Above
Skye bridge

Left
Our Lady of the Isles

Kellie Castle

religious beliefs can be seen in his work which also includes allegorical figures on the National Library of Scotland building on George IV Bridge in Edinburgh. There is a permanent exhibition of his work at his home, Kellie Castle in Fife. His father's notable works include the Scottish War Memorial at Edinburgh Castle.

North Uist is Presbyterian and South Uist is Catholic. On Heaval, the highest point of the island of Barra is a marble statue of Madonna, Lady Star of the Sea, erected in 1954 looking out to sea and placed there by the Welcome Home Fund for Seamen.

CHAPTER 6

Glasgow – City of Power

'Every Hero becomes a bore at last'
RALPH WALDO EMERSON

Glasgow has shaken off its critics. This imposing city on the Clyde, known as the Second City of the Empire during the industrial revolution, has had to live down certain aspects of its past. It was once perceived as a dark and dangerous city, associated with excessive drinking, knife fights, rioting football fans and Rab C. Nesbitt. It has taken time and effort to shake off this image; it wasn't helped in the 1970s by the M8 motorway ripping the heart out of Glasgow as the Kingston Bridge was constructed.

The renaissance really started between 1980 and 1984 under Lord Provost Michael Kelly who first launched the catchphrase 'Glasgow's Miles Better'. It worked. In 1991 it was made the European City of Culture and now it is reinventing itself as the City of Shopping and making a pitch for hosting The Commonwealth Games.

Glasgow entered the 21st century in upbeat mood with a growing reputation for its art endeavours and nightlife in addition to the best shopping in Scotland. It is known as The Friendly City and has recently been re-launched with yet another slogan: 'Glasgow – Scotland with Style'. Anywhere that is home to Charles Rennie Mackintosh is bound to have style.

Glaswegians certainly live for the present and don't dwell in the past. One of Mackintosh's most iconic works is The Willow Tearooms off Sauchiehall Street in the heart of the city. I once stood 300 yards from the Tearooms and asked six people where they were. Nobody knew. But they are certainly friendly people and do love their city. Especially Sauchiehall Street, the very

SAUCHIEHALL STREET
CITY CENTRE

mention of which is said to make exiled Scots all round the world misty-eyed. Appropriately just off this famous thoroughfare is a statue to **John Stewart** who founded the Glasgow Friendly Society in 1862. The work is by William Kellock Brown.

George Square is the heart of Glasgow. Rather typical of what some say is a rather ambivalent official attitude here towards statues was the City Council's suggestion in the 1990s of clearing George Square of all its statues. There was an outcry from some media and public who pointed out they were essential to the culture of the city and the idea was dropped. Glaswegians are

SIR JOHN MOORE
Soldiers figure on many Scottish statues and Sir John Moore had a particularly distinguished career.

fond of their statues – in old days the people of Glasgow were very generous in donating to the fund-raising to honour their heroes; donations for a Burns statue for example had to be restricted to one shilling per person such was the support.

Contemporary art is also making a comeback in Glasgow. On a pedestrian precinct south of St Vincent Street is a clever topographical relief map done in 1990 by Kathleen Chambers showing a map of centre of the city with street names also in Braille. However the bulk of the statuary in Glasgow reflects the rather 'serious' past of the city, more men of toil than eccentrics or romantics here. In common with other Scottish cities Glasgow's statuary probably reflects its distant past more than its present. It is painstakingly detailed in a wonderful book produced in 2002 by Ray McKenzie entitled *Public Sculpture of Glasgow*.

George Square is at the centre of Glasgow and is its major urban space. **Sir John Moore** (1761–1809) was on his own here in 1819 and had no company until 1832 when James Watt joined him. Top sculptor John Flaxman was chosen to produce the

Moore memorial, the first in the city for nearly one hundred years. Lieutenant General Sir John Moore was a British army officer who began military life in 1776 under the Duke of Hamilton. For a while he was also Member of Parliament for the burghs of Lanark, Selkirk, Peebles and Linlithgow but returned to the military. Moore saw action in many countries and became one of the greatest trainers of infantrymen in military history. In 1808 he was sent to combat Napoleon in the Peninsular War. During the retreat of his army to Corunna in 1809, Moore was mortally wounded in the hour of victory. His heroic death is commemorated in Rev. Charles Wolfe's poem *The Burial of Sir John Moore.*'

James Watt is remembered with a statue by Francis Leggatt Chantrey sculpted in 1830. Watt was born in Greenock in 1736 and began his career at the age of seventeen as a maker of mathematical instruments. In 1764 he became interested in steam engines and within five years had patented his own improved version. He went into partnership with Mathew Boulton, a successful businessman,

in Birmingham and marketed the first cylindrical steam engines which revolutionized industry. He surveyed the Forth and Clyde, Caledonian and other canals. Watts was awarded an honorary degree by Glasgow University, and the Royal Society in London recognized his overall work which also encompassed other areas. He was associated with the development of a pantograph used in letter copying and a bleaching process used in the textile industry. He died in 1819.

Sculptor George Edwin Ewing was given the job of

JAMES WATT
BORN 1736. DIED 1819.

JAMES WATT
There are many busts or statues to Watt all over Scotland, this one is in George Square by the renowned sculptor Francis Chantrey.

ROBERT BURNS

Seen with another great Scot, Sir Walter Scott on top of his pillar.

sculpting **Robert Burns,** unveiled in 1877. Public subscriptions were limited to a shilling each and there were over forty thousand subscribers producing a final fund of £2,000. They were not just Glasgow folk but men and women from all over Scotland, and other exiles who had emigrated to faraway shores. Glasgow proudly noted that it would overshadow the 'miserable monument' to Burns that Edinburgh had erected at Calton Hill, seen as not worthy of the National Poet of Scotland. In this bronze on a granite pedestal, Burns is represented as a 'superior Scottish peasant' with his broad Kilmarnock bonnet half crushed in the hollow of

his right elbow and holding the 'wee crimson-tipped flower' in his hand, in an easy and graceful attitude of poetic contemplation. Dressed in frock coat and knee breeches, the figure is supported from behind by a pillar concealed by a folded plaid with thistles growing from the rear. Pigeons seem to love this statue which is maintained by the Glasgow and District Burns Association.

Field Marshall Lord Clyde sculpted here by John Henry Foley in 1868 is an interesting character. Born in Glasgow the son of a joiner, he went to Grammar School then entered the 9th Regiment of Foot at the age of fifteen. He fought in the Peninsular War under Sir John Moore and was severely wounded. In further campaigns he reached the rank of Major and went on to conduct campaigns in India, China and the Crimean War attaining the rank of Field Marshall in command of the 42nd Black Watch who repulsed the Russians at the Battle of Balaclava in September 1854. In 1857 he was Commander-in-Chief of the Indian Army during the Mutiny there and took leading role in Relief of Lucknow. Known as 'Old Careful' by his men whom he treated very well, he was much admired by Queen Victoria who made him a lord in 1858. It is one of the finest bronze statues in the city although not everyone approved. The *Building News* correspondent at the time of the unveiling wrote... 'there is a melodramatic, not to say bumptious air, about it which is as alien to the highest class of art as it was to the character of the modest-minded soldier whose services it seeks to commemorate'.

Dominating the square is the **Scott Monument** by John Greenshields. It is said to be an excellent likeness of the great man but so high up on a column of twenty-five metres no one would know. However we can assume it to be the case as another Greenshields work of Sir Walter Scott in Edinburgh's Law Courts attracted the same response. The statue itself is over three metres tall and he is dressed in a cut-away coat, wearing a shepherd's plaid which passes diagonally across his chest and falls to the ground from his right shoulder, showing Scott as a man of the Borders not the Highlands.

Also in George Square can be seen other notables. **Thomas Campbell**, poet and historian, is by John

LORD CLYDE

Glasgow honours its military men, here Field Marshall Lord Clyde who fought under Sir John Moore in the Peninsular War.

SIR WALTER SCOTT

His monument dominates George Square, home to most of Glasgow's oldest statues.

THOMAS CAMPBELL
Poet and historian.

Mossman assisted by James Pittendrigh Macgillivray. Prime Minister **William Ewart Gladstone** appears facing the City Chambers in a work by William Hamo Thorneycroft. Chemist **Thomas Graham** is sculpted by William Brodie. Liberal politician and orator **James Oswald** from Auchincruive figures in a sculpture by Baron Carlo Marochetti.

The Baron is also responsible for the most iconic of the works in the square, **Victoria and Albert** on horseback. The Queen first visited Glasgow in the summer of 1849 and made such an impact that plans for a commemorative monument were discussed as soon as she left. Originally elsewhere in the city at St Vincent Place, it was moved here in 1866. This is a controversial work and there are all sorts of theories why it was moved. The sculptor came in for a lot of criticism – for the fact the queen should have been bigger, and the strangeness of the horse's legs. They were changed when the statue was moved. Also by the Baron is Prince Albert who joined his wife here in 1866. Inside both pedestals are time capsules with historical documents and papers.

James Watt is actually

JAMES OSWALD
His prominent top hat is the work of controversial sculptor Baron Carlo Marochetti.

SCOTLAND'S HEROES

Again the work of
Baron Marochetti
and when unveiled
drew widespread
criticism.

well remembered in Glasgow
apart from George Square;
there is an impressive marble
statue of him in the
Hunterian Museum at
Glasgow University (maybe
on loan to the National
Portrait Gallery in
Edinburgh) and he is also
high up on a building in
Elmbank Street with
neighbours Cicero, Galileo
and Homer making good
company. Here he is
commemorated by sculptor
John Mossman whose work
is all over the city. And for
many years there was even a
headless **James Watt** in
yellow sandstone at McPhun
Park in Bridgeton, Glasgow,
a division of Glasgow Green

JAMES WATT

In the grounds of the Winter Palace now, James Watt has been restored and moved from McPhun Park to this fine site near the impressive old Templeton Carpet Factory.

CHILDREN AT PLAY

Keeping Watt company is this bronze known as Peter Pan although it isn't the Barrie character really, just a boy with squirrels and a pipe.

ERECTED
BY TEMPERANCE REFORMERS
IN RECOGNITION OF
VALUABLE SERVICES
RENDERED TO
THE TEMPERANCE CAUSE
BY
SIR WILLIAM COLLINS
LORD PROVOST
OF THE CITY OF GLASGOW 1877-80
29th OCTOBER 1881.

SCOTLAND'S HEROES

where Watt used to enjoy walking. A major renovation plan for Glasgow Green in 2000 included plans to clean the statue which had clearly been attacked with a hammer and to replace the head with a fibreglass copy. In fact, in Christmas week 2005 the statue, originally by Charles Benham Grassby, was completely renovated with a new stone head, a new foot and new kneecaps. For security reasons it was also moved to the Winter Gardens enclosure near the People's Palace. Illustrating that vandalism is a continuing problem for modern statues, security fencing was put around the work. Nearby is the restored **Children at Play** statue with its bronze of a boy and squirrels known locally as Peter Pan, by Thomas Clapperton. Glasgow Green is said to be Europe's oldest public park with over eight hundred years of history. As you leave by the impressive gate near the Albert Bridge over the Clyde, you will notice a memorial to Sir William Collins who in the latter part of the 19th century had a big job trying to keep Glaswegians off the demon drink, a talent for the consumption of which they have enjoyed a worldwide reputation.

In Ingram Street outside the Hutcheson's Hall (Glasgow HQ of the National Trust for Scotland) are the Hutcheson brothers who were great benefactors to the city and the founder of Hutchesons' Hospital. **George and Thomas Hutcheson** is the work of James Colquhoun. **St Mungo,** who founded Glasgow, can also be admired in Ingram Street high up on the Trustee Savings Bank building in a statue by Sir George Frampton. You are not far away now from the famous weekend market the Barras, a spot for bargains and meeting locals.

A more recent work is by Andy Scott and Kenny Mackay at the Scottish Maritime Museum at Braehead Shopping Centre. It shows two shipyard workers hauling a ship by chains in the river Clyde, commemorating this industry which brought such prosperity to the city. The statue was unveiled in May 2000 by Govan native Sir Alex Ferguson of football fame.

Kelvingrove Park, originally known as West End Park, contains Kelvingrove Art Gallery and Museum. It was once seen as an overflow for statues from George Square. There is a stylish War Memorial to **Highland Light Infantry** by William Birnie Rhind, and a dramatic **Cameronians** (Scottish Rifles) monument by Philip Lindsey Clark. Lovers of Scott novels will be interested in the lady at the top of the Stewart Memorial Fountain. She is Ellen Douglas (sculpted by John Mossman again), the heroine of the poem *The Lady of the Lake*.

Field Marshall Earl Roberts (1832–1914). Unveiled in 1916 during the First World War this impressive monument to an earlier soldier shows him wearing a pith helmet and military uniform astride his Arab charger. Indian-born, he served with distinction there winning the VC at Khudaganj in 1858 and helped capture Lucknow in the same year. He also fought in the Boer War. He is buried in St Paul's Cathedral London. The sculptor was Harry Bates.

Thomas Carlyle is here too in another controversial work. Unveiled in November 1916, the sculptor William Kellock Brown had chiselled an effigy of Carlyle in a very unconvential manner after the style of Rodin's Monument to Balzac. The body is not shown; Carlyle's head and one arm emerge on top of the natural, untreated rock. His nose has been broken many times which adds to the strange appearance. It was certainly controversial putting this here during the War as Carlyle was linked with German culture; he was a great fan of Goethe whose works he translated. Some Glaswegians describe it as the worst statue in Glasgow.

Lord Joseph Lister of Lyme Regis (1827–1912) is represented in the park. This eminent surgeon and pioneer of antiseptics has saved the lives of many soldiers over the years. He was actually from Essex in England so after his death in 1912 there was a discussion on whether it was appropriate for a statue in Glasgow. He had been a surgeon at Edinburgh Royal Infirmary in 1856 and

THOMAS CARLYLE
Unveiled in 1916 and inspired by Rodin.

then Lecturer in Surgery at Glasgow University. He revolutionized modern surgery allowing operations previously unheard of because of the risk of infection. After his death the Lord Provost of Glasgow was lobbied by many people to erect a memorial to him in the city where he had done so much to relieve the suffering of the residents. At the same time London was considering something to commemorate the great man and the two cities combined thoughts on such ideas as a Lister Museum. Then the war interrupted matters and Lister was finally placed in Kelvingrove Park in 1924. The sculptor was George Henry Paulin. Incidentally, Lister is also remembered in Edinburgh with a plaque on the side of the Medical School in Teviot Place.

But perhaps the most appropriate resident here is the man behind the park, **Lord Kelvin.** Unveiled in 1913 the statue commemorates William Thomson (Lord Kelvin) who lived from 1824–1907. Born in Belfast he always considered himself Scottish, moving there when aged six. He entered Glasgow University at the age of ten, also studying at Cambridge University. He was a major figure at the Glasgow institution for over fifty years where he was professor of natural philosophy and an inspiration to scientists, writing countless scientific papers. His discoveries were many. The calculation that the point when atoms in motion come to a stop is absolute zero, the centigrade temperature scale, was named after him. His research led to the first

Trans-Atlantic cable being laid. Kelvin was a great mathematician like his father. He was knighted in 1866 and raised to the peerage in 1892 as Lord Kelvin of Largs where he settled in later life after his second marriage. He became President of Royal Society in 1890. The statue is by Archibald Macfarlane Shannan and shows Kelvin wearing an academic gown of Cambridge University.

Another park that owes its name to city benefactors is Elder Park. The Elders were great philanthropists who did so much for the Govan community. **John Elder** was an engineer born in Glasgow in 1824. On a plaque by the statue are the words 'to commemorate achievements of his genius and acknowledgement of his services to the community among whom he lived, this statue was erected by public subscription May 1888'. On the other side it reads 'by his unwearied efforts to promote the welfare of the working classes, his integrity of character, firmness of purpose and kindness of heart claim, equally with his genius, enduring remembrance. By his many inventions, particularly in connection with the compound engine, he effected a revolution in engineering second to that accomplished by James Watt and, in great measure, originated the developments in steam propulsion which have created modern commerce'.

After Glasgow University Elder was apprenticed to Napiers and later formed the firm of Randolph Elders & Co. (later the Fairfield Shipping Co.) He introduced the marine command steam engine which gave great economies in fuel consumption. This Clyde shipbuilder looked after the welfare of his workers setting up an accident fund to which he generously contributed himself. The sculptor was Joseph Edgar Boehm.

In 1857 he married Isabella, the daughter of Glasgow writer Alexander Ure. (**Mrs John Elder** 1828–1905). When the Govan shipyard opened they moved to a villa in Elmpark Road. In 1869 his health started to decline due to an abscess of the liver and he died in September that year. On the day of his funeral the works south of the river were closed and the ships displayed their flags at half mast. Isabella was left sole proprietor to the shipbuilding company. For nine months she carried on the business single-handed until partners were secured. She was a great benefactress both to relatives in trouble and to the public. She established a Chair of Civil Engineering at Glasgow University and the John Elder Chair of Naval Architecture. In 1883 she bought thirty-seven acres of land opposite the Elder shipyard to create a park for the people of Govan. In 1901, not long before her death she gave £27,000 to build and equip a library at the corner of Elder Park which was opened by Andrew Carnegie in 1903.

In 1902 the people of Govan made the decision to honour Isabella Elder with a statue. It was erected in the rose garden in Elder Park but she died on 18 November 1905 before the statue could be unveiled. She was a great champion of women's rights and her gifts to the city included the Queen Margaret College, the first college for women in Scotland. This statue, one of few to a woman in the country, is by Archibald Macfarlane Shannan.

In Govan Road there is a statue of **Sir William Pearce** by Edward Onslow Ford, a bronze on a pedestal of Peterhead granite. Pearce

(1833–1888) was a noted shipbuilder who served his apprenticeship at Chatham Naval Dockyard (he was born in Kent). He joined Lloyds Register and was appointed surveyor for the Clyde district. In 1870 he was persuaded by Mrs Elder to be one of three men running the Fairfield yard at Govan with a labour force of five thousand men. Pearce enjoyed a rather flamboyant lifestyle but did a lot of charitable work and became the first MP for Govan.

At Rangers' Football Ground is the **Ibrox Disaster** Monument by Andy Scott assisted by Alison Bell (2001) depicting a more than life-size replica of John Greig,

BROTHER WALFRID

BROTHER WALFRID
The man who founded Celtic Football Club is thanked with a statue at their ground.

former captain of Rangers. Wearing an armband, he looks towards the entrance where the disaster took place when sixty-six spectators were killed on Stairway 13 in the crush trying to leave a Rangers v Celtic game on 2 January 1971. The names of the victims are listed. The work also commemorates the earlier tragedies in April 1902 when twenty-five were killed, and in 1951 when two died.

In November 2005 a statue to Celtic's founder **Brother Walfrid** was erected outside their stadium. He was the man who made Celtic. For one hundred and twenty years there was no memorial here. Walfrid was born in Co. Sligo and went to Glasgow in the 1880s. Shocked by the poverty, he set up the charity which turned into Celtic Football Club. The cost of the statue was £30,000 and it is in granite by Kate Robertson.

Springburn Park remembers **James Reid** in a statue by William Goscombe John. Reid (1823–1894) was born in Ayrshire but formed a company here employing 2,500 workers and producing 200 locomotives a year in the 1890s. Another generous local benefactor, he collected many paintings which he left to the city.

The First Minister of Scotland has had to be moved to a higher spot after vandals kept damaging his statue outside the Buchanan Galleries.

One of the latest and most troubled statues in Glasgow is to **Donald Dewar** (1937–2000) 'Scotland Shall Have A Parliament', the plinth says and he was the man who delivered it. Dewar was born in the city, attended Glasgow University and qualified as a solicitor. He became an MP in Aberdeen first and then for a Glasgow seat at the 1978 General Election. As First Minister he took tremendous criticism for the greatly over-budget and behind-schedule Parliament building at the bottom of Edinburgh's Royal Mile. But at least he made it happen. An unusual green colour because of the patina chosen, it was placed outside the Royal Concert Hall by the main Buchanan Galleries

shopping arcade. This guaranteed a lot of people to admire the work by Kenny Hunter (May 2002) but the foundry warned that if it was not put on a higher plinth than suggested it would attract the efforts of vandals. They were right. Dewar's spectacles were broken so many times that even with an optician donating several pairs for replacement, it was eventually put on a higher pedestal and given steel spectacles at the end of 2005. In a seven-week makeover it was also recoloured, given a protective wax coating and the graffiti washed off. However his suit remains crumpled because it always was like that. A new positioning proved essential and the statue was moved slightly; the new plinth is two metres higher.

In Cathedral Square are several worthies. **James Lumsden** (by John Mossman) was Lord Provost of Glasgow, ran his father's stationery firm and was Chairman of the Clydesdale Bank. He also raised a lot of money for the Royal Infirmary and founded the Glasgow Native Benevolent Society. **David Livingston,** missionary and explorer is here – again by Mossman. **James White** of Overtoun was born in Glasgow, practised as a solicitor and became president of the Chamber of Commerce. The sculptor was Francis Leslie. **James Arthur** was a trader of note in the city. In 1849 he set up a retail business in Buchanan Street, Glasgow with Hugh Fraser, then taking over the wholesale side of the business and turning it into an internationally renowned Scottish company. The sculptor was George Lawson.

In Cathedral Square Gardens is **Reverend Dr Norman Macleod.** He was a Minister and influential liberal Presbyterian. Born in Campbeltown, Macleod was ordained in 1838 and was founder of the Evangelical Alliance. He was appointed Chaplain to the Queen in 1857 and Moderator of the Church of Scotland in 1869. He often preached abroad and was a brilliant public orator. This statue shows him in the act of preaching, bible in hand, books at his feet. This was the first statue to be erected in Cathedral Square after a major redesign of the area in the 1870s. A John Mossman work again.

On the grandiose Clydeport Building in Robertson Street in the City Centre look up at the impressive frontage and, above the columns, you will see many figures. Here is a

REVEREND NORMAN MACLEOD

A brilliant public speaker on religious matters.

DUNBAR is home to John Muir although he went off to America to find fame and fortune which he certainly did, becoming known as the father of world conservation – there is a John Muir Day ever year now in the United States.

THE MOVIE
Braveheart contained many historical inaccuracies but inspired triple heart-bypass survivor Tom Church to carve this thirteen-ton sandstone work in his spare time for placement at the Wallace Monument outside Stirling.

JOHN COWANE over Cowane's Hospital in Stirling. The legend is that at as the clock chimes twelve midnight on New Year morning the statue known as Auld Staney Breeks comes to dance in the courtyard and if children wonder why he didn't appear the parents say he was deafened by the ringing of the bells.

DON NESBIT of the Powderhall Foundry in Edinburgh in the Kilmany studio of sculptor David Annand putting coats of silicon rubber onto poet Robert Fergusson.

FLORA MACDONALD risked her life to help the young Pretender as his Jacobite cause ran out of steam and is rightly honoured in her home town of Inverness.

ROBERT BURNS has more statues spread around Scotland – and the world – than any other Scot and this tribute is in Dumfries where he died in 1796 a few days before the birth of his last son.

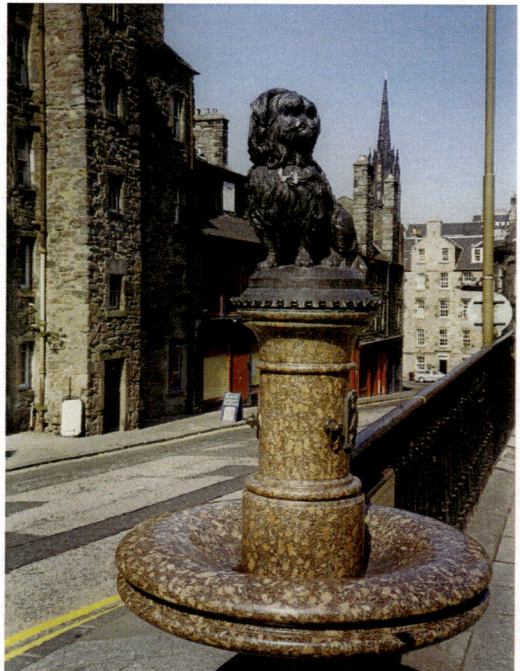

GREYFRIARS BOBBY was rewarded for loyalty to his master with this statue in Edinburgh.

DONALD DEWAR hasn't turned green with age or envy. An unusual green patina was used on this statue outside the Buchanan Galleries in Glasgow which has now had to be raised to try and thwart the vandals on a Saturday night who kept ripping off his spectacles.

THE BLACK WATCH statue in Perth commemorates one of Scotland's finest old regiments and was the spot for vigorous protests against the disbandment of some of the country's great regiments to form a new Royal Regiment of Scotland.

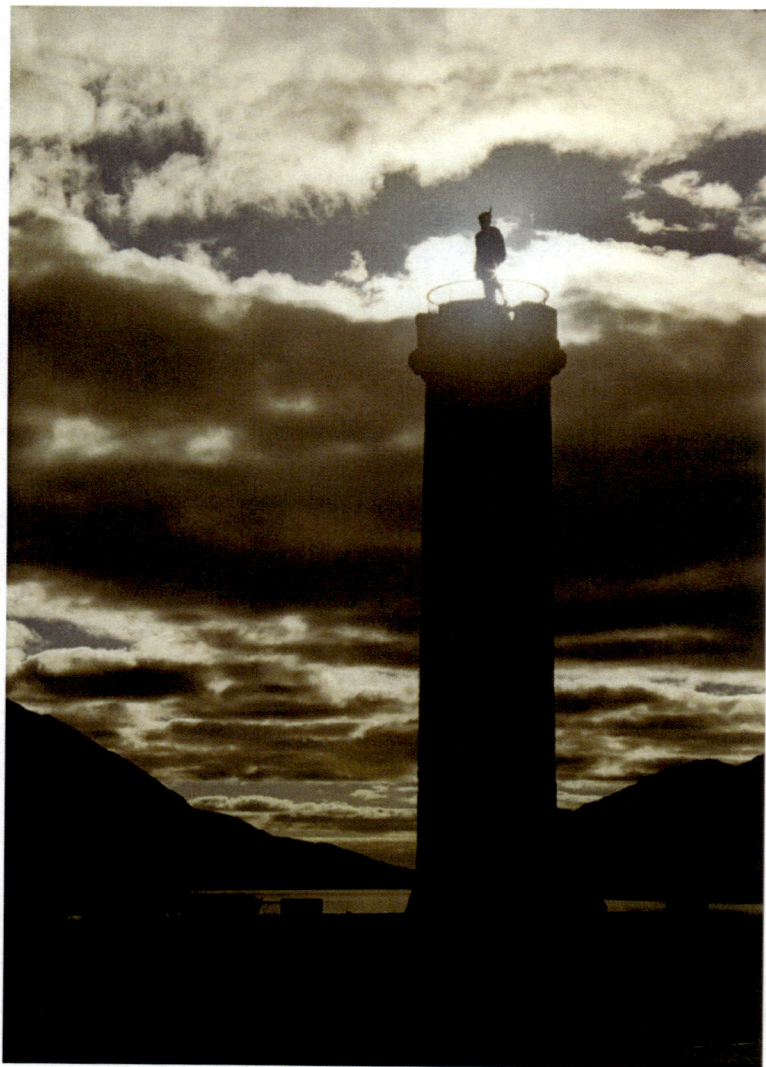

GLENFINNAN
and perhaps the
most stunning
location for a
statue anywhere
in Scotland. It
commemorates
Bonnie Prince
Charlie at the spot
where he landed
to get back
his crown
in 1745.

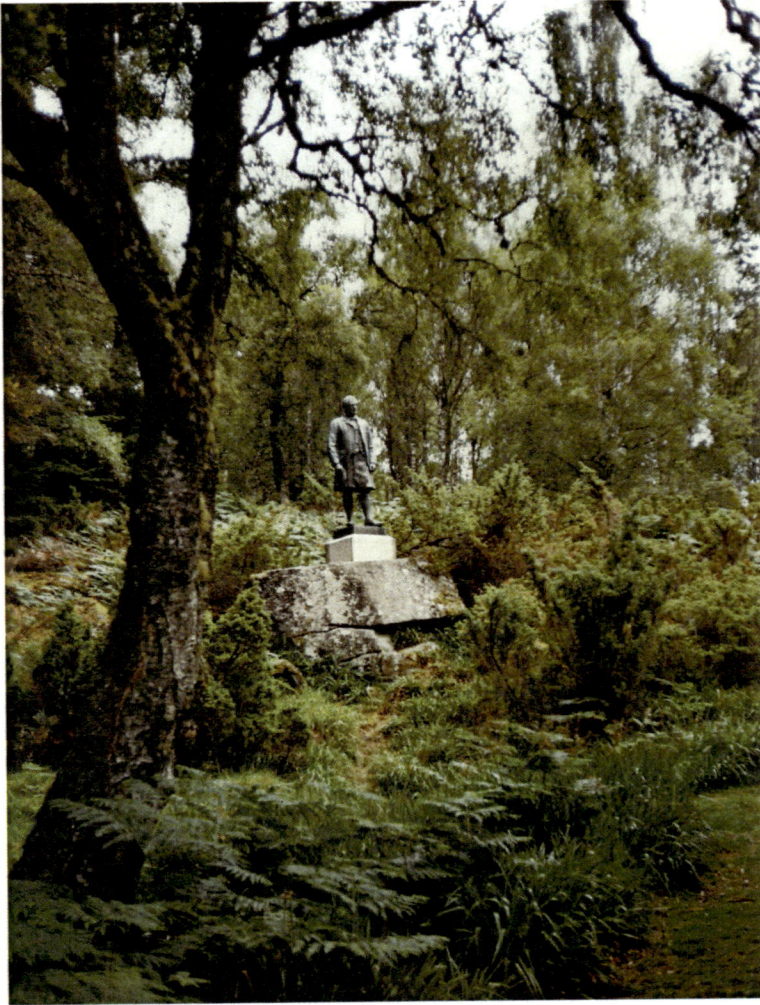

JOHN BROWN, faithful servant (some say more than that) to Queen Victoria stands amongst the greenery of Balmoral Castle grounds in a spot where some visitors say the Queen can sometimes be seen watching in a ghostly apparition in white among the trees immediately to Brown's left.

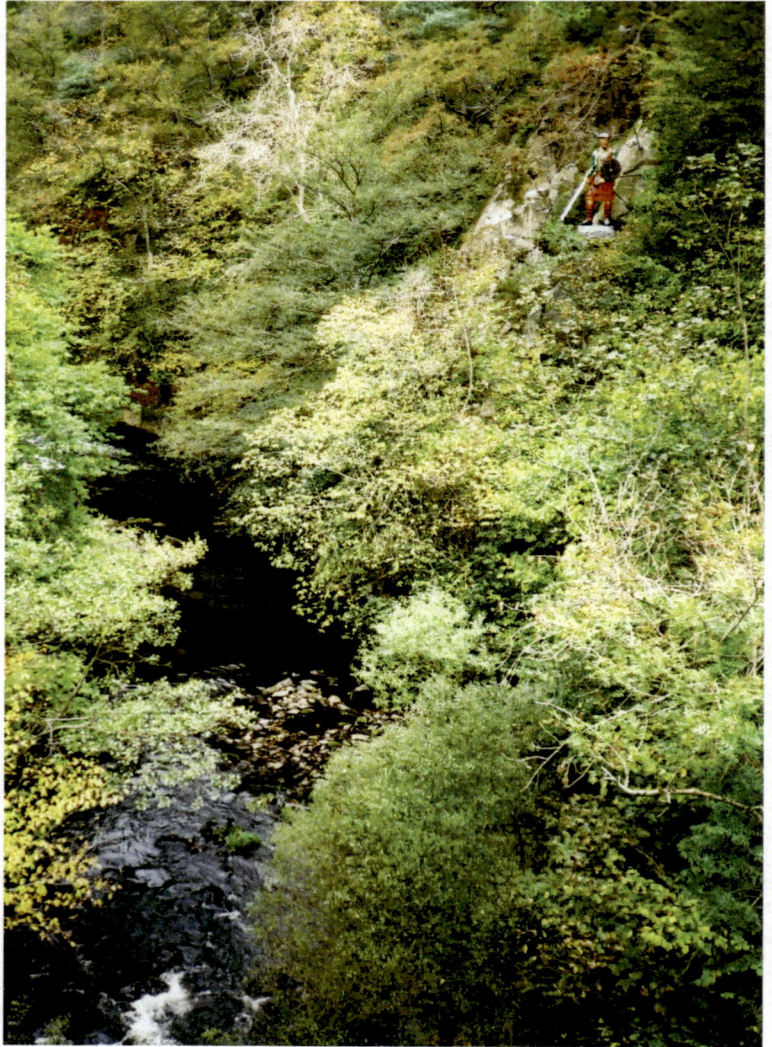

ROB ROY
was an outlaw
who found favour
with the public.
He is seen here in
the trees just visible
from the Leucher
Burn at Culter,
south of Aberdeen,
a burn he was said
to have jumped to
escape Redcoat
soldiers.

Scottish hero who is alongside some mythical figures from history. On the side of the pediment are three statues. They are of Henry Bell (right), an engineer from Torphichen near Linlithgow who in 1812 launched the first commercially successful steamship in the country. In the middle is our old friend James Watt and on the left is a man who deserves a more prominent spot and a wider audience, **Thomas Telford** (1757–1843). Telford was born at Westerkirk in Dumfriesshire, started life as a mason, then became an architect and in 1786 was appointed surveyor of Shropshire, a post which entailed building several bridges over the River Severn, including the famous cast iron one at Bewdley. He also designed and built aqueducts, harbours, roads and canals including the Caledonian Canal in the Scottish Highlands. He was also responsible for the Menai Straits Bridge in North Wales, one of the first to use wrought iron links to suspend the roadway. He was the first president of the Institute of Civil Engineers in 1828.

Mention of statues in Glasgow cannot go without reference to the Duke of Wellington in Royal Exchange Square in the City Centre – another equestrian work by Baron Marochetti. The Duke is in full field-marshal uniform on his horse, Copenhagen. For some reason it has become a Glasgow tradition for someone to put a traffic cone on his head. The statue stands in front of the Gallery of Modern Art who recently said they would like it removed as inappropriate to the building behind. But a storm of public protest made them back down, another example of the affection of Glaswegians towards their statues.

Outside Glasgow at Dumbarton, a man who gave employment to many at hard times is remembered. Outside the Municipal Buildings is a bronze statue of shipbuilder **Sir Peter Denny** by William

DUMBARTON
Sir Peter Denny deserves this memorial, his shipbuilding business employed many locals.

Hamo Thorneycroft. Denny was born here into a well-known shipbuilding family whose firm built the Cutty Sark in 1869 and were always pioneers in the industry, building the first all-welded ship amongst other 'firsts.' He was awarded the CBE in 1918.

Paisley near Glasgow was a centre of the textile industry in the 19th and 20th centuries. Nowadays it is a thriving shopping centre with the arts scene well served by the Paisley Arts Centre. It is home to busy sculptor Alexander Stoddart. In a booklet entitled Paisley's Public Sculptures he commented that "the public sculpture and statuary of Paisley stands as a civic

collection of the highest quality and widest stylistic span". Paisley people can recognize heroism when they see it. On the 700th anniversary of the death of William Wallace they staged an exhibition on the life of our national icon with just a one word title – 'Hero'.

The town has produced a number of deservedly famous people for its size and they are commemorated here with work from some of the country's best-known sculptors. They include two works by John Mossman: a sandstone statue of Rev. **Patrick Brewster** (1788–1859), minister of Paisley Abbey and champion of the poor, and a bronze statue of **Alexander Wilson** (1776–1813) weaver poet and father of North American ornithology near the Abbey. The money for this work was raised at open air choral concerts.

David Watson Stevenson, who produced a lot of work in Scotland, is responsible for a bronze to **Robert Tannahill** in a nearby spot on the lawns at Abbey Close. You may not know Mr Tannahill and, strangely, you won't learn much from the statue. It simply reads: Tannahill – born 1774 Died 1810. In fact he was a poet and songwriter

PAISLEY

Alexander Wilson is described as the father of North American ornithology.

as well as being a competent weaver and is much admired abroad in places like the United States and Australia who celebrate his anniversary. He has been compared to Burns himself and has many fans of his lyrical and traditional Scots folk music.

During the late nineteenth and early twentieth centuries Paisley's prosperity depended on the great mills owned by the Clark and Coats families where thousands of local people made sewing thread for all over the world. It made the mill owners very rich but the Coats gave a lot back to the town. By the Town Hall stand two statues by William Birnie Rhind, probably unique in Scotland as they are to brothers **Sir Peter and Thomas Coats** 'in memory of their many acts of generosity to their native town'.

The ubiquitous **Robert Burns** is here in Fountain Gardens with a bronze statue from F.W. Pomeroy, the London artist. Done in 1895 it has a relief panel with a scene from Tam O'Shanter on the base and shows the poet with hand on a plough.

In the High Street is the **Rev. John Witherspoon** (1723–94) Born in Gifford, East Lothian he was Minister

at Paisley before emigrating in 1768 to the United Sates of America to become President of the College of New Jersey (now the famous Princeton University). He produced many books and essays and helped frame the American Declaration of Independence in 1776, the only clergyman to sign the document. It was sculpted by Sandy Stoddart in 2001.

Stoddart is already considering his next two

PAISLEY
Enjoying the dramatic backdrop of Paisley Abbey is Robert Tannahill, poet and songwriter, but you wouldn't know it from the simple inscription.

PAISLEY
The Coats brothers were rewarded for their generous donations to the town.

John Witherspoon
helped frame the
American Declaration
of Independence.

states to Men of Paisley: a veteran MP and a man who helped build the iconic Sydney Harbour Bridge. Willie Gallagher (1881–1965) is remembered as a battling Communist Member of Parliament who was also a keen member of the temperance movement. He was a shop steward at a motor works and Clyde Workers Committee Chairman who joined the Social Democratic Federation and was active in converting it to the British Socialist Party. He was imprisoned for his strong views but in 1935 won West Fife as a Communist MP. He died in his Paisley council flat in 1965 and forty thousand mourners attended his funeral, his coffin draped in the Red Flag and with many tributes from the Soviet Bloc. Tony Benn is a supporter of this project.

Thomas Smith Tait (1882–1952) was the son of a Paisley stonemason who became the most prominent Scottish architect of the period between the Wars and a major voice in the Modernist Movement. Amongst his designs are the St Andrews House in Edinburgh (1934) and the piers for the bridge across Sydney Harbour which was started in 1924 and took one thousand four hundred men eight years to construct.

It is probably safe to say these men will be featured on a plinth: Stoddart has very definite views on the role of statues and the part a plinth plays saying: "it is not to elevate, but to make a division between our world and their world. Therefore the form of dress is important too and great care must be chosen in the final site, especially in relation to other nearby statues".

Just five miles from Glasgow is Blantyre, home to Scotland's most famous explorer and missionary who was born here in 1823. **David Livingstone** (1813–1873) is now remembered with a fascinating museum. Situated within twenty acres of gardens and once housing twenty-four families, the tenement of his birth is now a major exhibition charting his times in Africa. The David Livingstone Centre celebrates this man who at the age of ten was sent to work in a cotton mill but, studying hard, went on to study medicine in Glasgow with the idea of becoming a medical missionary. In 1841 he first went to South Africa as a missionary and, despite opposition from the Boers, travelled widely throughout the country. In an attempt to open up trade routes from east and west to the interior, he discovered the Victoria Falls on the Zambesi River. He returned to Britain, resigned as a missionary, and was sent back to Africa in 1858 by the British Government to lead another expedition. In 1862 his wife died at Shupunga.

Back in Britain, he exposed the truth about the slave trade. In 1866 he was back in Africa again to look for the source of the Nile but was in poor health when he reached Lake Tanganyika and this worried his friends back home. A party led by Henry Morton Stanley was sent to find him and did so in 1871 with the immortal

BLANTYRE

Robert Livingstone lost the use of one arm after this attack by a lion.

words: 'Dr Livingstone I presume?' He died at Chitambo in 1873; his body was embalmed and returned to England for burial in Westminster Abbey. The striking sculpture in the grounds of the centre is called Livingstone and the Lion. In 1844 Livingstone and men from Mabotsa (now in present day South Africa) went hunting lions which had killed a woman from the village. Livingstone shot and wounded one of the lions which then attacked him before suddenly dropping dead. He was lucky to survive and his arm was so badly injured he never regained full use of it. 'He shook me as a terrier does a rat,' he said. The original statuette was designed and modelled in wax by Ray Harryhausen from which the sculptor Gareth K. Knowles developed the striking bronze work. The project was sponsored by Ray and Diana Harryhausen on 7 April 2004.

CHAPTER 7

Towards Burns Country

*'See the conquering hero comes, sound the trumpets,
beat the drums'*

THOMAS MORELL

It is fitting to start this chapter with one of the great loves in the life of Robert Burns.

Only fragments of Dunoon Castle remain in a great position overlooking the Firth of Clyde and near the birthplace of **Highland Mary** (1764–1786). This is perhaps the most dramatic of the few statues of a woman in Scotland and she is depicted gazing across the water to the Ayrshire coast. The sculptor was D.W. Stevenson and contributions to its cost were invited from Burns followers all over the world. The site of the statue was gifted by Mrs Bouverie Campbell Wyndham and the bronze statue stands on a pedestal of Ballochmyle stone designed by R.A. Bryden of Glasgow. Lady Kelvin unveiled the statue on 1 August 1897.

The site is actually a mile from where Mary Campbell was born in a farmhouse at Auchamorer.

Her parents moved to Campbeltown when she was two years old and at the age of twelve she was employed as a domestic servant with a family there, later as a nursery maid. How she first met Burns is unclear, perhaps it was at church in Tarbolton where she was also in service. The relationship was undoubtedly serious although Burns made little mention of

DUNOON

The sad eyes of Highland Mary tell of her lost love, Robert Burns.

her, was not seen in her company and most of his poems of that time were about Jean Armour who was now Mrs Burns and carrying his child. But her father hated Burns and is reported to have said of Burns that he 'would rather hae seen the de'il himself coming to the hoose to coort his dochter than him.' This clash led Burns to 'unspeakable misery.'

Burns was failing to make his farm at Mossgiel pay and had decided to emigrate to Jamaica. When he learnt Jean was pregnant he gave her a written acknowledgement of marriage, believing this would make it all legal. But Mr Armour, a stonemason from Mauchline, was furious, took the document to his lawyer, and had it mutilated by cutting out the names. Burns was highly indignant and angry towards Jean. It was at this crisis in his life he met Mary and no doubt fell in love with her.

On the banks of the Fail they plighted their troth on 14 May 1786 by exchanging bibles, pronouncing their vows to be faithful to each other. After this they parted, never to meet again because tragically Mary died five months later in October of a malignant fever.

Did Burns intend to go to Jamaica with Mary? After her death her only sister Annie said that Burns sent Mary letters enclosing songs he had written for her but only two have survived. The Campbells destroyed all his correspondence after her death. They are *My Highland Lassie, O* and *Will Ye Go To the Indies, My Mary?* Many years after her death Burns said: "My Highland lassie was as warm hearted and charming a young creature as ever blessed a man with generous love."

There is not a lot new to say about Scotland's greatest romantic hero, **Robert Burns.**

Some of his characters such as Tam O'Shanter are immortalized. He is remembered not just with statues all over Scotland but all over the world, New Zealand and America notably and Burns Nights are celebrated every January in many countries.

Burns gave a great legacy to the Scottish people, a declaration of common

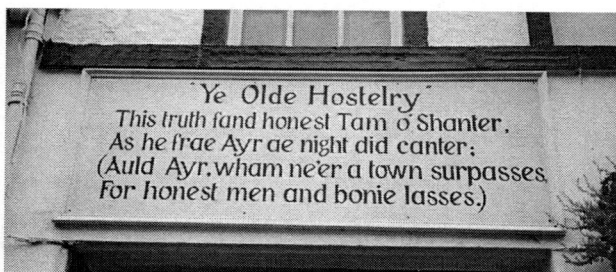

Ye Olde Hostelry
This truth fand honest Tam o Shanter,
As he frae Ayr ae night did canter:
(Auld Ayr, wham ne'er a town surpasses,
For honest men and bonie lasses.)

humanity and classlessness. *A Man's a Man for A' That*, first published anonymously had a radicalism and generosity of spirit, a true Scottish identity. It was typically brave writing at that time, a period of French and American revolutions. In 1773 he had visited in the Carron Ironworks near Falkirk and was horrified at the conditions.

The pride he shared in Scotland and wrote about has lasted through the centuries. In his poetry he praises our heroes such as Wallace, Bruce and Bonnie Prince Charlie. '*Scots wha hae wi' Wallace bled/Scots wham Bruce has often led/Welcome to your gory bed/Or to victorie.*' It was written (typically with a hangover) five years after a visit to Banockburn. Along with Sir Walter Scott he opened up Scotland to the world, not a bad tribute to a working man and agricultural worker.

On 1 July 1999 the first Scottish parliament for nearly three hundred years met in Edinburgh. The acclaimed folk singer Sheena Wallace sang, unaccompanied, *A Man's A Man* and there were genuine tears in the eyes of the whole house, united regardless of party. It was an iconic moment and a real tribute to Burns that some two hundred years after his death he could still unite a nation. Afterwards people suggested his poem become the Scottish national anthem.

The first of seven children, the national poet of Scotland was born on 25 January 1759 in a long low cottage (the auld clay biggin) with a thatched roof at Alloway, then a rural village but now almost a suburb of Ayr. At the age of seven he moved with his family to Mount Oliphant, a farm south-east of Alloway. He walked to school in Ayr for lessons in French and Latin.

Burns became chief farm labourer to his father who was a tenant farmer rendered penniless by a landlord. This state of affairs helped fashion Burns' writings. When his father died Burns moved to a farm at Mossgiel, near Mauchline and began to write in earnest. Kilmarnock was his first publisher and the early poems met with much praise. Robert Burns was twenty-seven when he arrived in Edinburgh in November 1786 after the successful publication of his poetry and the literary establishment took him to their heart. Despite the success, he at times felt trapped, unable to make enough money from writing to leave farming and hobnobbing with the establishment whilst writing against them.

Burns often boasted of his sexual conquests and he fathered several illegitimate children but in 1788 he eventually married Jean Armour with whom he already had two children. His writing became prodigious He moved to Ellisland Farm near Dumfries, living there for the last three years of his life. He died there aged thirty-seven on 21 July 1796. Over ten thousand people attended his funeral. On the day he was buried Bonnie Jean produced a son.

The Immortal Memory of Robert Burns lives on with work like *Auld Lang Syne, O My Love is Like a Red Red Rose, Charlie is my Darling; The Selkirk Grace; Tam O'Shanter* (maybe his greatest effort) and the *Address to the Haggis.*

Many towns in this region are associated with Burns – Ayr, Irvine, Kilmarnock; Mauchline, Dumfries, Alloway. At Alloway is the Burns Monument and in the gardens the Statue House and humorous statues of Burns' cronies, **Tam O'Shanter and Souter Johnny**, the work of James Thom in 1897. Both Thom and Burns liked a drink so maybe it is no surprise to also see here Thom's statue of **Nance Tinnock**, an innkeeper from a hostelry in Mauchline they frequented.

The Burns Monument is one of many memorials to the great poet around the world. The foundation stone was paid on 25 January 1820 and completed 4 July 1823. It stands 70 feet high and has a copy of a bust to Burns by the great sculptor Sir John Steel; the original is in Poets Corner in Westminster Abbey, London.

The foundation stone of the Burns Monument was laid by Sir Alexander Boswell, son of James Boswell the famous diarist and biographer. Ayrshire's two great literary figures, Burns and Boswell were contemporaries but never met.

The Auld Kirk at Alloway, a ruin even in Burns' day, is

GALLOWAY

In the Statue House by the Burns Monument are James Thom's figures of Tam O' Shanter and Souter Johnny, carved out of the local stone which makes them look like characters from that old Lurpak butter TV advert.

Left
GALLOWAY

Also in the Statue House by Thom is Nance Tinnock, an innkeeper from Mauchline.

Right
MAUCHLINE

Jean Armour, wife of Robert Burns, born Mauchline 25 February 1765. Died Dumfries 26 March 1834. Erected by the Mauchline Burns Club assisted by funding from Score Environment Ltd.

to be renovated. The old haunted church, where Burns' father is buried and which is the setting for Tam O'Shanter, will get a £250,000 facelift by 2009 in time for the 250th anniversary of Burns birth. Certainly some work is required to fully celebrate the national bard; the Burns National Heritage Park at Alloway has seen damp and rainwater in the museum threatening some Burns memorabilia. Marketing expert Alison McRae has been appointed to head a worldwide drive – aimed particularly at the fifty million strong Scots diaspora – using the Burns celebrations to promote Scotland to a worldwide audience.

At Mauchline, eleven miles east of Ayr is the National Burns Memorial Tower erected on the centenary of the poet's death. Also here is the Burns House Museum on Castle Street where Burns lived at the time of his marriage to **Jean Armour.** On the statue is the lovely inscription: 'Of a' the airts the winds can blow, I dearly like the West, For there the bonny lassie lives, The lassie I lo'e best'.

Dumfries is a real Burns town with probably more sites, stones, relics, monuments, statues etc. than anywhere in the world. At the northern end of the High Street, by a floral roundabout, is the Burns statue, a sentimental piece of

Victorian frippery in white Carrara marble, featuring the great man holding a posy in one hand while the other clutches at his heart. His faithful hound, Luath, lies curled around his feet – though it doesn't look much like a Border collie (as Luath was). The statue is by Amelia Hill and was unveiled in 1882.

Further down the High Street, Burns' body lay in state at the Midsteeple building. Nearby is the Globe Inn, Burns' favourite drinking place and now HQ of the local Burns Society – one of the few surviving 17th-century buildings. There is a small statue of Burns by Steve Niblock here. Burns had a fling with Annie Park, a barmaid at the Inn, and the resultant child was taken into the Burns household by the long-suffering Jean Armour, who apparently opined that 'our Robbie should have had twa wives.' In Burns Street stands Burns House where he died of rheumatic heart disease in 1796 a few days before the birth of his last son, Maxwell. Burns only lived here for three years but his wife Jean stayed on until her own death thirty-eight years later. He was buried by St. Michael's Church but in 1815 was dug up and moved across the graveyard

to a purpose-built Mausoleum which houses a slightly ludicrous statue of Burns being accosted by the Poetic Muse.

Although Burns dominates this region there are other personalities of note recalled. Kilmarnock is noted for first bringing Burns to prominence with the 1786 first publication of his poems but also here is a statue to **Sir James Shaw** (1764–1844). He was Lord Mayor of London and a real-life Dick Whittington. Shaw was a humble farmer's son from Mosshead but his father died when he was only five and his mother moved to Kilmarnock. He emigrated to America aged fifteen but returned to London five years later for a job in commerce. He was appointed Lord Mayor of London in 1805, a position that saw him at the head of the funeral to the great hero, Admiral Lord Nelson. In 1806 he entered Parliament as an MP. His marble statue was made possible through public subscription of £1,000 and was unveiled in 1848. It is by James Fillans.

The Burns Monument in Kilmarnock, was a large and, some said, rather ugly red sandstone affair by Robert S. Ingram, first erected in 1879 in Kay Park. Shortly after the death of his father, Robert Ingram was present at the formal opening of what was the crowning point of his career. This 80ft high Gothic tower was slowly disintegrating as the twenty-first century was reached. Sadly vandals completed the job as the whole monument was burnt to the ground in November 2004 in an arson attack that left two firefighters badly injured and saw three young men convicted. The good statue of the bard in the monument was done by W.G. Stevenson and thankfully survived the fire to form the centrepiece of the £3million refurbishment due for completion in the autumn or winter of 2007. The monument is to be strengthened and partially rebuilt and in the centre will be an open courtyard containing the statue. The premises will include a local heritage and genealogy centre, even a registry office. No doubt a romantic Burns would have approved of that; Kay Park is popular with courting couples. There is also a recent statue to Burns in the town centre, at the junction of Foregate and Portlandgate, celebrating the Kilmarnock Edition –

KILMARNOCK
The Burns Monument was largely destroyed by fire in an arson attack in 2004 but there are ambitious redevelopment plans.

by Alexander Stoddart (1995). Yet another statue to Burns is in nearby Irvine and was sculpted by Pittendrigh Macgillivray.

Here also, in the Irvine Valley is not a statue as such to the great William Wallace but the latest tribute to him in Scotland. Wallace's name has been linked with this area since his defeat of the English at Loudoun Hill in 1297. There used to be a cairn here marking the burial place of the English dead but this has gone. Now there is a Spirit of Scotland Sculpture by local artist Richard Price erected in September 2004 in the form of a five-metre steel arch in the very rough outline of a figure with a suitable inscription on it. It is a variant from other more traditional memorials

One of the newest
depictions of Burns
is in this shopping
centre, in a design by
sculptor David
Annand he is seen
with his dog Luath.

of Wallace but this modern
artwork shows Scotland's
greatest hero is still being
remembered in different ways.

Incidentally, West Kilbride
is renowned locally as the
Scots village named as the
Country's UFO Capital, with

more sightings of strange
sightings in the sky than
anywhere else. Scotland, in
fact, has more sightings of
UFOs than any other country
in the world.

The historic town of Ayr
has been in existence for over
eight hundred years and
closely linked with Burns
who spent his early years
here, his poems *Tam
O'Shanter* and *The Brigs of
Ayr* are set in the town.
Burns extolled Ayr as
'unsurpassed for honest men
and bonnie lasses'.

In a small garden in Burns
Statue Square near the
railway station is George
Lawson's renowned bronze
sculpture, considered one of
the very finest of the poet. It
was presented by the Ayr
Burns Club and unveiled on

AYR

George Lawson's
depiction of Robert
Burns is one of the
finest of the bard
and copied all over
the world.

8 July 1891 before a crowd of forty thousand people. Standing over nine feet tall, Burns is looking towards his birthplace, Alloway. It stands on a granite pedestal designed by Ayr architect James A. Morris with four bronze plaques. These show Burns' parting from Highland Mary and scenes from *Tam O'Shanter, The Cottar's Saturday Night,* and *The Jolly Beggars.*

In the summer of 2006 Ayr had another Burns statue, in a new £70 million shopping mall at Ayr Central. The work of David Annand, it is an innovative design based on Burns' poem *'The Twa Dogs'*, a circular bench with the sculptures and excerpts from the poem on it, allowing shoppers and pedestrians to sit alongside the great Bard and his faithful border collie Luath.

There are two rather undistinguished statues of William Wallace in Ayr. One is in a niche at the corner of Newmarket Street and High Street. It was erected in the 19th century to commemorate his imprisonment in the Tollboth of Ayr but locals maintain that the statue was taller than expected and the legs had to be shortened to fit the niche!

The other is on the Wallace Tower in the High Street. This is the work of James Thom but did not meet with universal approval with one comment being: 'it is more like an angry

AYR

Left

William Wallace in Newmarket Street. . .

Right

. . . and on the nearby Wallace Tower.

schoolmaster than the champion of his race.' Further up the High Street is a modern bronze statue of a fisherman by Malcolm Robertson (1995) recalling the old fish market site. The old Meal Market nearby was demolished in 1841 and on the wide part of the pavement outside a bank is a bronze sculpture by Doug Cocker, 'The Poet and the World.' This was placed here in 1996 on the bicentenary of the death of Robert Burns.

Wellington Square was built for 'county people, gentlemen of rich fortune and retired army officers.' It houses three statues, one in particular probably displaying how our view towards heroes has changed over the decades, if not centuries. It commemorates **James George Smith Neill** (1810–1857), a soldier who was one of the heroes of the 1857 Indian Mutiny.

Born in Wellington Square in 1810, he studied at Ayr Academy and Glasgow University and then joined the East India Company. He was known as fearless, a religious zealot, but a considerate leader to the men under him. He could be ruthless if crossed and there is a story told of him preventing a train from

leaving Calcutta railway station without his men on board by threatening to shoot the station master. He served in Burma and in the Crimean war and quickly rose to the rank of Brigadier General. In India he commanded the Madras Fusiliers to secure Allahabad but was superseded in command of the force to relieve Cawnpore and Lucknow by Brigadier General Havelock. He took this badly and arrived in Cawnpore in a bad mood. But historians now say nothing can excuse the revolting retribution handed out to those mutineers deemed responsible for the massacre and terrible atrocities against British women and children in

AYR

James Neill would today probably be tried for war crimes but was a hero of the Indian Mutiny.

Cawnpore. Neill ordered them to clean the house where the butchery had occurred by licking up every last drop of blood whilst being lashed unmercifully. They were then hanged. Neill was subsequently killed in action at Lucknow in September 1857.

The 10ft high statue on a 12ft pedestal commemorating him is by Matthew Noble and was erected soon afterwards by public subscription in 1859. The inscription describes him as 'a brave, resolute, self-reliant soldier, universally acknowledged as the first who stemmed the torrent of rebellion in Bengal.....he fell gloriously at the Relief of Lucknow 25 September 1857 aged 47'. Below the statue is a relief of the fighting. There are also other memorials to Neill in India. This son of Ayr is buried in the Auld Kirkyard. However his deeds are now seen as wanton brutality.

An even bigger memorial by Matthew Noble is to **The 13th Earl of Eglinton** (1812–1861) and was erected in 1865 to commemorate a family heavily involved in 18th-century town planning. He became the Lord Lieutenant of Ayrshire and Viceroy of Ireland. He loved horse-racing and is remembered as the man behind the famous jousting event, the Eglinton Tournament at Eglinton Castle held in 1839 at a huge financial loss. The Earl was a generous benefactor to many sports in Ayrshire and curling teams still compete for a trophy donated by him. This large statue is notable for a typical flowery eulogy Victorians loved to write. It states: '....erected by public testimony of admiration for his public character, of affectionate remembrance of his private virtues and of universal regret for the loss occasioned to his friends by his early death'.

Sir James Fergusson (1832–1907) was a

statesman and MP for Ayrshire who held various government posts abroad in Australia, New Zealand and India. He was killed in an earthquake in 1907 in Kingston, Jamaica and this work is by Sir William Goscombe John (1910). The garden in the square also remembers locally-born **John Loudoun McAdam,** the road surveyor and engineer with a tablet erected in 1936 to mark the centenary of his death. In the opposite corner of the garden is the Kennedy Fountain commemorating Primrose William Kennedy, a banker, landowner and ex-Provost of Ayr who played a major role in civic affairs in Ayr in the mid-nineteenth century.

Behind the County Building is Pilkington Jackson's **Royal Scottish Fusiliers Memorial** described at the time as 'coy and of a mannered sentimentality' but honouring the County's regiment from its formation in 1678 until its amalgamation with the Highland Light Infantry in 1959 to form the Royal Highland Fusiliers. The bronze dates from 1960 and commemorates soldiers of the regiment who died in the Second World War. There is another earlier statue to the regiment across town to the men who died in various

AYR
Statues to
The Royal Scots
Fusiliers.

SCOTLAND'S HEROES

19th century campaigns with the line: 'Ye Babbling Winds in Silence Sweep – Disturb Ye Not the Hero's Sleep.'

At Ayr Racecourse is the legendary steeplechaser **Red Rum**, more associated with the sands at Southport but winner here of the Scottish Grand National in 1974, the year he did the unique 'double' winning the Grand National at Aintree as well. The sculpture was done in 1975 by Annette Yarrow. The Scottish Grand National has been held here since 1966.

At Wallacetown south of Ayr is a statue in the cemetery to local coal owner **Dr John Taylor** (1805–1842) who was considered a dangerous Chartist by the Government for his fiery pronouncements and views. He stood unsuccessfully for Ayr Burghs in 1832. He was once arrested in 1839 for inciting a riot in Birmingham but released after a month in jail. His health suffered thereafter and he died three years later.

At Cumnock in front of the Town Hall there is a bust by Benno Schotz to **James Keir Hardie** (1856–1915), founder of the Scottish Labour Party. He was born at Legbrannock in Ayrshire and at the age of ten was working down the mines where he stayed for twelve years, falling foul of the mine owners for trying to recruit the workers into a union. He moved to Hamilton and worked as a journalist but the cause of the working man was still dear to him and he was involved in the creation of the Scottish Miners' Federation. In 1888 he was founding Chairman of the Scottish Labour Party and went on to become an MP for both English and Welsh constituencies but oddly never in Scotland. At Kirkconnel there is a **Miner's Bust**, a Memorial erected in 1983–4 after the closure of the last pit in the area. And in June 2004 the mining town of Muirkirk remembered their mining brothers. Between 1892 and 1964 eighty lives were lost in pit disasters. The First Minister unveiled a seven-foot high bronze of a miner in his hat and Davy lamp on a black granite plinth bearing the names of all the dead miners. The artist of the **Miners' Monument** was Kirti Mandir.

On the southern tip of the country here is another creature associated with Scotland but now returning to parts of England as well. **The Otter**, a much-loved Scottish aquatic mammal, is in memory of Gavin

Robert the Bruce
in the place where he
is said to have been
born.

Maxwell, author of *Ring of Bright Water*, who lived here for a time. This sculpture by Penny Wheatley is at Monreith by Kirkmaiden and was placed here in 1909.

Lochmaben is associated with **Robert the Bruce** whose 1879 statue here by John Hutchison shows Bruce in full armour. It stands, 8ft high on a 10ft pedestal of Dalbeattie granite, in the centre of town on the site of the old Mercat Cross. Lochmaben was founded in the 13th century as a burgh of barony by the Bruces of Annandale and finally gained its charter as a royal burgh in 1605. On the south side you can see the site of the 12th-century Castle of the Bruce. Bruce himself was probably born here in 1274

although there is an alternative view that he was born in Turnberry Castle.

Near the Mercat Cross is a statue of local historian the **Rev. William Graham**, by sculptor John Dodds.

Dumfries is quirky little town as shown by their decision not just to remember Burns but to put a statue of a rhinoceros on top of a bus shelter! Why a rhinoceros? Well, in the late 80s a mobile art project in the town created the animal sculpture on the suggestion of local schoolchildren and with grants from the local council. A bypass being built meant moving from its original site to its current position that is pretty vandal-proof and serves as a bit of a landmark. Also here, near the Dumfries Museum is a figure of Old Mortality and his Horse from Sir Walter Scott's *Old Mortality*. It is known as the Sinclair Memorial because the 1841 sculpture by Andrew Currie was won in a lottery by Dr. Sinclair, a surgeon with the Royal Navy at Chatham. However he was killed the day after the lottery and it was presented here.

Another Currie statue is **Henry Duncan** (1774–1846) founder of the savings bank movement. He is in Church Crescent on the wall of an appropriate bank. Duncan was a clergyman, born in Lochrutton, who became Minister at Ruthwell where he established the first idea of a savings bank. He also founded the *Dumfries & Galloway Courier* and during the 1843 Disruption joined the Free Church.

Edward Irving (1792–1834) is in Annan, south-east of Dumfries. He was assistant to Thomas Chalmers who founded the Free Church of Scotland and was born here. After Edinburgh University, he became a successful preacher in London but in 1825 announced the Second Coming of Jesus Christ was imminent, to the alarm of many. He was convicted of heresy and deposed from the church in 1833, turning him into a rather eccentric mystic. However his congregation largely followed him and a new communion was formed to be known as the Irvingite or Catholic Apostolic Church.

The latest statue to be erected in Dumfries takes us back to where we started. **Jean Armour** was granted the honour of a statue in 2004 in St Michael's Street appropriately near the Burns Mausoleum and near the man she looked after so faithfully and loyally for so many years. It is fitting she is

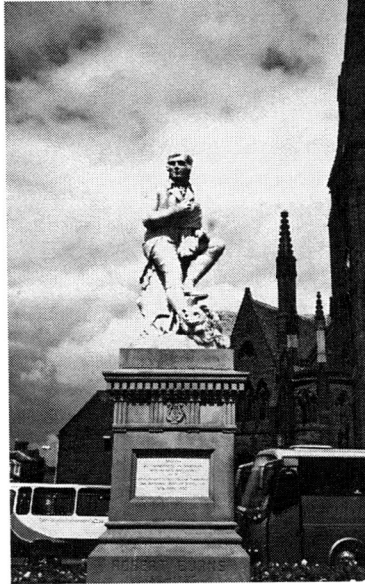

DUMFRIES
A real Robert Burns town with many memorabilia.

recalled in the town where she died as well as the town where she was born, Mauchline. It is by Jim Guy from Cornwall, life-and-a-quarter size, and cast by Art

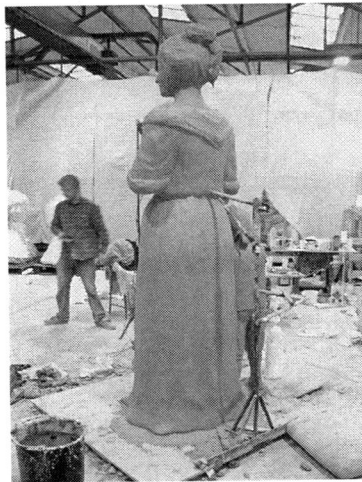

DUMFRIES
The last woman to have a statue erected to her in Scotland – Jean Armour, seen here in the foundry before her unveiling in St Michael's Street.

Founders Limited of Essex. Jean was a patient woman but can rest in her grave assured that she was once the love of the greatest Scottish hero this small country has ever produced, whose work lives on as strongly as ever nearly two hundred and fifty years after his death at a tragically young age.

CHAPTER 8

Forgotten and Flawed Heroes – and a Few Heroines

'Here's tae us. Wha's Like us – Damn Few and they're 'a Deid'

NEW YEAR TOAST

If any Scot still feels an inferiority complex towards the English the following lines will certainly put them right:

The Average Englishman, in the home he calls his castle, slips into his national costume – a shabby raincoat – patented by chemist Charles Macintosh from Glasgow, Scotland. En route to his office he strides along the English lane, surfaced by John McAdam of Ayr, Scotland. He drives an English car fitted with tyres invented by John Boyd Dunlop of Dreghorn, Scotland. At the office he receives the mail bearing adhesive stamps invented by James Chalmers of Dundee, Scotland. During the day he uses the telephone invented by Alexander Graham Bell, born in Edinburgh, Scotland. At home in the evening his daughter pedals her bicycle invented by Kirkpatrick MacMillan, blacksmith of Dumfries, Scotland. He watches the news on TV, an invention of John Logie Baird of Helensburgh, Scotland, and hears an item about the US Navy, founded by John Paul Jones of Kirkbean, Scotland. He has now been reminded too much of Scotland and in desperation he picks up the bible, only to find the first man mentioned in the good book is a Scot – King James VI – who authorized its translation. Nowhere can an Englishman turn to escape the ingenuity of the Scots. He could take to drink, but the Scots make the best in the world. He could take a rifle and end it all, but the breech-loading rifle was invented by Captain Patrick Ferguson of Pitfours, Scotland. If he escapes death, he could find himself on an operating table injected with penicillin, discovered by Alexander Fleming of Darvel, Scotland, and given an anaesthetic, discovered by Sir James Young Simpson of Bathgate, Scotland. Out of the anaesthetic he would find no comfort in learning that he was as safe as the Bank of England, founded by William Paterson of Dumfries, Scotland. Perhaps his only remaining hope would be to get a transfusion of guid Scottish blood which would entitle him to ask...

Wha's Like Us! Damn Few and they're 'a Deid!

Inventors do figure large amongst Scottish heroes over the centuries but these heroes come from all walks of life. If you list the most famous ever Scots, past and present, it might run to over three thousand names. An attempt is made in the Appendix to list a Top 100 but for the complete roll call the invaluable Chambers Scottish Biographical Dictionary is a must. It helpfully lists its biographies by subject, from Academia through to Zoology. When you see the wide range you realize how many Great Scots there are and have been. There are six William Wallaces alone in the book!

Politics is the biggest category which will probably disappoint, and maybe surprise, many people.

Alongside it is literature, religion and medicine – certainly areas where Scots have made a lasting impact across the world. The smallest category is just five names. Anyone believing they are related to a Scottish hero will probably be aware the most common Scottish names for the famous are Anderson (fifteen), Brown (twenty), Campbell (fifteen), Hamilton (twenty-three), Macdonald (twenty-six albeit with different spellings), Robertson (fifteen), Scott (fifteen), Smith (twenty seven), Stewart (twenty-three), Thomson (eighteen) and Wilson (twenty).

Not all are heroes of course – or heroines. As we have said one man's meat is another man's poison but some names stand out and, if not entirely forgotten to the Scottish public, have been largely overlooked by those capable of perpetuating their memory with a statue. Some men and women from the past are clearly recalled with pride and affection in some way in their home town or area, maybe a plaque or bust, but perhaps surprisingly not on a national level. Surely some of these men and women deserve more than a commemorative bust in some dusty hall away from public gaze, they warrant a public statue in a central and identifiable position – and not just on top of an eighty foot high building!

Inventors

Alexander Graham Bell (1847–1922) Surely one of the greatest Scotsmen of all time and someone 'remembered' every day. He invented the telephone as anyone who has ever said 'give me a bell' knows. He was born in Edinburgh, the son of Alexander Melville Bell, founder of the science of phonetics, who taught his son the mechanics of speech and problems of the deaf. In 1870 he emigrated to Canada and a year later to America where at Boston University he became Professor of Vocal Physiology. As well as helping deaf children communicate through speech he was obsessed with the idea of transmitting speech. His theory was that it was possible to transmit sound through telegraph wires and in 1875 his assistant in a different room heard the words through a crude apparatus: 'Watson, come here, I want you.' His design was patented in 1876 and the Bell Telephone Company was formed the following year.

He returned to Scotland on occasions and founded a school for the deaf in Greenock. He kept on inventing and with Thomas Edison came up with the photophone and also developed a form of iron lung and a metal detector machine. Scots were among the first to pick up the phone, Lord Kelvin being the first person in the UK to install one, and Glasgow had the UK's first telephone exchange. Bell died in Nova Scotia in the summer of 1922.

We might not have won the War without **Sir Robert Watson-Watt** (1892–1973). This son of Brechin in Angus was born in 1892 and attended University in Dundee and St Andrews before embarking on a career with the British Government in several research departments,

St Andrews University.

soon becoming expert on military uses of the radio. By the mid 1930s he had produced a short wave device that could locate aircraft by night or day. He had invented radar ('radio detection and ranging' to give it its full name). Daringly, he and his wife covertly toured Germany in the years before World War II to see what the Germans were up to in this field whilst in Britain an effective early warning system was being created with the building of many radar stations. He also helped America set up a system in 1941 that gave them advance warning of Japanese planes approaching Pearl Harbor. The Americans took no notice and we all know the result. He received a knighthood for his work in 1942. He died in Inverness in 1973. Currently campaigners in Brechin are looking for £50,000 to erect a well-merited statue there.

John Boyd Dunlop

(1840–1921) was born in Dreghorn, Ayrshire. After training to be a vet he worked in Edinburgh for a short time but then moved to Ireland, settling in Belfast in 1867. Playing with his child's tricycle one day he fitted home-made tyres using a length of hosepipe he had inflated with air. He realised the germ of an idea and was buoyed by the thought that another Scot, Robert William Thomson from Stonehaven, had patented the pneumatic tyre over many years beforehand, the high price of rubber preventing development. Thomson was, in fact, a serial inventor; amongst his many inventions was the first self-acting fountain pen. Dunlop started a business to produce pneumatic tyres for bicycles and later cars. They were a massive success, protecting sore bottoms all over the country and the Dunlop Rubber Company became known worldwide.

John Logie Baird

(1888–1946) was the son of a Helensburgh minister and invented television. He never really achieved the recognition he deserved during his lifetime and, rarely in great health, died in 1946 aged fifty-eight. Always keen on inventions he started out setting up a telephone exchange and electric light system at his parents' home. He was employed by the Clyde Valley Electric Power Company and became obsessed with the idea of sending pictures by sound

Robert Stevenson (1772–1850). Born in Glasgow the son of a merchant, he was the father of The Lighthouse Family in Scotland as they were called. In 1791 he started as an apprentice to this stepfather who was working for the Northern Lighthouse Board as an engineer. Stevenson loved the work and forgot all idea of his original career in the ministry eventually taking over from his stepfather and, in his capacity as a lighthouse engineer, built over twenty lighthouses. He was an innovative designer and invented the revolving light to make the beam visible from all directions. In 1800 with fellow Scottish engineer John Rennie he began work on the massive Bell Rock Lighthouse, his masterpiece that required him inventing new tools to work on the forbidding rock. On its completion he was truly a national hero. His three sons followed him into the business but relative Robert Louis Stevenson preferred a different life although he said: "whenever I smell seawater I know I am not far from one of the works of my ancestors".

waves. He was down to his last £50 when, in October 1925, he transmitted a dummy's head onto a receiver. Moments later office boy William Taynton became the first human face ever seen on TV and Baird paid him two shillings and sixpence for his trouble. He was a genius who also invented the first video recorder and the first fax machine. Perhaps lesser known is the invention to cure his permanently cold feet – the Baird Undersock. There is a bust of him in a Helensburgh street but many believe this is the man above all others we have reason to give thanks for every day and he should have more public recognition.

Sir Alexander Fleming
(1881–1955) was born near
Darvel, Ayrshire, the seventh
of eight children. Aged
fourteen he joined his
brothers in London as a
shipping clerk and in 1902
started his medical studies at
St Mary's Medical School.
He was a brilliant student,
specialising in bacteriology
and pioneered the use of
anti-typhoid vaccines on
humans. During World War
One he worked in a
battlefield hospital laboratory
in France and continued his
research, determined to find
a drug that would tackle the
infections to which so many
wounded soldiers succumbed.
He returned to become
Professor of Bacteriology at
St Mary's and discovered
penicillin quite by accident.
Returning from holiday in
1928 he saw mould on an
unwashed dish and noticed
all the bacteria in the area
had been killed. Amazingly,
when he announced his
discovery – which later

turned out to be the most
remarkable antibiotic ever
seen anywhere in the world –
the reaction was very
lukewarm as he couldn't
produce penicillin in a pure
enough form or in large
enough quantities.

He started to concentrate
on other things but the
Second World War brought
up the problem again and
two pharmaceutical
researchers Howard Florey
and Ernst (sic) Chain finally
produced it in quantity.
Fleming never made a penny
from his discovery as it
could not be patented in the
UK being a 'national'
substance although it was in
the USA. Fleming was
awarded a knighthood for
his work in 1944 and the
three men were awarded the
Nobel Prize for Medicine in
1945. On his death he was
cremated and the remains
put in St Paul's Cathedral in
London. There is a bust of
him at Darvel in the town
square near the war
memorial and a memorial
lecture each year but no
statue to remember this
great man. However, the
prostitutes of Barcelona did
remember him, deciding to
erect a statue to the man
they said saved their
business. A plant in Irvine
producing penicillin does

bear the name of a man who helped eradicate scarlet fever and diphtheria.

You might not know the name **James Chalmers** (1782–1853) but you probably have cause to recall him every day. This son of Arbroath invented the first adhesive postage stamp in 1834 when working as a printer in Dundee. Letters were originally paid for by the receiver rather than the sender which caused much confusion and cost to the Post Office. His stamp bore the slogan General Postage – Not Exceeding Half an Ounce' and he suggested different coloured stamps for different weights. Parliament liked the idea and in 1840 the Penny Black was launched. His granddaughter erected a plaque to the originator of the first adhesive postage stamp on his bookshop in Dundee.

China has reason to thank Dumfriesshire blacksmith **Kirkpatrick Macmillan** (1813–1878) for he invented the bicycle without which many Chinese couldn't get around. In 1837, after much fiddling to the amusement of his village neighbours, he came up with a machine that weighed fifty-seven lb with a wooden frame and wheels with iron tyres. He put a carved horse's head on the front to show his trade. He wasn't a great businessman and just wanted it to ride the short journeys around his home and work although in 1842 he rode it the seventy miles from Keir to Glasgow. The Glaswegians loved it. His niece, Mary Marchbank, became the world's first woman cyclist. The Museum of Transport in Glasgow has a copy of his original machine. Macmillan didn't patent his invention.

If it is raining as you read this then you might say a silent prayer of thanks to **Charles Macintosh** (1766–1843). Born in Glasgow in 1766 he was the son of a chemical manufacturer and soon established his own works, rapidly becoming the country's largest producer of alum which is used in colour dyeing. He needed human urine for the process as demand outstripped supply and urine had to be shipped in from London and elsewhere. Experimenting to find a use for the naphtha gas produced he came up with a waterproof fabric consisting of two layers of cloth glued together with an

India rubber solution. Edinburgh medical student James Syme helped and Macintosh patented the process that became the Mac as it is still known today. Early items were heavy, smelly, not always waterproof, and maybe melted in hot weather (!) but he persevered. He also went on to make the first inflatable lifejacket.

The Arts, Literature, Poetry and Painting

Anyone with a sense of wonder recalls Toad, Ratty, Mole and Badger. But who recalls **Kenneth Grahame** (1859–1932)? Born in Edinburgh, the son of as lawyer, he went on to write

Kenneth Grahame's house in Edinburgh.

possibly the greatest children's book of all time and become Secretary of the Bank of England. Not a bad double. *The Wind in the Willows* came from bedtime stories he read to his young son. It was published in 1908 the year he had to retire from the bank for ill-health. Later the noted children's author A.A. Milne wrote a dramatised version of the book called *Toad of Toad Hall*, the play that is still performed to the delight of children all over the world. Grahame's life was not altogether a happy one and his son who was very troubled, finally committed suicide by lying down in front of a train. Kenneth Grahame died in 1932 and is buried in Oxford. The elegant town house at 32 Castle Street, by Princes Street Gardens, where he was born was sold in September 2006. A plaque outside recognizes his birth there on March 8th 1859.

John Buchan (1875–1940), the 1st Baron Tweedsmuir was born in Perth, the son of a Minister. After attending Glasgow and Oxford Universities he studied for the law and become private secretary to Lord Milner, the High Commissioner for

South Africa. Returning to Scotland in 1903 he practised as a barrister whilst continuing with his first love, writing. He wrote over 100 books, many good adventure stories, the best known being *Prester John* and the *Thirty-Nine Steps*. He also wrote a good biography of Sir Walter Scott (1932) and James Graham, Marquis of Montrose (1928). He started working for the British Government during World War I and became Director of Information in 1917. In 1927 he became MP for the Scottish Universities, and in 1933 was appointed Lord High Commissioner to the General Assembly of the Church of Scotland. In 1935 he also became Governor General of Canada, and in 1937 Chancellor of Edinburgh University, all the time writing whilst holding these prestigious jobs, works, fiction and non-fiction. He was a fierce Scottish patriot when young but Oxford University widened his outlook.

Sir Henry Raeburn
(1756–1823) is Scotland's best-known painter, his famous *Rev Robert Walker Skating* painting used by Edinburgh Galleries in their promotional literature and perhaps the country's most

famous painting. From Edinburgh, he was orphaned at an early age and as a teenager was apprenticed to the goldsmith James Gilland where he taught himself to paint. He worked in the studio of the leading Scottish portrait painter of the time, David Martin. He started on watercolour miniatures but progressed to oils; his style was fast, no sketches or preliminary drawings, using bold sweeps. Marrying a wealthy widow meant he could show his work in London where he came under the influence of Sir Joshua Reynolds. From his studio in Edinburgh's famous George Street he produced great portraits of men like Boswell, Sir Walter Scott and David Hume. In 1822 he was knighted and appointed King's Limner and Painter for Scotland shortly before his death.

Charles Rennie Mackintosh
(1868–1928), was architect, designer, painter and the man who brought Art Nouveau to Scotland. The son of a police superintendent in Glasgow he studied at the Glasgow School of Art evening classes whilst apprenticed to architect John Hutcheson in the city. His distinctive style of work is represented in

Glasgow School
of Art.

many mediums, strong
structures mixed with subtle
curves and lines. He
perfected this Glasgow style
in interior design, furniture,
textiles etc. but in 1914
turned his back on
architecture for painting
and moved to the South of
France becoming a gifted
watercolour painter. His
architectural output in the
city is seen most notably
with the Glasgow School
of Art and on the Hill
House in Helensburgh.
His stylish motifs now adorn
many 'souvenir' items and
he is recognised as a true
genius. His first ever
commission was for a
headstone in the Necropolis,
the city's massive graveyard,
to the Chief Constable of
Glasgow Police.

James Boswell (1740–1795)
is usually recalled along
with Dr Samuel Johnson
with whom his name is
always linked. Boswell was
in fact born in Edinburgh
and his father was Lord
Auchinleck, a judge who
soon began to despair of
his wayward son who
became a bit of a playboy
and libertine. He had made
friends with Dr Samuel
Johnson in 1763 but under
threat of disinheritance he
went on a tour of Europe
and had several love affairs.
He returned to Edinburgh
and marriage in 1769 but
Edinburgh didn't hold the
attractions of London for
him and he met up again
with Johnson. The two men
embarked on a tour of the
Highlands and Hebrides

SCOTLAND'S HEROES

which introduced Scotland to a new audience. Always a heavy drinker, after his wife died in 1789 he drank even more and died in London in May 1795. His biography of Johnson, finally published in 1791, remains his best work and some describe it as the greatest biography ever written.

Someone now who is hardly a hero, more a heroic failure: whatever you think of the poetry of **William McGonagall** (1830–1902), described as Scotland's Worst Ever Poet, you have to admit people know about him. Born in 1830 in Edinburgh to an Irish immigrant weaver he spent his childhood in the Orkney Islands, Glasgow and at the age of eleven went to Dundee, the city that was eventually to make him famous or infamous depending on your love of his poetry. He devoted his spare time to the theatre where he was known as a very bad actor and wrote lots of poems, some say to the same standard. He knew he was bad, so did Queen Victoria. He once walked from Dundee to Balmoral with a poem for her but she refused to see him. McGonagall toured England and America reading his

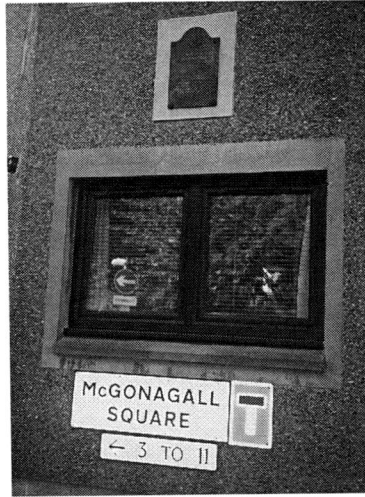

poems with no success. Then some kind of worldwide notoriety came with his ode penned to the Tay Bridge Disaster which brought even greater amusement amongst his new audiences. There is a plaque to the poet in McGonagall Square which isn't on some maps as it is a quite new development and overlooks the bridge. Don't let the Tourist Board tell you it is in Step Row. It isn't, it is actually in the next street, Paton's Lane and, almost as if the city doesn't want to reward McGonagall, it is high up on a building and hard to read. But if you look carefully you will see the inscription: William McGonagall, Dundee Poet and Tragedian circa

1825–29.09.02. In June 1877 sitting in his back room at 19 Paton's Lane William McGonagall was visited by the 'Muse' which inspired him to write his unique poetry. Sept 2000.

Hugh MacDiarmid

(1892–1978) on the other hand was a genuine poet – and a great Scots nationalist to boot. He was born Christopher Murray Grieve in Langholm, Dumfriesshire. His father was a postman but he trained as a teacher before becoming a journalist with the *Edinburgh Evening News*. Whilst serving in World War I he wrote prose and verse. After the War he married Peggy Skinner and

Hugh MacDiarmid

moved to Montrose where he wrote poetry and edited the Scottish *Chapbook* magazine. He became a founder member of the National Party in 1928 and, as Hugh MacDiarmid heavily pushed Scottish culture, writing in Scots and promoting it as a literary language. On moving to London his marriage collapsed; his work didn't find so much favour. He married again, started writing better, embraced communism for a while, and lived the last twenty-five years of his life in Biggar.

Sir Compton Mackenzie

(1883–1972) English-born writer who settled on Island of Barra in Outer Hebrides and became one of the major forces in early Scottish national politics. A prolific output including the revered *Whisky Galore* (1947) turned into a popular film.

Alistair Maclean (1922–1987) Greatest selling Scots author of all time – if you accept that J.K. Rowling and her Harry Potter creation is English. Born in Glasgow and educated at Inverness Royal Academy, and Glasgow University. He served in the Royal Navy from 1941–1946. In 1954, as a schoolteacher, he won a *Glasgow Herald* competition with a tale of adventures at sea, drawing on his own experiences. HMS *Ulysses* followed; an epic tale of wartime bravery which became a best-seller and was followed in 1957 by *The Guns of Navarone*. He gave up teaching and became a full time and very successful writer with many of his adventure stories turned into successful films. *Guns of Navarone, Ice Station Zebra* and *Where Eagles Dare* are still admired as movies today. He also found time to write biographies of T.E. Lawrence and Captain Cook.

Allan Ramsay (1713–1784) Leading Scottish portrait painter and elder son of the poet Allan Ramsay whose statue graces Princes Street in Edinburgh. Trained in Italy, he worked at first in Edinburgh but then moved to London in 1762. Soon became established and within five years had been appointed portrait painter to King George III. His work was fine, simple work and he specialized in the portraits of women. Along the way he made friends with Dr Samuel Johnson.

Engineers

Thomas Telford (1757–1834) made an enormous contribution to Scottish life. From Westerkirk, Langholm, Dumfriesshire, he was the

Edinburgh New Town and Telford.

son of a shepherd but when fourteen was apprenticed to a stonemason in Edinburgh. Then in 1782 he moved to London on the way to becoming a major engineer in the Industrial revolution. His work is legendary. He was appointed Surveyor of Public Works in Shropshire in 1788 and a distinguished career started – he built canals, docks, bridges. His work on the Ellesmere Canal with nineteen locks and two aqueducts won such acclaim that he was asked to do the Caledonian Canal. He also laid down nearly a thousand miles of new roads, over a thousand bridges and many public buildings and harbours. He worked fast and won many international contracts and truly helped open up the Highlands of Scotland. He even had a hand in Edinburgh's burgeoning New Town. Known as The Colossus of Roads, he is buried in Westminster Abbey. There is a statue on a high building in Glasgow but you would never know it is Telford.

John Loudoun McAdam (1756–1836) Maybe another contender for the title Colossus of Roads this Muirkirk-born engineer spent his early years in America as a merchant but returned to Scotland aged twenty-seven with plenty of money in his pocket. This enabled him to fund some of his own research into improving road construction from his base at Sauchrie. In 1816 he was appointed surveyor to the Bristol Turnpike Trust and put his theories into practice e.g. the 'term 'macadamised' – laying down a thick layer of crushed stones with gravel thus levelling the road which was raised, giving it a camber to improve drainage. In 1822 the first highway in America was macadamised to be followed by similar efforts in London. His method was much admired but oddly his work had cost him much money and, after petitioning Parliament he was awarded

£2000 in 1825. Two years later he was appointed Surveyor General of Metropolitan Roads. He turned down a knighthood and died at Moffat in Dumfriesshire. He is remembered in Wellington Square, Ayr.

Sir William Arrol (1839–1913) was from Houston in Renfrewshire and two of his most famous projects stand as Scottish icons to this day – the Forth Railway Bridge and the new Tay Railway Bridge. From a poor family, he started life as bobbin-boy in a thread works and then a blacksmith. But engineering was his great passion and he studied at night school to learn the trade. He was able to set up his own engineering business in 1868 and in 1872 began construction of the massive Dalmarnock Ironworks in Glasgow. Although his company was also involved in the building of Tower Bridge in London it is the two Scottish bridges he is best known for. His 85-span Tay Bridge (1881–1887) replaced the earlier one lost in the great disaster. The cantilever Forth Railway Bridge (1883–1890), was the world's first all-steel bridge of that length, the longest in the world when opened in 1890. It was first thought a total of fifty-seven men had died working on the bridge, including a thirteen-year-old boy. That was later revised to seventy-nine but new research shows the final figure could be even higher, possibly ninety-eight. Arrol became MP for South Ayrshire from 1892–1906. At the end of 2006 the Memorial Arts Trust decided to campaign for a permanent memorial – a statue, laser light or whatever, to be erected on this Forth engineering marvel. Back in Ayr, his beautiful old home Seaford House *(pictured)* is now derelict after years of NHS usage.

Sport

Sport and Scotland are synonymous with football, golf and motor racing probably producing the most celebrated performers over the decades. Especially football where Bill Shankly, Sir Matt Busby and Billy Bremner are all remembered with statues in England where they spent much of their careers.

Jock Stein (1922–1985). Born in the Lanarkshire coal-mining fraternity of Burnbank he found more fame as a football manager than player. His first job was at Dunfermline Athletic where they won the Scottish Cup. He moved to Hibernian after that but made his name at Celtic where he is much loved. Visitors on the club tour can see a bust of him but the founder of the club is the only one with a statue outside. Stein went there in 1965 and in his thirteen years with a club he had once played for brought them many trophies. His team won all domestic honours but perhaps his greatest triumph was the European Cup win in 1967. They became the first British club to ever win this major European trophy and became known as the

Lisbon Lions after defeating Inter Milan in the Portuguese capital. They reached the final again in 1970, losing to Feyenoord of the Netherlands. In 1978 he left Celtic for Leeds United but soon returned to Scotland to take over the national team helping them qualify for the World Cup Finals in 1982. He was regarded as a tactical genius, streetwise, and understood the psychology of footballers better than any other manager of his time. Stein, a big man, died of a heart attack at a Scotland versus Wales match at Cardiff in 1985.

Donald Ross (1872–1948) A true man of Dornoch although he made his reputation in the United States. The leader of the emigrant Scots who did so much for the game in America, he was responsible for designing over 500 courses in that country. The son of a stonemason he began life as a journeyman carpenter but golf was his love and he studied under Old Tom Morris at St Andrews before becoming the professional and greenkeeper at Dornoch. He emigrated in 1898 with two dollars in his pocket and never forgot his Scottish roots although he went on to become supreme amongst golf course architects in the USA. There are statues of Ross in the USA. They are at Pinehurst Resort and Country Club overlooking the final green of their Number Two Course; an impressive wooden statue at Brook Lea Country Club in Rochester, New York carved from a damaged tree, and a statue at Grove Park Inn Golf Course in Asheville, North Carolina – a life-size bronze done in May 2005 by local artist James K. Spratt.

Medicine

Scots have a well-deserved reputation for medicine. Here are women worthy of public recognition in Scotland, one perhaps about to receive it and one who pretended she wasn't a woman and deceived everyone(!).

Marie Carmichael Stopes
(1880–1958) Born in Edinburgh, her father was an archaeologist and her mother a suffragist. She studied science at university with some success. Her first marriage was unconsummated and after its annulment she found herself devoting her life to sex education. Always fighting the Catholic Church,

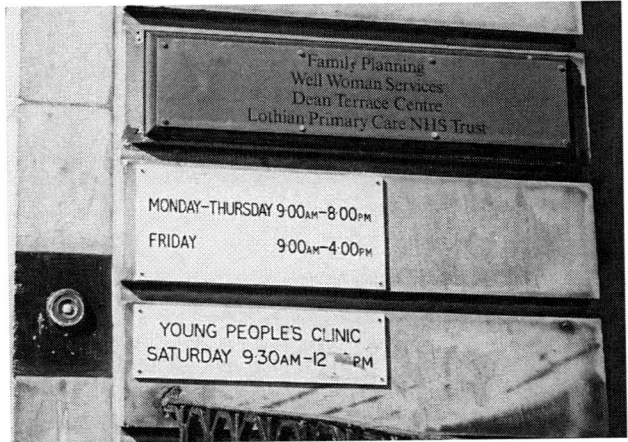

she went on to establish Britain's first birth control clinic and became a prolific writer on sex advice for women. With the full backing of her second husband, her work led to the foundation of the National Birth Control Association, the forerunner of the Family Planning Association in 1931. She produced newspapers and other crusading issues regarding women although her progressive ideas continued to run into conflict.

Elsie Maud Inglis
(1864–1917). Actually born in India, she was a pioneer in women's medicine, one of the first medical students at Edinburgh and Glasgow. After qualifying in 1892 she moved to London. A committed suffragette she

Elsie Maud Inglis

returned to Edinburgh two years later and started her own practice with another woman doctor. She opened a maternity hospital completely staffed by women and became founder of the Scottish Women's Suffragette Federation in 1906. During World War 1 she served in Serbia setting up hospitals – again all run by women – helping fight the dreadful disease of typhoid which was prevalent at that time. She ran other hospitals in Russia until the Revolution, when she returned to Britain where she died of cancer a few weeks later. Elsie may not be forgotten for long. The Lord Provosts of Edinburgh and Glasgow co-operated in their

desire to see a statue remembering not just this heroine but all women nurses in wartime, probably in Edinburgh's Royal Mile – funding permitting. In the meantime there is a bust of her in Edinburgh's National Portrait Gallery, by Ivan Mestrovic (1918).

James Stuart Miranda Barry (c.1790–1865) was the world's first woman doctor – pretending to be a man, a pretence she kept until she died, becoming Surgeon and Inspector General of the Army in 1858 and retiring on half pay in 1859. It was said it might have been love for an army surgeon and wanting to be near him that made her keep up the disguise all her life. After training as a doctor in Edinburgh Barry went on to serve in the army around the world, including a period in Corfu where she treated casualties of the Crimean War, rising to the rank of Inspector General of Military Hospitals in Canada. A skilled surgeon, M. Barry had a high-pitched voice and a terrible temper, regularly rowing with colleagues and the military authorities. Florence Nightingale described Barry during the Crimean War as 'the most hardened creature I have ever met.' When Barry died and the corpse was laid out it was claimed not only that Barry was a woman but had also given birth. She took her secret to the grave and nobody will ever know the true story. There is no record of the name or birthplace. Some colleagues did say they thought 'he was rather effeminate.'

Politics

Scotland continues to produce many top politicians, leading to the charge that Westminster is governed by a Scottish mafia. A number of these have been rewarded with a prominent statue in the past but much less so these days, Donald Dewar being an exception. Perhaps Robert Burns was right when he penned the lines 'such a parcel of rogues in a nation' referring to the members of the Scottish Parliament who signed the Act of Union with England in 1707.

James Ramsay Macdonald (1866–1937) Born at Lossiemouth in Morayshire (where there is actually a stone memorial), he went on to become Labour politician and first Labour Prime Minister of Great Britain. A voracious reader when

Ramsay Macdonald

young, he moved to London where he met and married Margaret Ethel Gladstone and became actively involved in the Labour movement, becoming secretary of the Independent Labour Party. In 1906 he became MP for Leicester and Chairman of the Parliamentary Labour Party in 1911. The War brought a halt to his career and he lost his seat in 1918, returning in the 1922 Election as MP for Aberavon and becoming Leader of the party. Two years later and he was PM and Foreign Secretary of the first-ever Labour party government. It lasted less than a year but again Labour was returned to power in 1929 when he became the first British PM to visit the USA. In 1931 with the Depression on he formed a coalition with the Conservatives which held power until 1935, bringing about economic reform, when he resigned as premier. He died two years later. Visitors to Edinburgh's National Portrait Gallery can see a likeness of him in a striking bust by the talented Jacob Epstein.

Entertainers

Sir Harry Lauder

(1870–1950) Born in Portobello, Edinburgh, he described himself as a simple Scots comic but went on to become the highest paid entertainer of his day mixing with royalty and American presidents. A comedian and singer on the music-hall circuits his songs have become classics. Many were his own compositions including the famous *Roamin' in the Gloamin,* *I Love a Lassie* and the classic *Keep Right On to the End of The Road* which entertained many during World War 1 but covered a deep personal sadness – he wrote it in honour of his son who was killed in action. His real name was Henry Maclennan. He toured extensively at home and overseas and became a big international star, especially with exiled Scots. He was knighted in 1919.

Will Fyfe (1885–1947)

Another music hall favourite, born in Dundee, he started as an actor, first appearing on the stage as a child and didn't become a singer touring the halls until around 1916. He had written several sketches for Harry Lauder who rejected them so he decided to perform them himself. By 1921 he was topping the bill at the London Palladium and was a special favourite with the Royal Variety Performances. Also appeared in many films and was King Rat of that show-business charity for six years. He played on the romantic vision many have of Scotland and his song *I*

Known as Glasgow's family theatre, the Pavilion opened in 1904 in Renfrew Street for music-hall and where Harry Lauder played to full houses – the pub next door commemorates the fact.

belong to Glasgow reduced exiled Glaswegians all over the world to tears of nostalgia. He died falling out of a third-floor window at Rusacks Hotel in St Andrews, some said it was suicide.

Chic Murray (1919–1985) Charles (Chic) Murray was born in Greenock. His father had been gassed during the War and died when Chic was only fourteen. He was an accomplished musician who could play many instruments and left school aged fifteen to begin an apprenticeship in marine engineering on the Clyde where formed a band. During the War he missed military service on medical grounds and in 1943 met his future wife Maidie who was performing at the Greenock

Empire. They married in 1945. She made him join her in a double act which gave Chic new-found confidence and whilst they both sang he also told jokes and funny stories. They were very successful in Britain, the United States and Australia and their fame and wealth allowed them to buy two houses in Edinburgh's Bruntsfield Terrace to convert into a hotel. But Chic's 'wanderings' and love of drink led to divorce although he continued to work in television and films such as *Gregory's Girl*. He was much loved and the world of entertainment was well represented at his funeral in 1985.

Chic Murray was one of the famous names to thrill audiences at the Glasgow Empire – it was also the graveyard of English comedians who came to dread the boozy responses of the second house crowd on a Friday night. It closed in 1963 and is sadly only remembered with a small and dirty plaque high on a wall outside a pizza restaurant.

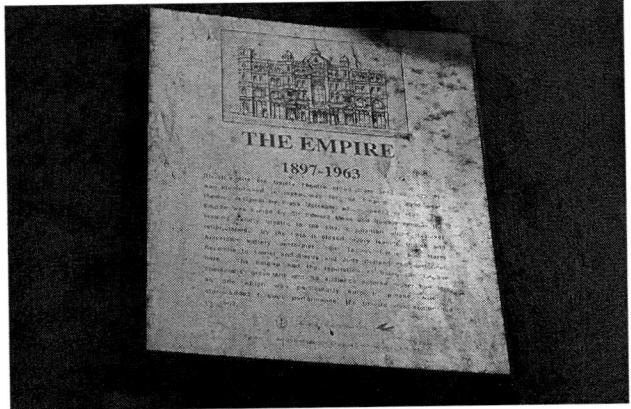

Businessmen

Lord Reith (1889–1971)
John Charles Walsham, 1st Baron of Stonehaven was born in that Kincardine port, the son of a minister. Considering his success as a businessman it is surprising he didn't go to university but served an apprenticeship as an engineer. After the First World War, where he was wounded, he worked as a manager for an engineering firm and in 1922 was appointed General Manager of the British Broadcasting Corporation, a new and private company. He became Director General in 1927 having forcefully proposed the aims of that great institution – to inform and educate. During his time at the BBC, television first went on air. In 1938 he left the BBC to become chairman of Imperial Airways, the pre-runner of BOAC when merged with British Airways. He was MP for Southampton for many years and in 1940 became Churchill's Minister for Works and Building. He also served in many other business posts and was known for building the foundations of public service broadcasting. He died in Edinburgh.

Robert Napier (1791–1876)
From Dumbarton. At the age of twenty-one he moved to Edinburgh and worked for Robert Stevenson, the lighthouse builder. Within a few years he set up his own blacksmith business in Glasgow but really wanted to be a marine engineer like his cousin David. He built very successful marine engines that won many steamboat races and his talents reached the ears of the Government. Samuel Cunard approached him to build his first ship, the *Britannia* and in the early 1840s he moved into shipbuilding in a big way, his yard at Govan building steamers for the Royal Navy. Many of his workforce went on to open their own famous yards on the Clyde developing a worldwide reputation for Clydeside. In 1842 he built the world's first train ferry carrying passengers and freight across the Forth.

Thomas Lipton (1850–1931)
Breakfast in many a Scottish household has cause to remember some great Scots. Thomas Lipton helped turn tea into the everyday drink of millions. Born in a Glasgow Gorbals tenement (10 Crown Street) to Irish parents, at age

nine he started as an errand boy and in 1865 went to USA where amongst other menial jobs worked in a grocers' shop. Returned to Scotland and in 1870 opened his first shop in Finnieston area of Glasgow, becoming a millionaire by the time he was thirty. Using bold advertising he became an instant success with this relatively new product from India instead of the more established China. Soon he had branches throughout England and the USA. He was the first to package tea in airtight containers to keep it fresh and used different attractive blends. To challenge the coffee dominance in the USA was a great achievement. He also brought out his own version of Bovril. His great wealth also enabled him to compete for the famous yachting trophy the Americas Cup five times but with no success, although the Americans liked him very much. His business interests in Italy led him to stage a football World Cup in Turin in 1909, over twenty years before the one we know today started. He gifted £10,000 to the City of Glasgow. Lipton probably had cause to thank Janet Keiller, wife of a Dundee merchant, for

commercialising marmalade in this country to make an ideal breakfast companion. He died unmarried at the age of eighty-one and is buried in The Necropolis.

Crown Street in the Gorbals is much changed and improved from Lipton's day.

Mathematics

John Napier (1550–1617) From Merchiston Castle in Edinburgh, he went to St Andrews University at the age of thirteen where he became a staunch Protestant and supporter of the Reformation. He started designing instruments of war to defend the country from any Spanish invasion after the execution of Mary Queen of Scots. Among these were a primitive submarine and an armoured tank. He travelled widely in Europe producing religious publications. Back home in Scotland he discovered that all numbers could be expressed as fractional powers of a base number. Multiplications could then be done by adding the fractions and division done by subtracting them. He called them logarithms. He also came up with the primitive computer or calculating machine. Called Napier's Bones, he showed how calculations could be made using bone or ivory rods and metal plates.

James Clerk Maxwell (1831–1879) was a genius who proved Robert Bruce's theory of try and try again, having been turned down by Aberdeen and Edinburgh Universities. Maxwell was from a wealthy landowning family Glenlair in Galloway and became one of the greatest theoretical physicists the world has known although nicknamed 'Dafty' by Edinburgh Academy schoolmates. At the age of fifteen a paper on geometry was read before the highly-respected Royal Society of Edinburgh. He went to Cambridge University becoming one of the Twelve Apostles, membership restricted to the twelve brightest scholars at the university. Many achievements throughout his lifetime include organizing the Cavendish Laboratory at Cambridge. He published many papers on subjects such as the kinetic theory of gases, Saturn's rings, and

Edinburgh University.

SCOTLAND'S HEROES

demonstrated colour photography with the aid of a picture of a tartan ribbon in 1861, taking the world's first colour photograph. He is said to have laid the foundation for development of 20th-century electronics with his work on atoms and electromagnetic fields as anyone who knows about long and short wave radio or x-rays can testify. He has a measure of magnetic flex named after him – the maxwell (Mx). His most important work was on the theory of electromagnetic radiation. His work was an inspiration for Albert Einstein.

Musicians

Whenever or wherever you mention Scotland, people think of bagpipes and there are two great exponents of this art who are worthy of remembrance.

Pipe-Major George Stewart McLennan (1884–1929) was born in Edinburgh but a childhood illness left him unable to walk until he was four-and-a-half. At the age of nine he won the Amateur Championship for March, Strathspey and Reel, the start of a great career. Queen Victoria brought him to Balmoral to play. He enlisted in 1899 in the Gordon Highlanders and, serving in South Africa, became the youngest army Pipe-Major at the age of twenty-one. In his life he won over two thousand piping awards but he caught fluid on the lung in World War One and was discharged from the army on pension in 1922 to set up his own bagpipe-making business in Aberdeen. He died in 1929 with a chanter in his hand and over twenty thousand people attended his funeral in Aberdeen.

Pipe-Major Bob Brown MBE (1906–1972) was born in Strachan, Kincardineshire and began learning the pipes at ten, winning prizes from the age of twelve. In 1926 he started working on the Balmoral Estate as a ghillie and piper to the Royal Family. As well as a great piper he was a master ghillie, teaching the young Prince Charles to fish for salmon on the River Dee. When war was declared in 1939, Bob joined the Gordon

BAGPIPES GALORE

Highlanders becoming Pipe-Major and serving in North Africa and the Middle East. After the war he returned to Balmoral where he stayed until his death, travelling worldwide teaching, judging and becoming a much-respected authority on the Pibroch. His funeral at Crathie Church was attended by the Queen, Queen Mother and Prince of Wales.

Military

Hugh Caswell Dowding (1882–1970) Air Force chief, born in Moffat, educated at Winchester and Royal Military Academy at Woolwich. He was decorated for efforts with Royal Flying Corps in World War One but better known for his work in World War Two as Commander-in-Chief of Fighter Command when he led 'The Few' to victory against a superior German air force attack in the Battle of Britain, between August and September 1940. That turned the tide of the war in Britain's favour. He was created a peer in 1943.

Sir Hector Macdonald (1853–1903) was said by many to be the British Army's greatest soldier but unrecognized, as his career

and life ended in disgrace. In childhood he worked as a tailor in his native Dingwall and there met soldiers in Inverness, seeing a possibility of a military career with the British Empire. There is a monument to him at Dingwall. In 1870 he enlisted with the Gordon Highlanders and gained renown in the Egyptian, Sudan and Boer Wars. His first battle was in Afghanistan where he was mentioned in dispatches and promoted to lieutenant afterwards. He fought with great bravery in India and Sudan. In the Boer War he was captured but released as a hero and given his sword back. He would return to battle with wounds unhealed and when he ran out of bullets he used to throw stones at the enemy. He was knighted by Queen Victoria who described him as one of the Scots who had made the biggest impact on the British Empire. It was said Kitchener was jealous of him. He was later made Governor of

Sir Hector Macdonald

Ceylon but rumours of a sexual nature involving young boys surfaced and he faced a court martial. He died alone in a Paris hotel room of a gunshot. Suicide was the verdict but many still believe he was murdered by one of his regiment for bringing them into disrepute. His wife (who few knew he had) buried him secretly at six o'clock one morning in Dean Park Cemetery in Edinburgh. There are said to be letters in a Dingwall lawyer's office which could throw light on the case.

authorities in Boston, Massachusetts believing he would get a pardon. He was wrong and was hanged for piracy in England in May 1701.

Famous but Notorious

William Kidd (c. 1645–1701) was a pirate from Greenock at the end of the 17th century. A seafarer from a young age he owned several ships in the United States and then England, who in a move it may have regretted, commissioned him to fight the pirates attacking trading vessels in the Indian Ocean. He sailed for Madagascar but decided he would rather become a pirate than catch them and started attacking merchant ships. A warrant was soon put out for his capture and in the Caribbean he became a romantic figure with a price on his head. He gave himself up to the

Burke and Hare are part of Edinburgh folklore although they were in fact from Ireland. These 19th-century grave-robbers and murderers found a kind of infamy through sixteen murders around the city by selling the bodies to anatomist Dr. Robert Knox for assisting his work with anatomy students. They enjoyed a profitable period before police captured them with Hare offered immunity if he testified against Burke. He did; Burke was found guilty and sentenced to death by hanging in 1828. Hare was released the following year and quietly disappeared.

William Deacon Brodie
(1741–1788) Originally a
cabinet-maker, Brodie was a
respectable member of
Edinburgh society by day and
a burglar by night. He took
over his family business and
was made a freeman of the
city of Edinburgh, but spent
his nights gambling and
robbing properties. He
attempted a robbery at the
Excise Office in Canongate
but the gang only got away
with a paltry sum. One of the
burglars confessed and
Brodie fled to Europe where
he was eventually captured in
Amsterdam and returned to
Edinburgh. He was found
guilty and hung on a gibbet
of his own making as
devotees of the film *The
Prime of Miss Jean Brodie*
will know.

Drinkers at an Edinburgh
Royal Mile pub can raise a
glass to his memory.

Scotland has several notable
rebels: **Robert Baillie**
(1634–1684, a nationalist
leader and conspirator from
Lanarkshire and **John Baird**
(1878–1820) a radical martyr
from Condorrat,
Dunbartonshire were hanged
for treason. **John Balfour** (c.
1675) a conspirator chiefly
responsible for Archbishop
Sharp's assassination in 1679,
died in Holland, avoiding the
hangman's noose to the end.

Andrew Hardie (1791–1820)
was a Glasgow weaver and
radical martyr who fought
against Napoleon. He
supported the call to arms
urging insurrection, mutiny

and strike action and was hanged for treason. **Joseph Smith** (d. 1780) was a cobbler and leader of the Edinburgh mobs. By beating a drum on the High Street of the city it was said he could have at his command a crowd of ten thousand within an hour. It was said he always acted in good causes to ensure fair play, he was just against unscrupulous landlords and crooked traders. He died falling off a stagecoach whilst drunk.

Miscellaneous

Thomas Glover (1838–1911) The Scottish Samurai. He was the son of a Fraserburgh coastguard officer who at the age of nineteen went to Shanghai to form his own trading company. He soon moved on to Japan to the trading port of Nagasaki. Japan was still a feudal society controlled by the shogun and when the samurai rebelled against the authority of the shogun he began importing arms to assist the rebels. After the war he became a successful trader in ships and after a brief time as a bankrupt was involved in modernising the coal mines in the country. In 1908 he was presented with the Order of the Rising Sun,

the country's highest civilian honour and he is still remembered with honour in Japan. His house overlooking Nagasaki Harbour is popular with tourists.

James Hutton (1726–1797) He was the man who really introduced geology as a proper subject. From Edinburgh, he trained as a doctor but never practised. Whilst a student he produced sal ammoniac from Edinburgh's plentiful supplies of soot. He later started a profitable chemical business from that discovery, then started farming in Berwickshire, but soon sold all his business interests and returned to his first love in Edinburgh. Before him, nobody had any theories of where the earth came from; the prevailing view of the preachers was it was all down to God. His time as a farmer convinced him the earth's surface had evolved over an immense period. He proved it was the action of fire that developed the earth's crust, inspired by the rock formations at Arthur's Seat and Salisbury Crags in his native town. In 1785 he published The Theory of the Earth which, understandably, was not well received by the church. It was really badly written which didn't help and it took his University friend John Playfair to produce (five years after Hutton's death) his *Illustrations of the Huttonian Theory of the Earth*, a classic of geological writing, to confirm the soundness of Hutton's theory. Hutton lived in Edinburgh all his life, he never married and lived with his three sisters. He can be seen very high up on the outside wall of the National Portrait Gallery in Edinburgh but you would never know it was him.

And finally. . . .

Missionary **Mary Slessor** (1845–1915) was born into poverty and hardship in Aberdeen, the family moving to Dundee where at the age of eleven she was a weaver in a jute mill. Her two elder brothers had died young. Her father, an alcoholic, died soon after, and with her mother also in poor health she became responsible for looking after the three remaining girls. Mary was a deeply religious woman which kept her going. She became a missionary of the United Presbyterian Church and in 1876 was posted to West Africa, the Calabar district of Nigeria. Very independently minded she

went even further to areas where no white man had been and, living like the natives, became adopted by them. Eventually ill health and the conditions got to her and she died from malaria and dysentery in 1915. Slessor is buried in Africa, the land she loved and there is a statue to her already in Calabar.

However there won't be a statue to her in Aberdeen. A committee with a budget of around £15,000 and comprising representatives from the Council, Mary Slessor Society, and Aberdeen Art Gallery decided to remember Mary Slessor with a memorial in Union Terrace Gardens. Four submissions made the final selection process, two were figurative but the final choice was a 'container' by sculptor Mary Bourne, who grew up in Aberdeen but now works and

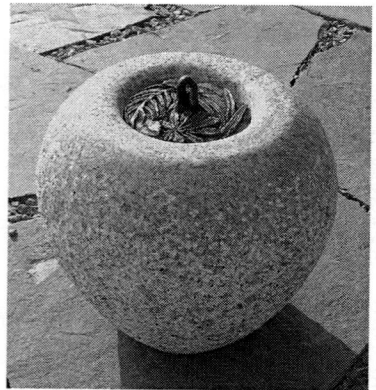

lives in Dufftown. So there will not now be a figure statue of this Scots heroine in her own country. The limited budget, not unusual for a local authority, obviously was a factor but as Dr Jennifer Melville of the Art Gallery says: "Art has moved on from Victorian times, I am not sure public sculpture is the way to do it now. The more enlightened cities don't like triumphal statues of politicians, military men, even missionaries."

The sculpture will certainly be impressive – Mary Bourne's varied work can be seen throughout Scotland – and the people of Aberdeen will be able to judge from around May 2007. The bowl sculpture will be made of Kemnay granite, predominately grey but with a subtle flush of pink through it, the material used for the floor of the new Scottish Parliament. Words from a letter of Slessor to her great friend Charles Partridge – 'the bush with its myriad voices calls you' – will be sandblasted into the rim in Mary's own handwriting. Within the container will lie a modelled circle of leaves from plants from the Nigerian bush cast in bronze. The choice of a dicotyledonous plant shoot that grows twin leaves is a reference to the many twin babies rescued by Mary from ritual murder. Her statue in Calabar shows her cradling two babies.

The work will no doubt be imposing on its site and will be the first one in the lovely Gardens, central in the city and enjoyed by many. However it is hoped a plaque with full explanation will be part of the sculpture. The

Mary Slessor even appears on a Scottish bank note.

artist worked closely with local playwright Mike Gibb who has written a play on Slessor and together they have produced a meaningful memorial. Let us hope the meaning will not be lost on those who may seek to use it just to stub out their cigarettes. However if it gets people thinking about Mary Slessor, is that not a good use of commemorative public art?

CHAPTER 9

You Don't Have to be Dead but it Helps

'I'm not the heroic type really, I was beaten up by Quakers'

WOODY ALLEN

There seems an unwritten convention that until you depart this mortal coil you are unlikely to have a memorial put up to you on the basis that memorials are meant to remember and that is certainly easier when someone has departed.

There are exceptions – Olympic gold medal rowers Steve Redgrave and Matthew Pinsent are there in statue form for all to see in Henley, a town where they have contributed so much through their rowing exploits. And at Wentworth Golf Club in Surrey golfers tee off under the watchful gaze of club professional Bernard Gallacher. But they are exceptions. Many more famous Scots will no doubt have the collecting tins rattling for them when they

Olympic rowing gold medallists Steven Redgrave and Matthew Pinsent are honoured in Henley where they perfected their sport.

have passed on but it seems a pity more are not remembered in their lifetime.

Two names who have done so much for promoting the image of Scotland abroad immediately come to mind, Sean Connery and Billy Connolly. Both had very humble beginnings and what better way to illustrate how you can progress in life from a poor beginning than to remember these two who started with nothing. Connolly – perhaps in that magnificent costume of black leotard and oversized tee-shirt with unkempt beard and hair as he pranced around the Albert Hall stage – would make a great statue. If erected in the Clyde shipyards it would show that with talent and hard work you can get out of the poor beginning to a lifestyle far away.

Connery has similar humble beginnings. He started as a milkman in Edinburgh earning £1 a week; again what an opportunity to show how you do not necessarily have to be trapped by your environment. Everyone will have their own view of our most famous living Scotsmen and women but here is a selection. A statue whilst they are alive would be both just

reward and an inspiration to others – a proper use for sculpture surely?

Sean Connery was born in 1930 in the Fountainbridge area of Edinburgh. With his father a lorry driver he had a poor childhood and, after school, joined the Royal Navy only to be discharged on medical grounds. He then did a number of various jobs including modelling for life-classes. He enjoyed bodybuilding and at the age of twenty-three was runner-up in the British Mr Universe contest. He soon secured a part in the chorus line of the *South Pacific* stage show running in London at that time. Bit parts in TV and films followed but then in 1962 his life changed when he was offered the role of the first (and some say still the best) James Bond. The film was *Dr No* and the film and the character became a massive hit. He did another four Bond movies soon after and that led to other successful parts he took to shake off the Bond image. But the lure of the character

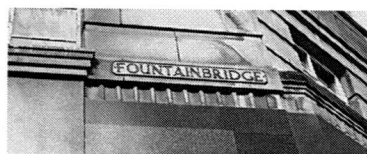

was such that he returned to the role later in *Diamonds are Forever* and his final part as Bond in *Never Say Never Again*. One of the world's great movie stars, his distinctive Scottish burr has brought him many fans and many awards as well as being voted the sexiest man on the planet. An ardent Scots nationalist (although living in Spain) he has campaigned for an independent Scotland for many years. He was awarded the freedom of Edinburgh in 1991 and although his politics might stop him getting a knighthood or recognition at national level surely a statue to him is overdue in his home city.

Billy Connolly: another rags to riches story. He was born in Anderston in Glasgow in 1941 and after school worked as a baker's delivery boy before taking up an apprenticeship in the shipyards. He played the banjo and soon adapted to the quickfire wit of Clyde shipyards which produced some of the great comedians of that time. He toured folk clubs but his jokes were as popular as his playing, although his group the Humblebums were loved in his native city. The Big Yin took to stand-up comedy and his outrageous homely tales and colourful language won him nationwide acclaim, particularly after his first appearance on the Michael Parkinson TV chat show. He wasn't without problems as too much work and too much drink played havoc with his first marriage and in 1978 he moved to London and took up with comedienne Pamela Stephenson. In 1988 they moved to America where he tried, with differing amounts of success, to be a TV star and adjust to the American way of life. He returned to Scotland in 1994 and bought an estate in Aberdeenshire. He has been in many successful TV shows, touring performances and films. Perhaps the most memorable was with Dame Judi Dench as Queen Victoria where he played the faithful servant John Brown in the film *Mrs Brown*.

Evelyn Glennie is an inspiring tale of triumphing over adversity. Born in 1965 in Aberdeen she was a child prodigy at music and began studying timpani and percussion at the age of twelve, at which time she went profoundly deaf. Whilst still a teenager she was accepted into the Royal Academy of Music in

Women figure in few statues in Scotland, Evelyn Glennie would be a suitable addition – maybe in Aberdeen?

London where she won the Queen's Commendation for All Round Excellence, the top honour. Many top composers have written for her and she tours extensively worldwide giving well over one hundred concerts a year. She is a full-time solo percussionist of exceptional talent, regardless of her disability which makes it all the more amazing. She plays many percussion instruments, some she makes herself and also composes music. She was voted Scots Woman of the Decade in 1990 and awarded the OBE in 1993. Her autobiography is called *Good Vibrations*.

In November 2004 The Scottish Football Association Hall of Fame was created initially honouring twenty footballing greats – some alive and some, alas, gone. They were players and managers alike. The full list was Jim Baxter, Billy Bremner, Sir Matt Busby, Kenny Dalglish, Sir Alex Ferguson, Patsy Gallagher, John Greig, Jimmy Johnstone, Denis Law, Dave Mackay, Danny McGrain, Jimmy McGrory, Billy McNeill, Willie Miller, Bobby Murdoch, Bill Shankly, Gordon Smith, Graeme Souness, Jock Stein and Willie Woodburn.

Many who choose football as their life go to England to pursue their career so Jim Baxter is the only one of this list remembered in his homeland with a full statue after his death. Also dead but remembered in England are Billy Bremner who is remembered with a statue at Leeds (a stone engraved memorial listing his achievements was unveiled at Raploch, Stirling in August 2006), Bill Shankly at Liverpool's Anfield Stadium (there's a plaque at Glenbuck where he was born) and Sir Matt Busby at Old Trafford. Manchester United could have a problem because Sir Alex Ferguson is described as United's greatest-ever manager so can hardly take second place to the legendary Sir Matt! Maybe Aberdeen, where he made his name, should erect a statue to him.

SCOTLAND'S HEROES

Sir Alex Ferguson: Born in Govan, Glasgow in 1941 and became an apprentice toolmaker. Enjoyed his football as an amateur and in 1964 he turned professional playing for Dunfermline, Glasgow Rangers, Falkirk and Ayr. Football management was a natural progression and he had several famous names to inspire him. He enjoyed spells at East Stirling and St Mirren but it was with Aberdeen he really made his name, taking them to the Scottish League Championship in 1978. Further League and Cup successes followed and he is revered on Aberdeen turf for his victory in the European Cup Winners Cup in 1983. He was Scotland manager for a short spell and took over the world's most famous club, Manchester United in 1986 where, after an initial uninspired start, he went onto win every honour in the game. In 1999 the Reds won the European Cup as well as the two domestic trophies, the FA Cup and League Cup. He followed Sir Matt Busby as a great of British football and was knighted in 1999.

Kenny Dalglish: Another from the Glasgow stable of great footballers. He was born there in 1951 and Jock Stein saw his talent, signing him for Celtic at the age of 17. He played for them for ten years and became a legend in the green part of that city. In 1977 he set the British transfer fee moving to Liverpool where he won every award going as Liverpool triumphed across Europe. He was the first player to score one hundred goals in both English and Scottish football. He played for Scotland one hundred and two times and, with Denis Law, holds the record thirty goals scored for the national side. He followed his career with successful manager periods at clubs including Blackburn and Liverpool, Newcastle and Celtic. Now a TV commentator and keen golfer over the Royal Birkdale links with friend Alan Hansen, another Liverpool and Scotland great.

Denis Law: Born in Aberdeen in 1940 he started his career in England with Huddersfield Town before joining the team that he is best known for, Manchester City, in 1959. He was one of the first British footballers to ply his trade in Europe, joining Torino in Italy in 1961. However Sir Matt Busby wanted him back in

Manchester and he returned to play for City's great rivals, Manchester United for a record-breaking transfer fee, helping them to great successes. He was capped fifty-five times for Scotland and shares the record of thirty goals for Scotland with Dalglish. He ended his career back at Manchester City and although not always in the best of health, is a popular TV and newspaper pundit. A passionate Scot, when England won the World Cup in 1966 he couldn't bear to watch the final and played golf instead – a round he said was ruined by someone telling him the result as he walked off the 18th!

Bill McLaren: The Voice of Rugby is admired wherever the game is played and probably where it isn't played too. He was born in 1923 in Hawick in the Borders where he was a PE teacher, and his love for the area has certainly endeared him to the Borders Tourist Board. He has loved rugby all his life and played for the famous Hawick side although the War interrupted his rugby career. He was playing for them with ambitions to play for Scotland when he was diagnosed with tuberculosis

in 1948 finishing his career. Two years in hospital followed and on recovery he became a sports reporter with his local paper. He gave his first radio commentary in 1952 and in the 1960s moved into television to make his name with his amazing research using cards to remember all the players. His commentaries were unbiased although he is passionately Scots. Loved by the players especially David Campese who considered him always to be fair and impartial. McLaren retired in 2004 after over forty years of broadcasting.

Jackie Stewart was born in Dumbartonshire in June 1939 into a motor-racing family, his father and brother were keen motor cycle racers. He inherited their love of speed and, although also a talented target shooter up to Olympic standard, made his Formula One debut with BRM. A natural talent, he won the Italian Grand Prix at Monza. In 1968 he won three Grand Prix and became world champion three times in 1969, 1970 and 1973. During his career he won twenty-seven Grand Prix, sometimes sharing the podium with Jim Clark in a unique Celtic double and after the last win retired to keep an interest in the sport. He is involved with the Silverstone Racetrack and the British Grand Prix. For a while he had his own tartan racing team with son Paul, called Stewart Grand Prix.

Bernard Gallacher: This Bathgate Boy is synonymous with the Wentworth Golf Club at Virginia Water having been professional there for over 20 years. The PGA European Tour also has its headquarters there. The Ryder Cup Committee took a decision to appoint a European Ryder Cup Captain for only two terms – a home and an away match. But after their favourite son lost the first two encounters with the Americans in 1991 and 1993 they gave him a third term in 1995 which he duly won. Gallacher now competes on the Seniors Tour.

J. K. ROWLING
Wrote some of the early chapters of HARRY POTTER in the rooms on the First Floor of this building

Edinburgh is a literary hotspot, made hotter recently by the Harry Potter phenomenon, the creation of **J.K. Rowling** – always known by the initials – who was actually born on 31 July 1965 in Chipping Sodbury, Gloucestershire. There was no real sign of the great fame to come although she says she was writing stories from a very early age. Aged twenty-six she moved to Portugal to teach English where she began working on a story about a 'wizard' that eventually turned out to be Harry Potter. She married a Portuguese but was divorced shortly after and with an infant daughter moved to Edinburgh to be near her sister. She is now an 'adopted Scot' and revered by the Edinburgh authorities. Continuing her writing in the town's cafes, she received a

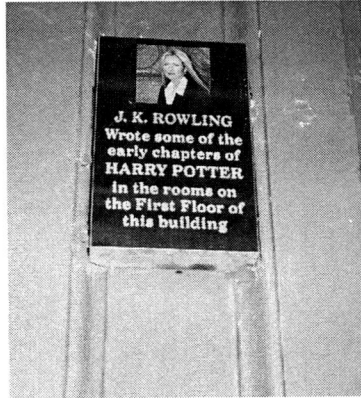

BERNARD GALLACHER checks out the swings of golfers on the smart Wentworth course in Surrey.

grant from the Scottish Arts Council and after several rejections sold her novel *Harry Potter and the Philosopher's Stone.*

She began working as a French teacher but soon the rewards came and her first three books zoomed to the top of the Best Seller charts in both UK and USA, selling over thirty million copies and making her a very rich woman. Initial print runs of nearly ten million copies were unheard of before in the publishing business. The Harry Potter books, loved by children and adults alike, have to date sold well over three hundred million copies and the films grossed over £1billion at the box office. In October 2006 a small plaque was erected in Edinburgh, corner of Nicholson and Drummond Streets opposite Edinburgh University, marking the spot where she first created Harry Potter.

And finally . . .

Love him or loathe him you can't ignore **Tony Blair.** Anthony Charles Lynton Blair was born in Edinburgh on 6 May 1953. His family moved to Adelaide, South Australia soon afterwards but he returned to England at the age of five and never emphasized his Scottish roots. Perhaps it was because at the time of his leadership the English complained Whitehall was run by a Scottish Mafia. He won three successive terms for a Labour government as Leader, a historic achievement which had seemed almost inconceivable during long years of Tory rule. He also, a few days before his 44th birthday, became Britain's youngest Prime Minister since the Napoleonic Wars. It seems unlikely that there will ever be a statue to him in Scotland however. Certainly not at Fettes College which he attended but said he didn't really enjoy and Scotland overall can appear more Old Labour than New Labour. He will probably also never be forgiven by a large section of the country for leading Britain into a war they thought unnecessary and then presiding over dismemberment of the Black Watch. Knowing the penchant for vandalising political statues *a la* Donald Dewar it seems he will probably remain 'a prophet forgotten in his own country.'

CHAPTER 10

Sculpture in Scotland Finds an Identity

'Remember . . . a statue has never been put up in honour of a critic'

JEAN SIBELIUS

The tradition of sculpture in Scotland has never been that strong. Why that is depends partly on religion and partly on economics. Sculpture can be difficult and expensive to produce. The Scottish Kirk has no track record on commissioning sculpture and the great Scottish landowners tended to keep their best stuff in their London houses. Sculpture and architecture are frequently and closely related, with the latter recalled more fondly.

It wasn't until the second quarter of the nineteenth century that an independent Scottish School really became recognized. Until then a Scottish mason wishing to become a sculptor had to go abroad to learn to handle marble and bronze and carve it. Wealthy Scots would hire the best sculptors either from London or Rome. In 1991 at the Royal Scottish Academy

in Edinburgh there was an exhibition entitled Virtue and Vision, Sculpture and Scotland 1540–1990. Its purpose was to reassess sculpture in Scotland and explore Scotland's native sculptural tradition. The work of men from this period such as Brodie, Burnett, Campbell, Fillans, Park, Ritchie and Steell was given due recognition by the exhibition.

The 19th century was the golden age of monumental sculpture in Britain. The London-based sculptors Sir Francis Leggat Chantrey and John Flaxman executed major figures and statues prior to 1840 for places such as Edinburgh, Glasgow and Sutherland. The southern dominance of commissions was broken in 1838 by the first public subscription for a monument to a Scot of international renown, Sir

Walter Scott, and the choice of the young Sir John Steell was a breakthrough. A home-grown school of sculpture was taking shape.

The presence in Scotland of the Queen's Sculptor, Sir Joseph Edgar Boehm helped. He portrayed Thomas Carlyle, the guardian of the nation's morals, and this impressive work in marble can be seen in the National Portrait Gallery in Edinburgh. It was royal patronage that gave Steell the opportunity, by then a Queen's Sculptor for Scotland, to create in his final years the Consort Memorial in Edinburgh.

In the early 19th century the first art academies and societies for the promotion of fine art were established throughout Scotland and it was Edinburgh and Glasgow that led the way in identifying a Scottish identity. The Glasgow Institute of Fine Arts, started by John Mossman in 1861 still exists today.

Edinburgh outdid Glasgow and the English monopoly of public commissions in that city was largely discontinued during the 1820s. In comparison Glasgow was notably less progressive. The merchant class which predominated in the city took little interest in sculpture during the early part of the century; they were more interested in making money than spending it. Edinburgh had introduced competitions to allocate public commissions, Glasgow relied more on private patronage and there wasn't all that much of that. The city of Glasgow really didn't really favour national monuments, electing instead to erect local memorials. Theoretically this should have provided work for Glasgow's resident sculptors but it didn't in practice. Glasgow committees remained convinced of the worth of the best English craftsmen and asked Sir Francis Chantrey to commemorate James Watt, and John Flaxman to sculpt works on William Pitt and

Chantrey's marble depiction of James Watt was done in 1830 for the University of Glasgow.

Sir John Moore. Baron Marochetti was also a favourite, producing likenesses of James Oswald, Queen Victoria, The Duke of Wellington and the Prince Consort. Only after the 1870s did local sculptors get their fair share of the commissions going. Any prejudice against artists working locally began to decline towards the middle of the century and James Fillans (1831) and then Patric Park (1833) established studios in Glasgow, although never really cracking the really big public monument commission.

Around this time William Mossman started a family practice that would dominate sculpture in the West of Scotland during the second half of the century. In 1831 William Mossman set up as a sculptor in Glasgow, the first sculptor studio of real significance. His bust of James Clelands done the same year is reputed to be the first bust professionally sculpted in Glasgow. He did a lot of funerary monuments and his sons followed him into the business. The Mossman family received a challenge in the west of Scotland in 1859 from the Ewing brothers of Birmingham who started their own studio and did a lot of portrait busts.

However, George and younger brother James only took one public commission from Mossman, that of the Burns statue in 1873 in George Square. George Ewing left for the USA afterwards to try his luck there.

In 1888 the first Glasgow International Exhibition of Art was held. With Mossman's death English sculptors again came back on the scene and as building increased in Glasgow so they got a lot of work. However it wasn't long into the 20th century that Pittendrigh Macgillivray, Kellock Brown and others led a revival. Macgillivray was an outstanding sculptor working in Glasgow and is recognized as undoubtedly the finest sculptor resident in Scotland at this time, making a major contribution to sculpture in both Glasgow and Edinburgh.

The eldest son of a mason sculptor, Macgillivray was apprenticed to William Brodie in Edinburgh for six years before working in the studios of James Steell and John Mossman in Glasgow. After helping Mossman with his statues of Thomas Campbell and David Livingstone he set up on his own in 1881 with only five pounds to his name. He achieved his greatest success

Top

PITTENDRIGH MACGILLIVRAY was one of Scotland's greatest sculptors and his massive Gladstone Monument in Edinburgh is recognised as one of his finest statues.

Bottom

Another Macgillvray statue much admired, now in St Giles Cathedral Edinburgh is his tribute to John Knox.

in the 1890s and the early 20th century. In this period he won at least twelve major commissions.

The massive Gladstone Monument in Edinburgh took up a lot of his time and is his greatest work. In 1917 it was unveiled, a statue at 9ft 6 in high and with eight other figures around the sides, each life-size. The Edinburgh College of Art was his concept. He had many talents besides sculpture – music and painting for example but preferred life in Scotland to the obvious move to London. He was a passionate advocate of Scottish nationalism In a lecture to the Edinburgh Architectural Association in 1917 he lamented that Scotland was 'still without sculpture in a national and characteristic sense' and deplored what he described as 'the wretchedly neglected condition of sculpture in Scotland.'

During his lifetime Scottish sculpture advanced leaps and bounds becoming comparable to its English counterparts. John Knox in Edinburgh's St Giles Cathedral is also a fine example of his work.

Kellock Brown's monument to Thomas Carlyle in Kelvingrove Park done in 1916, with an obvious nod to Rodin, is almost unique among public monuments in Scotland with the head and shoulders emerging out of a large, crudely chiselled, granite pillar. There is no torso or legs. Towards the end of the 19th century bronze started to replace marble in popularity as a form for statues.

From the middle of the 20th century onwards modern art became more prevalent – a means of making money; pickled sharks and unmade beds making good money for less apparent effort. Then came a resurgence of figure work in the late twentieth century and early twenty-first Scottish sculptors like Sir Eduardo Paolozzi and William Turnbull exhibited works but men like Alexander Stoddart, David Annand, and Kenny McKay keep up the tradition of honouring famous Scots in sculpture form. Sculpture became more common in urban areas and city streets, away from the usual public parks and gardens, with vandalism sadly becoming an increasing problem as society standards dropped. The Scottish Arts Council began to get behind sculpture in the late 1960s and started to push for it to be seen in urban spaces for the enjoyment of the public at large.

The body looking at Scotland's contribution to sculpture along with the whole of the United Kingdom is the Public Monuments and Sculpture Association in London. Created to unite people with a mutual interest in public monuments and sculpture, the PMSA is recording, preserving and promoting our sculptural heritage. It was started in 1991 with £470,000 worth of Lottery money topped up to a million by interested organizations, sponsors etc. Its works falls into four categories – recording, preserving, promoting, and providing information. The National Recording Project established in 1997 aims to catalogue every piece of public sculpture and every public monument in the British Isles in digital form for public access. Nearly three-quarters are now already recorded with some at great risk. This unique record contains nearly ten thousand entries. The organization also produces newsletters, the magazine *Sculpture Journal*, and a companion series of books listing public sculptures. Six are already published including City of London and City of Glasgow and eleven more are in preparation. The National Archive Centre has rooms at the Courtauld Institute of Art in London headed by Jo Darke, founder member and driving force behind the operation. There are fifteen regional archive centres including two in Scotland – at the Glasgow School of Art and in Edinburgh, originally based at Edinburgh College of Art but now in Bernard Terrace.

In Scotland those wishing to find out more about our heritage head for Bernard Terrace. Based there is the Royal Commission on the Ancient and Historical Monuments of Scotland, a body financed by the Scottish Office under the sponsorship of Historic Scotland. It records and interprets the sites, monuments and buildings of Scotland's past maintaining a National Monuments Record. Established in 1908, it has extensive information on all types of monuments at sites throughout Scotland.

Two modern Scottish sculptors of this period are remembered with gratitude. Fred Bushe founded the Scottish Sculptor Workshop at Lumsden in West Aberdeen in 1979 which has inspired open-air exhibitions in Aberdeen and at Kildrummy Castle at Strathdon, as well as establishing contacts abroad which have brought sculptors to work at Lumsden from overseas.

Andrew Mylious inspired the Scottish Sculpture Trust which was set up in 1976 to promote contemporary sculpture on public sites in Scotland. Anyone visiting the Highlands and passing Glenshee can see an interesting sample of their work and there is also a Highland Sculpture Park at Carrbridge. Sadly the Trust is now gone but their work can live on. The Trust ceased activity in 2004 with some bitterness and stated they "will no longer be able to contact anyone with regard to the work it carried out in support of sculptors, the arts community and the creative life of Scotland. The decision was taken with great sadness as a result of the failure of the Scottish Arts Council to proceed with any interest or energy towards the creation of the Public Arts Development Agency which the Trust was asked to undertake in partnership with the Glasgow School of Art over two years ago. The Trust's archive material has been donated to the National Library of Scotland and is available for consultation or research."

The Gerald Laing Art Foundation at his studio in Kinkell Castle in the Highlands was set up by the renowned sculptor to "promote the understanding, appreciation and practice of figurative public sculpture". The Foundation is dedicated to promoting the understanding of the social and historical significance of public sculpture and teaching the necessary skills for its creation. It is assembling a collection of original drawings, maquettes and plaster casts for study and display as well as a studio teaching practical subjects of various kinds. Full-time residential and part-time courses at professional and amateur levels are available. The Foundation, which works in conjunction with the Public Monuments and Sculpture Association, is expanding all the time.

Says Gerald Laing: "Public sculpture escapes the vagaries and exploitations of the art market because it is not for sale and is therefore of no interest to dealers. Their drawings and plaster casts are often forgotten and one of the objectives of the Gerald Laing Art Foundation is to provide a refuge for these artefacts in order to preserve them and make them available for study."

Some of this work is in America where Save Outdoor Sculpture (SOS) is a joint project of Heritage Preservation and the Smithsonian American Art Museum to document and help preserve all monuments and outdoor sculptures in the United States. In Phase One of this operation to save the country's sculptural heritage some seven thousand volunteers reported thirty thousand publicly accessible outdoor sculptures to the Inventory of American Sculpture database at the Museum, with forty-five per cent found to be in critical need of attention and nine per cent requiring urgent treatment to survive. It now has a database of ninety thousand entries as it seeks to save the country's vast sculptural heritage. They have uncovered examples of the more common Scottish heroes and the more unusual such as a Loch Ness Monster at Wichita Falls, as well as other work by Scottish sculptors, men who are often overlooked but are remembered here.

Leading Figure Sculptors in Scotland

David Annand (b.1948) Scotland's leading figure sculptor whose credits include Jim Clark, Jimmy Shand, Robert Fergusson. He trained at Dundee Art College and after a lot of private commissions created the Deer Leap in Dundee, and now has many animal sculptures around the country. He recently completed a bronze of Robert Burns for a new shopping mall in Ayr but also has work all over Britain.

Sir Joseph Edgar Boehm (1834–1890) Leading sculptor of Victorian era, an Austrian and favourite of the Queen. Appointed Sculptor to Her Majesty in 1881. Responsible for Carlyle on Chelsea embankment and John Brown at Balmoral.

William Brodie (1815–1881) Born Banff. Educated in Aberdeen and one of the best Scottish – if not British – sculptors. Another who studied in Rome. Moved to Edinburgh in 1847 where many busts and statues are to be seen. His bust of Carlyle is in the National Portrait Gallery of Scotland and Lord Cockburn statue is in Parliament House. Also produced Sir James Simpson in Edinburgh and Sir David Brewster in Edinburgh. Greyfriars Bobby was his and some work on the Scott Monument. He was Secretary of Royal Scottish Academy in 1859.

Thomas Stuart Burnett (1853–1888) He did the statue of General Gordon of Khartoum in Aberdeen. A resident of Glasgow and member of well-known family of architects in that city.

Sir Francis Legatt Chantrey (1781–1841) Born near Sheffield, the Godfather of British Sculptors, son of a small farmer from Derbyshire. Was first a

The sun sets on Chelsea Embankment in London and Boehm's bronze of Thomas Carlyle, also seen in Ecclefechan.

portrait painter but became a full-time sculptor and at start of 19th century was in London exhibiting at the Royal Academy. Produced many busts but full-size statues are what he is known for. In 1835 he was knighted. Chantrey was good at asking for money with commissions and became very wealthy although he was given a head start by marrying a rich cousin and building his own studio. He later built his own foundry at 13 Eccleston Place in London for bronze casting. He said his statue of James Watt (1824) at Handsworth Parish Church was his finest statue. Chantrey also created Watt in Westminster Abbey in 1819. His favourite bust was of Sir Walter Scott – he made two replicas for Sir Robert Peel and the Duke of Wellington. In 1814 he went to Paris for five years and then Rome. His statues include President Blair (Edinburgh 1815), Lord Melville (Sessions House Edinburgh 1818), Robert Dundas, Sessions House Edinburgh 1824, James Watt (Greenock 1830 and Hunterian Museum (1830), George IV (Edinburgh 1831), James Watt (Glasgow 1832), William Pitt (Edinburgh 1833) and Duke of Sutherland (Dornoch 1837).

His death mask of Sir Walter Scott is in the National Portrait Gallery in Edinburgh (done in 1832) and a monument to Rev. David Wilkie (1812) in Cults, Fife. He died of a heart attack on November 25 1841 leaving a fortune of £150,000. After his death his wife gave all original models of busts and statues to Oxford University. After she died the Chantrey Bequest to the Royal Academy was established.

Thomas Clapperton (1879–1862) Born in Galashiels, he won a travelling scholarship at the Royal Academy which enabled him to study in Paris and Rome. He set up studios in London and in 1913 made the Flodden and Mungo Park Memorials in Selkirk. He also did a number of War

GEORGE IV in George Street, Edinburgh is another Chantrey work and popular with tourists who like to have themselves photographed next to the plaque saying "visited Scotland."

THOMAS JOHN CLAPPERTON
1879-1962

The Old Gala House in Galashiels displays work of Thomas Clapperton who was from the town.

Memorials after WWI and a massive frieze for Liberty's store in London. Clapperton was responsible for The Reivers in Galashiels and Robert the Bruce at the entrance to Edinburgh Castle.

Andrew Currie (c.1810–1879) Self-taught Scottish sculptor, native of Dumfries. He carved a statue of Mungo Park in 1839 in Selkirk. In 1860 he made a statue of James Hogg, The Ettrick Shepherd, on banks of St Mary's Loch. He also executed a sandstone figure of Old Mortality which he decided to raffle. The winner, a Dr Sinclair, was killed in Chatham on the very day of the draw and his executors presented the work to Dumfries Observatory where an octagonal temple was built to receive it.

Sir William Reid Dick (1879–1961) Born in Glasgow, studied in London and one-time President of the Royal Society of Sculptors. Prodigious output, a lot of royalty and statue of Livingstone at Victoria Falls.

David Dunbar The Younger (died 1866). Son of David The Elder who from 1815–1823 exhibited at the Royal Academy. David Junior studied in Rome and on his return to England was employed by Sir Francis Chantrey. In 1844 he exhibited a statue of Robert Burns in Westminster Hall which according to the *Literary Gazette* 'would have been pleasing had the execution been equal to the intention.' The statue had been started by his father.

James Fillans (1802–1852) Noted Scots sculptor born in

Wilsontown in Lanarkshire. Started as a weaver. Trained in Paris and Rome and did many portrait busts including Sir Walter Scott and massive statue of Sir James Shaw at Kilmarnock. One of the best known Scottish sculptors, he is buried in Paisley.

John Flaxman (1755–1826) World-renowned sculptor from York. He was the son of a caster and model maker. He is second in the British School of Sculpture only to Chantrey. In 1787 he visited Rome. Born York, taken to London by parents when only six months old. He created Sir John Moore in George Square Glasgow and a marble of William Pitt the Younger in Glasgow Art Gallery. Interested in art all his life from a young age, at age twenty he joined his father working for Wedgwood as a designer and model-maker. Wedgwood took him to Rome where, now married, he spent seven years. The Statue of Burns in the National Portrait Gallery Edinburgh is his. His funerary works are his best work – notably Lord Nelson in St Paul's Cathedral London.

Robert Forrest (1791–1852) Self-taught, from Carluke in Lanarkshire, he began life as a stone-mason in Clydesdale quarries. His main work was a statue of Wallace for Lanark at 7ft 6 in high and unusually shows the national hero of Scotland dressed in a Roman costume with sword and buckler. The people of Lanark loved it however and after the unveiling carried the sculptor 'in triumph through the streets, preceded by music and the banners of the different trades.' Other statues include a huge one of Lord Melville (1822) in Edinburgh, John Knox in Glasgow Necropolis (1825) and Duke of Wellington in Falkirk (1843). The Melville statue was executed from a design by Chantrey. In 1832 he started on huge equestrian statues of, among others, Mary Queen of Scots and Robert Burns each carved from a single block of sandstone and weighing twenty tons. They were well

One way of seeing Robert Forrest's depiction of John Knox dominating the Necropolis in Glasgow is to take to the air (see right).

received and he was known as Scotland's national sculptor. But it financially crippled him and another unfinished work was his statue of the Duke of Wellington for the summit of Arthur's Seat in Edinburgh.

John Greenshields (1792–1838) A mason by trade born in Lesmahagow, aged thirty he turned to sculpting and had a studio near Carluke Lanarkshire after doing apprenticeship with Forrest. He started with a small statue of Lord Byron and one of Burns for an Australian client. One of King George IV so impressed Sir Walter Scott that the writer went to visit him in his cottage in 1829 and Greenshields then did a statue of Sir Walter Scott in 1831 for Cadell, an Edinburgh publisher. Carved in freestone, friends of Scott say it is the best likeness of the master.

Amelia Hill (19th c.) wife of David Octavius Hill, notable Scottish landscape painter (1802–1870) did mainly portrait busts including two of Thomas Carlyle and one of David Livingstone – one of the best women sculptors. She sculpted the much-admired Burns statue in Dumfries.

John Hutchison (1833–1910) Born in Edinburgh and sculptor of some fine busts and many statues including Adam Black, Robert the Bruce and John Knox. One of finest Scottish sculptors of his day, the Lochmaben statue of Bruce is his work.

Samuel Joseph (1791–1850) One of the most eminent of Scottish School of Sculptors although his place of birth is unknown (probably English) However he saw himself as Scottish and Scotland claims him as one of their own. Did mainly busts of eminent people including Scott and the Duke of Argyll. In 1823 he went to Edinburgh and in 1826 in Edinburgh became one of the founder members of the Royal Scottish Academy. The Wilberforce statue in Westminster Abbey is his masterpiece.

Gerald Laing (b.1936) Born in Newcastle he studied in London and lived in the USA before making his name in Scotland with many exhibitions of his work and the establishment of a bronze foundry at Kinkell Castle. He did the Conan Doyle statue in Edinburgh and is respected as a contemporary artist with a body of work that spans the Pop movement of the sixties before converting to more representational bronze sculptures.

William Lamb (1893–1951) A native of Montrose, he set up a studio in the town which now has a number of his statues on display particularly 'working characters' such as The Minesweeper, The Fisherwomen, The Smith, and the Seafarer. His fame grew from the north-east of Scotland and attracted the attention of the Royal Family who commissioned him to produce portrait busts of the then Duchess of York, subsequently Queen Elizabeth and her two Princesses.

James Pittendrigh Macgillivray (1856–1938) born in Inverurie near Aberdeen, son of a sculptor he trained in William Brodie's Edinburgh studio. Afterwards he worked with John Mossman before striking out on his own. Admired for a great statue of John Knox in St Giles Cathedral Edinburgh. His monument to Robert Burns (Irvine 1895) and elaborate Monument to William Ewart Gladstone in Edinburgh (1899–1917) are other good examples of his craft. He was Co-founder of *Scottish Art Review*. The Aberdeen Gallery displays some of his work.

Baron Carlo Marochetti (1805–1867) From Turin in Italy, he became a naturalized French citizen studying in Paris. He fled Paris at the time of the 1848 Revolution and reached London where his flamboyant personality and links with the Italian and French courts endeared him to our Royal family. He was known for his equestrian statues – even although they attracted much criticism for their flamboyant style – and the Duke of Wellington and Victoria and Albert in Glasgow are his work. Always controversial, his figures were never less than 'lively.'

The name **Mossman** is strongly linked with sculpture in Scotland. J. & G. Mossman is a firm of architectural

Lamb's depiction of The Smith in Montrose.

sculptors and monumental masons founded in Leith by William Mossman Senior with sons John, George and William as successors. They moved to Glasgow in 1828 making their reputation with the recently opened Necropolis. **John G. Mossman** (1817–1890) is a name synonymous with statues in Glasgow. He studied with his father and Baron Marochetti and early on produced many busts of society figures. He was the most important maker of statues of his generation in the West of Scotland. At his workshop the young James Pittendrigh Macgillivray trained. Amongst many, statues of Peel (George Square Glasgow 1853), David Livingstone (Cathedral Square 1876), Thomas

Mossman is a famous name in Glasgow – and Scottish – sculpture and his work is everywhere. Here David Livingstone looks out on a Glasgow street.

Campbell (George Square 1873) and Norman Macleod Cathedral Square Gardens 1881) are his.

Anthony Morrow (b.1954) Studied Fine Art at Duncan of Jordanstone College of Art in Dundee. Responsible for Desperate Dan (with his wife Susie doing Minnie the Minx) and he also produced the Dragon in Murraygate, Dundee and restored the bronze statue of Peter Pan in Kirriemuir in 1994. Now Head of Sculpture at Dundee College.

Sir Eduardo Paolozzi (1924–2005) One of the foremost sculptors of his generation and an important influence on Pop Art. Born at Leith, Edinburgh, the son of Italian parents, his work influenced many young modern Scottish sculptors. His best-known work is probably a 10ft bronze of Sir Isaac Newton for the new British Library in London. A reproduction of his London studio is at the Dean Gallery in London. In 1986 he was appointed the Queen's Sculptor in Ordinary for Scotland and was knighted in 1989. He was Patron of the Public Monuments and Sculpture Association.

Patric Park (1811–1855). Born in Glasgow, he started work as a decorative stonecarver at Hamilton Palace. Mostly in demand for portrait busts but also sculpted a fine Charles Tennant statue in Glasgow's Necropolis. In 1850 Park started a project of erecting a huge statue of Wallace on Edinburgh hills to stand fifteen feet high requiring ten tons of clay. Lack of encouragement led to him abandoning the project and destroying the model with his own mallet.

Alexander Handyside Ritchie (1804–1870) Born at Musselburgh, the son of a brickmaker. He studied at Edinburgh School of Arts and trained in Rome but back home in his native city was employed on many public works throughout Scotland including a monument to the Duke of Hamilton, in Glasgow. He carved many statues including Sir Walter Scott (1839) at Selkirk, Prince Charles Edward Stuart (1844) for the Scott Monument in Edinburgh, Hugh Miller (1858) at Cromarty and Wallace (1858) at Lanark In 1845 he also made a number of statues for the New Physicians Hall in Edinburgh and in 1858 those of Knox, Melville, Henderson, Renwick and Ebenezer Erskine for Stirling Cemetery. In a large output, he also was responsible for Charles Marjoribanks at Coldstream in 1836.

Sir John Steell (1804–1891)Born in Aberdeen, he worked in Edinburgh and Rome. He was also the first to introduce artistic bronze casting into Scotland and, at his own expense, built a foundry so that works of his and other artists could be reproduced in metal. Knighted by Queen Victoria when she unveiled his statue of the Prince Consort in Edinburgh in 1876. Amongst many fine works including the Alexander and

Handyside Ritchie had a large output including Ebenezer Erskine in Stirling Cemetery.

Bucephalus figure outside Edinburgh City Chambers were statues of Queen Victoria (Royal Institution Edinburgh 1844), Allan Ramsay (Edinburgh 1850), Wellington (Edinburgh 1852), Lord Jeffrey (Parliament House, Edinburgh 1855), Professor Wilson (Princes St, Edinburgh 1856), Lord President Boyle (Parliament House Edinburgh 1856), Lord Melville (Edinburgh 1857) and Sir David Baxter (Dundee 1863). He worked on Burns in New York (1874), Burns in Dundee (1880) and Burns on London Embankment (1884). The Burns bust in Westminster Abbey is his, made in 1885.

David Watson Stevenson (1842–1904) From Edinburgh, Trained at studio of William Brodie, mostly portrait busts including Robert Louis Stevenson but also statues of Labour and Learning on side of Prince Albert Memorial in Edinburgh. Best known for William Wallace on the Wallace Monument in Stirling. He also sculpted Highland Mary at Dunoon in 1896.

William Grant Stevenson (1849–1919) Brother of above. Born at Ratho, he lived and worked in Edinburgh. Responsible for original Burns in Kilmarnock and Wallace in Aberdeen. He also painted in oil.

Alexander Stoddart (b. 1959) Born in Edinburgh, wrote his undergraduate thesis on the life and work of John

Sir John Steell produced many great statues and a great statue deserves a great location such as here outside the McManus Galleries in Dundee originally built as a memorial to Prince Albert.

Mossman. A vocal advocate of Neo-classical monumentalism with strong views on 'the mandarins of contemporary art.' His monument to David Hume on Royal Mile in 1997 with the figure dressed in a classical toga was criticised by some but admired by many. He lives and works in Paisley where his statue to Rev. Dr. John Witherspoon (2001) can be seen. Kidnapped in Edinburgh is a recent work and was chosen for the statue of Adam Smith to be erected in Edinburgh's Canongate.

James Thom (1802–1850) Born at Lochlee in Ayrshire. His work was very Scottish, homely. He was an apprentice in Kilmarnock, then Glasgow and finally Ayr where he copied a portrait

he'd seen of Burns for a stone bust in 1827 which was much praised. So he then hewed out of local stone life-size figures of Tam O'Shanter and Souter Johnnie which were sent on tour to raise funds for a Burns Monument in Alloway. He produced another Old Mortality and a statue of Wallace at Ayr. His studio was much visited and Americans took an increasing interest in his

Above
Alexander Stoddart with the torso of Adam Smith.

Left
John Witherspoon.

work, particularly his works on Burns. He died in New York on 17 April 1850 having made his reputation on the great poet.

Peter Turnerelli (1774–1839) An Irishman from Dublin he was a favourite of the Royal Family for whom he became Sculptor-in-Ordinary. He created the statue of Robert Burns in 1816 at the Dumfries National Monument. He turned down a possible knighthood.

CHAPTER 11

How Does It Happen?

'A pretty girl who naked is – is worth a million statues'

e.e. CUMMINGS

How do statues appear? It has to start somewhere and often not with councils who are naturally reluctant to spend taxpayers' money in memory of someone who may not be universally popular. This might not be a good vote-winner and it is usually left to public-spirited individuals to prompt them to remember their local heroes with a prominent site. Men such as Bob Watt, an experienced campaigner in raising money for statues of notable figures from the past and the man behind the recent Fergusson statue in Edinburgh.

Bob lives in an elegant wide street in the Colinton district of Edinburgh and is known in that city for his forceful fund-raising. It started when he decided to take his wife on a round-the-world tour to celebrate their fortieth wedding anniversary. In Samoa, impressed with the house of Robert Louis Stevenson and how his life was recalled there, he got to thinking of how Scotland didn't always remember her heroes in their own land.

On his return he started raising money for a bronze plaque and head of William McGonagall to be erected in Greyfriars Graveyard. 'Stone plaques are actually better,' he says, "vandalism can be a big problem and metal ones get stolen for the metal." This was followed by monuments in Peebles to celebrate the centenary of

Lord Provost Drummond. For this Bob put on a competition for Edinburgh schoolchildren, a typical example of how he tries to get as many people and organizations involved as possible to gather the necessary groundswell of support before an approach is made to the local authority for a fitting site for a good memorial.

A visit to San Diego (twinned with Edinburgh) followed. He was Twin Cities Chairman at the time and at a conference in Los Angeles was impressed by Americans in the audience waving their greenback dollars in the air. America is a country noted for its fund-raising from individuals and companies and back in Scotland he returned to fund-raising for statues with definite thoughts on the way he wanted to proceed.

He had started work as a lab-boy at Edinburgh University and on retiring from a career in industry as a chemist was able to take up charity work using his undoubted energy. Bob calls himself a fund-raiser and problem solver. "I like it," he says, "you see the best in people, the best of human nature." He is a big, bluff, non-drinker who speaks his mind saying about his methods: "Look, if you are trapped in the jungle, I'll get you out. You might not like me at the end of it but I'll get you out. I can be a hard-nosed street-fighter who could argue for my country, as proudly Scottish as you can get."

Using his unique brand of charm and intimidation – Bob is not a committee man – he set about raising the £40,000 needed for the Fergusson statue with aims to exceed the target so the remainder could be set aside for maintenance and renovation work. A grant of £2,000 from the City of Edinburgh started it off and with a committee of heavyweights including sculptor George Wylie and Brian Caster of the Edinburgh Powderhall Foundry he ran a competition to find a sculptor.

Most sculptors produce a maquette (miniature) of what they envisage and Bob sought

Bob Watt is joined by Robert Burns at the unveiling of the Fergusson statue in Edinburgh's Royal mile.

to get these displayed in major galleries and art centres in Glasgow, Edinburgh, Aberdeen, Inverness and Dundee alongside a voting box so the public could have their say. A total of fifteen thousand votes were cast with Fife sculptor David Annand winning eighty per cent of the total. It also was another opportunity for donations – in the end the smallest donation from this source was fifty pence, the largest overall was several thousand pounds.

Bob was off and running. He collected money from Burns Clubs, shops in Edinburgh, art and poetry bodies, major and minor companies, and individuals with a love of poetry. The maquette was sold to St Andrews University where Fergusson studied. An appeal for help went out on Fergusson's birthday. A series of 'Words With the Watts' evenings were held at his house with wife Pat doing the catering which brought in some generous sums.

The idea to remember Fergusson in this way had come out of a number of discussions with his friend George Philp, a Glasgow doctor and Scots language and poetry historian. Says Bob: "If George was the mother then I was the midwife." Philp gave his fees for his Scotstoun lectures to the cause as did other artists. A raffle was organized and Bob wrote to every Scottish Member of Parliament and Scottish Society. He thought it would take five years (they started in 2000 which was the 250th anniversary of Fergusson's birth) to get the money, in fact it took four and there was a surplus.

Most statues in olden times were pretty rigid figures. Not only was Fergusson a 'moving' piece striding along the Canongate pavement but Bob organised for a time capsule to be put under the spot where the poet stands. It will contain tapes of his poems; newspaper reports of the unveiling; information about the Edinburgh Cape Society, the arts and poetry club of which the poet was a member; photographs, list of the major contributors, a Scottish dictionary of the time, and memorabilia about the City of Edinburgh who were so happy to back the scheme. The statue in fact was unveiled just as Edinburgh had been awarded the title of the first City of Literature by the United Nations. It is proving very popular with tourists to have their photographs alongside or hugging the poet. Unlike most statues which tend to be high up on a plinth it is reachable.

Another casket is planned, to be placed in the city archives and not to be opened for one hundred years, containing work from all the city's primary, state and private school pupils who had the opportunity to write four lines of poetry about Edinburgh. To commemorate Fergusson they had to contain three Scottish words. As 2006 ended there were plans for a plaque to be fixed to the bottom of the statue with a telephone number so people could call up on the internet information on the poet and old views of Edinburgh at the time he was there etc., the money raised going to charity.

His foresight is bringing new life to the question of figurative statues, and plaques, with ideas such as plaques in Braille. He admired a year-long exhibition of sculpture outside the Scottish Parliament at the bottom of Edinburgh's Royal Mile, especially a forty-ton red granite Lion of Scotland, by Ronald Rae. When the exhibition closed on 20 May 2007 he was petitioning the Parliament to have it moved thirty yards, turned one-hundred-and-eighty degrees and campaigning to have it there permanently as a

This lion of Scotland may end up permanently outside the new Scottish Parliament if Bob Watt has his way.

symbol of Scotland. Rae was born in Ayr in 1946 and hand carves granite sculptures and the Lion is his largest in the pink and grey granite from the Corrennie quarry in Aberdeenshire.

Edinburgh already has a Holy Corner with numerous churches; Bob Watt is trying for a Writer's Corner – "near the University, lots of writers went there." In October 2006 he saw the unveiling of a plaque he had organized to one of Edinburgh's newer, and world-respected, authors. The plaque explains that J.K. Rowling wrote the early chapters of Harry Potter on the first floor of the building at the corner of Drummond and Nicholson Streets. It is small so look carefully; on the opposite corner of Drummond Street is a plaque to Robert Louis Stevenson. "Literature doesn't have to be remote, I want to bring it to as many people as possible."

He again raised the money from various fund-raising efforts put on by Bob and Pat. The corner already has a plaque to where William McGonagall died. Bob is a fan of the poet best known for his Tay Bridge Disaster Ode and has applied to Edinburgh Council and The Saltire Society to remember McGonagall by

the Writers Museum in Edinburgh. That will not be easy, he will be surrounded by men of the ilk of Burns, Stevenson, Scott etc.

His energy and distinctive fund-raising efforts are now turned towards his desire to put statues along the Forth and Clyde Canal. He envisages scientists and inventors at the Glasgow end and literary figures at the Edinburgh end being a good mix. This energetic man, with the correct concept for both remembering our heroes and making statues interesting, is already also turning his thoughts to how best to raise money for two great Edinburgh men of the past. He says: "James Hutton was the Albert Einstein of his day, in fact he is said to have inspired the great man and turned geology into a popular subject. Hutton was inspired by the rocks on Arthur's Seat. I wanted to see the face of Hutton coming out of the rocks there, Edinburgh's Mt. Rushmore if you like. But the Royal Parks, perhaps not surprisingly, didn't like the idea. But on the canal, his head hewed from granite rock, now that would be good."

His mind races ahead. 'And James Clerk Maxwell is talked of in the same breath as Isaac Newton you know – what a man, a great mathematician and more.' And maybe Telford at the Glasgow end; that would be good.'

There is no stopping him. It's a popular misconception that councils fund statues. They don't. They do control the eventual location of a statue but not the funding.

Indeed, Edinburgh, with approaching two hundred 'memorials' in some form of which around thirty are statues to its favourite sons and daughters in their image, has historically only ever funded two. And that was some while ago, Charles II and former city provost in the mid-nineteenth century, William Chambers. They get approached by many well-meaning individuals who are good at campaigning for statues of their particular hero but aren't so good at fund-raising. Current 'suggestions' include Elsie Inglis, women at war, and the men who died building the Forth Road Bridge. It is men like Bob Watt who have to find the money and guarantee Scotland's heroes are remembered.

CHAPTER 12

How a Statue is Made

'Mathematics rightly viewed possesses not only truth but supreme beauty – a beauty cold and austere like that of sculpture'

BERTRAND RUSSELL

It took over four years for Robert Fergusson to reach the Edinburgh foundry of husband and wife team Brian Caster and Kerry Hammond and another three months for him to take his place on the Royal Mile. That is about the average time for a statue of this size and complexity and all that fund-raising effort and all the skills of the sculptor are dependent on the finishing talents of the final part of the process – the foundry.

There are three fine art foundries in Scotland, one in Peebles and another in the Black Isle but the biggest is Powderhall Bronze in Edinburgh, owned and run by husband-and-wife team Brian Caster and Kerry Hammond since 1989. They had met as students at the Royal College of Art in London and started the business in a former bakery behind the old dog track at the Powderhall Stadium. Says

Kerry: "The local blacksmith around the corner was a bit of an historian and told us it was the first area north of the Tweed granted a licence to make gunpowder. The name was reminiscent of explosions, gunfire etc. so we felt it was perfect for the business we were setting up."

Now, after a couple of moves, the pair have a staff of four and are happily ensconced in purpose-built premises in Graham Street, Leith where they have just opened the first foundry-based teaching school and

The foundry floor at Powderhall in Edinburgh.

exhibition area. Kerry again: "We will be running evening classes, short three-day courses etc. in response to the number of people who have asked how they can learn this fascinating subject." The foundry will, however, remain the core of Powderhall's business and in recent years they have worked with all the major Scottish sculptors, probably twenty or thirty in number. Their work ranges from the small private commission for the individual to major public statue work.

Among notable Scots they are responsible for are Jimmy Shand, Donald Dewar , Robert Fergusson, John Muir, David Hume, Jim Clark, the Marquis of Montrose (a particular favourite) and the innovative Desperate Dan statue in Dundee.

Kilmany sculptor David Annand won the commission to turn Fergusson into bronze and Powderhall waited for the call to say the work was complete and the project was now in their hands. The first step in the process is for the foundry to either travel to the sculptor's studio or receive the statue at their workplace to make a mould.

Three coats of silicon rubber are put on the sculptor's work, the early ones are like runny yoghurt but it gradually thickens the last one carefully applied with a spatula. A thixotropic paste is added to the 2nd and 3rd coat to make it spreadable. The rubber sets within 30 minutes and is valuable stuff, an expensive part of the whole process and, unlike some other materials, cannot be used

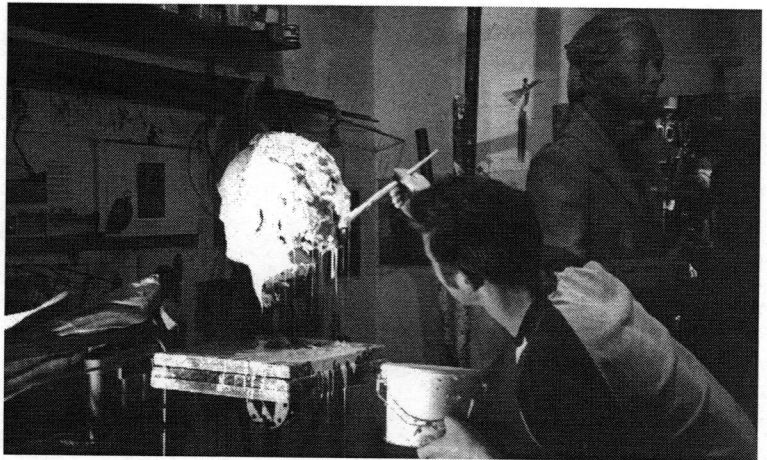

Three coats of silicon rubber are put on the sculptor's work.

again. Maybe 50 kilos of rubber can be used on a big statue. Rubber moulds can work on clay, metal or wooden subjects.

Once all the rubber work is completed, rigid plaster of Paris 'jackets' are made in sections to support the flexible rubber and to fit in the kiln. Once they are all in place they are removed one at a time and the rubber cut to fit the corresponding jackets. Hot wax (usually green but sometimes red) is carefully painted onto the surface of the mould, painted more thickly over the high points. A quantity of wax (enough to fill the mould to the top) is put to one side to cool slightly until it has a thin skin on the surface. This is then poured into the mould and kept in for around one minute. During this time it will cool and thicken onto the surface of the mould. It is then tipped out leaving a wax skin on the surface of around 1/8 to 1/4 of an inch. This gives the casting thickness required. The rubber is not thrown away, it will be used again for any further editions.

Now it is a bit like an Easter egg. Once cool, the smaller moulds are opened and the waxes taken out hollow. The moulds now lie on the floor, the larger ones pinned to keep the structure from moving about. The larger waxes are filled with a hardening material of plaster or ludo (recycled core material) and grog (broken up brick dust). The seam lines on the waxes are carefully worked with fine dental tools and soft wax until there is no evidence of them. The

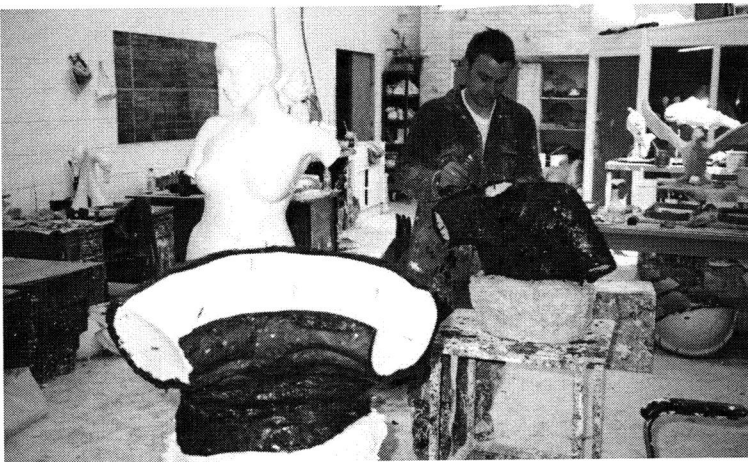

Jackets from plaster of Paris support the rubber ready for the kiln.

sculptor is usually invited to inspect the work at this stage.

The seams the foundry have inserted to separate the various pieces are cut back and smoothed off, back to the finish the sculptor required. These pieces are determined by the complexity of the statue, Fergusson was in fifteen pieces. A runner and riser system is put on which is a method for the wax to exit and the metal to enter the piece. Runners are the method by which the molten bronze enters the mould. Risers are the method by which the wax, air and any gases leave the mould. Steel nails are put in to hold the inner core material in its correct position within the investment mould as once the wax is melted away the core needs to keep its position in the void.

The investment material

Robert Fergusson's torso goes into the kiln which is heated to about 600 degrees.

goes in, thin creamy stuff to fill any small space and faithfully capture the skill of the sculptor. The investment is built up to a strong cylindrical shape, following the contours of the sculpture. The kiln is heated up to about six hundred degrees and in she goes, staying there maybe for two days depending on the individual size. When the kiln has cooled it is taken out very carefully and all the wax has disappeared – hence the process is known as 'lost wax casting.'

The next stage is rather enjoyable to watch. Molten metal is poured into a hole at the top of the mould and air holes inserted. The whole mould gives off a red glow rather like the dying extra-terrestial in the film ET and the air holes give the impression of twinkling lights. Nail holes are welded over, and areas where the runner and riser system had been attached are finished. It takes a day to cool down properly. The next day the investment material is knocked off, the runners and risers are cut off and the steel pins taken out. The holes are welded over and the original surface required by the sculptor recreated so there is no evidence of where the foundry has cut up the statue. The various sections are then welded together.

The overall finishing is now completed and it is ready for the patina process, a mix of chemicals depending on the choice of finish wanted by the sculptor. The metal surface of the statue is warmed with a blow torch and the patina painted on, very deliberately, in layers, with a brush. A final coating of wax for protection – two if the statue is going outside – a quick buff and that's it. Another bronze statue is ready for the unveiling.

Bronze is expensive and getting more so thanks to the Chinese who are starting to use it at a fast rate. The average bronze ingot weighs about 18lb each. It is made up largely of copper (eighty-five per cent); tin (five per cent); Zinc (five per cent) and lead (five per cent). Powderhall tend to use Bronze LG2 gun metal which has a higher than usual lead content. The lead is there to reduce the boiling point and the zinc reduces the retention of gases which can affect the surface. The bronze is melted at a temperature of 2,200 degrees c. The bronze ingots used for Fergusson actually came from Rotherham so there is a little bit of England in one of Scotland's greatest poets.

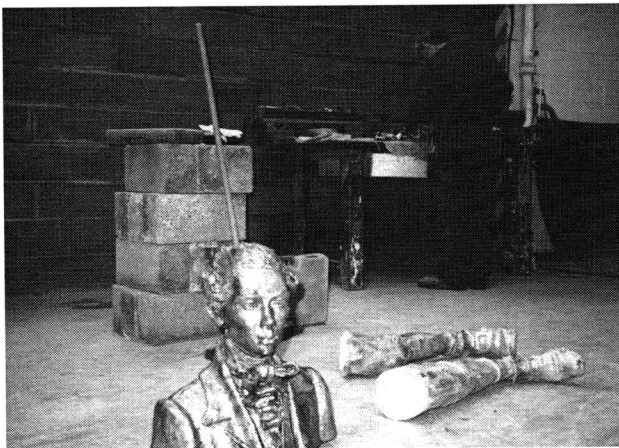

Fergusson is now in pieces ready to be welded together.

The decision on how the statue is patinated (coloured) is the sculptor's in nearly all cases, and depending on the various acid or chemical compounds used is usually light brown but can be shades of green as with Donald Dewar. The foundry men are craftsmen and some sculptors will actually allow them to choose the finish and colour of the statue.

Bronze casting has been around for several thousands of years. The discovery of copper, the principal ingredient of bronze, in Mesopotamia (now Iraq) around 8,000 BC started the whole business. It was then Egyptian craftsmen who developed techniques of turning it into figurines by beating the copper into shape but the Chinese are responsible for the first cast metal objects. In 1522 the people of Benin, an ancient African kingdom, began trading slaves, ivory and pepper with the Portuguese in return for bronze. They saw the reddish-brown colour of the bronze representing fire and blood giving the bronze the power to destroy and create as the ore came from the earth. They started the use of wax (actually mutton or beef fat in their case) in casting and bronze casting assumed an almost ritualistic and mystical importance. A goat or cockerel would be sacrificed over the shape, a practice no longer used thankfully although some workers have been known to break a bottle of wine over the piece as it enters the mould!

But the unveiling of Mr

The new teaching and display area at the Powderhall Foundry.

Fergusson probably isn't the last Powderhall will see of the poet. Says Brian Caster: "We do a lot of repair and restoration work all over Scotland, especially war memorials coming up to Remembrance Day in November and, sadly, where vandalism has occurred. The cleaning has to be done sensitively, it cannot be scrubbed and often the work is re-waxed for further protection and to keep the original colour.

London alone has ten or eleven foundries but in Scotland there are just three. Alongside Powderhall there is another, Beltane in Peebles, set up by ex-Edinburgh folk, who made the Jim Baxter statue. The third, the Black Isle Foundry was set up with Highlands Development Board money in Nairn and is run by the son of sculptor Gerald Laing. Brian and Kerry met when actually producing their own sculpture – Kerry studied sculpture in London whilst Brian studied glass. But in no way are they frustrated sculptors. They love their work and the challenges it brings and are happy to pass on their knowledge to another generation through their new display and training area.

CHAPTER 13

What's The Problem?
A Personal View

'Show me a Hero and I will write you a tragedy'
F. SCOTT FITZGERALD

W hy is it always such a problem? What is the difficulty in erecting a simple life-size representative likeness of some famous person when they are gone? Surely people in one hundred years would like to know what someone looked like over and above one-dimensional photographs?

We seem to make things hard for ourselves in this modern, politically-conscious world trying to live up to the reputation Tony Blair tried to forge of Cool Britannia. What is wrong with tradition? Famous people have had statues erected to them for centuries and although, thankfully, in Scotland there does seem to be a revival in figure sculptures, it is not the same in other parts of the British Isles. Trying to remember someone with a memorial or statue can prove very troublesome. We look in this chapter at examples from many countries but start at home with arguably the most famous figure of the 20th century.

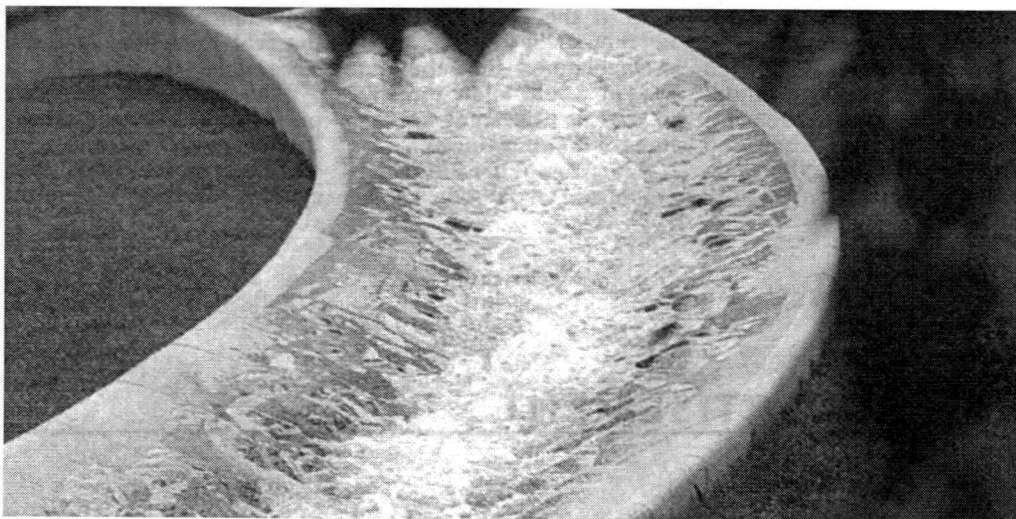

Princess Diana, once called the most beautiful woman in the world, is remembered with this storm drain in a London park.

Diana, Princess of Wales, one of the most beautiful women in the world, is not remembered with a statue at all but is celebrated with a glorified storm drain in a London park that is closed more often than it is open.

The memorial fountain in Hyde Park has been plagued with problems since it opened in July 2004. It was two years late and the budget had jumped hugely to £3.6 million. Kathryn Gustafson, the American behind the project, defended criticism of her 'Drainage Ditch' but the problems continued with regular closures. This 260ft by 165ft ring of granite with flowing water was meant to be a hit with children but they were soon asked not to paddle in it as there were design flaws and safety concerns. It closed within two weeks of opening with the Secretary of State for Culture Media and Sport blaming the public for its irresponsible behaviour. There is no public statue to Diana for her many legions of fans to admire.

Another much-loved and departed Royal is the Queen Mother. Universally admired, she lived to the age of one hundred and one and died in 2002. The Queen Mother's Memorial Fund for Scotland sought £1million to build a national memorial in the Royal Botanic Gardens in Edinburgh and memorial gates at Glamis in Angus. The focus of the garden is a pavilion, decorated inside with shells and pebbles gathered by primary schoolchildren throughout Scotland. Within the pavilion is a bronze relief, head and shoulders of the Queen Mother.

However there is a statue of George VI, husband of the Queen Mother, on The Mall in London overlooking Horse Guards Parade and some form of memory of the Queen Mother will be placed there. It is unlikely to be a formal statue as commemorative statues are said not to find favour with the current Royal Family. The £2million monument (why is so much needed?) will be financed by proceeds from a commemorative coin to mark the current Queen's 80th birthday in the spring of 2006. Potential designers have been told to avoid the use of water following the fiasco of the Diana memorial fountain.

Winning Sculptor Philip Jackson has many 'royal' commissions so hopefully it will be a faithful likeness, he is against abstract designs. Due in 2007.

Some towns are quick off the mark; the seaside resort of Morecambe, struggling to compete for holidaymakers with cheap flights to Spain and Portugal were pretty quick to erect a lovely statue of their favourite son, comedian Eric of Morecambe and Wise fame. Plans are also afoot for a prominent memorial to former Goon Spike Milligan, a man who gave pleasure to millions. Actor Michael Palin and poet Roger McGough rightly say he deserves to be remembered. They are heading a fund-raising campaign to find £30,000 to erect a bronze statue of Milligan sitting on a park bench and turning as if to speak to an imaginary person. It will go in Finchley where the comic genius lived for nineteen years. So why isn't there a statue in the middle of Glasgow to Chic Murray? Billy Connolly acknowledges him as one of the greats. He came from a long line of Shipyard Clyde comedians. He could stand as a tribute to them all. Of course Councils will say it is an inappropriate use of taxpayers' money but how many councils spend money on obscure other arts appealing to a small percentage of the population? Statues are permanent memorials attracting interest from both locals and tourists.

Of course when you recall that in our country's capital city an empty plinth stood on the north side of Trafalgar Square awaiting a statue for one hundred and sixty years until recently, you have to wonder at the speed of decision-making. The plinth, designed by Sir Charles Barry, was intended for a statue of King William IV in 1841 but remained empty until 1998. Only in recent years with the arrival of a new Mayor of London has it been used. Before that, various suggestions were put forward for who should be there. Back in the 1990s the Royal Society of Arts asked people their opinions as to who should be on the plinth. Nelson Mandela (it is near South Africa House), Mahatma Gandhi, George Orwell, The Queen Mother, Princess Diana, a British Bulldog, Red Rum the racehorse, Ronald Reagan and David Beckham were names touted about.

Then in 1998 the Royal Society of Architects commissioned three sculptures to stand temporarily on the plinth. They were to be a statue of Jesus Christ; a combination of a book, tree and human head; and what looked like a giant fibreglass resin lavatory cistern. The latter, by fashionable artists Rachel Whiteread, actually did appear to much derisory comment and some praise, and then a gullible American offered to buy it. That was controversial enough but then in 2001 a review group chaired by author John Mortimer decided the plinth will not have a permanent statue after all. By 2004 Mayor Ken Livingstone, known for his love of newts and saying he would like to see the Saudi Royal Family swinging from lampposts, had organised a competition for contemporary sculptors to give temporary displays. The shortlist of six comprised a car covered in pigeon droppings; a group of anti-war marchers; two cruise missiles; a pregnant deformed lady; a perspex pigeon hotel; and the framework for two skyscrapers. The public were able to vote on which they

The Fourth Plinth, Trafalgar Square
Join the debate...

Chris Burden
Toy Skyscraper as Tall
as a Real Building

Sokari Douglas Camp
No-o-war-r No-o-war-r

Stefan Gec
Mannequin

Sarah Lucas
This One's for the Pigeons
(Oi! Pigeons, over here!)

Marc Quinn
Alison Lapper pregnant

Thomas Schütte
Hotel for the Birds

www.fourthplinth.co.uk

with thanks to   Arup Associates   FedEx   NATIONAL GALLERY   ARTS COUNCIL ENGLAND   fourthplinth

wanted. Two questions were asked – what do you think about having contemporary art on the fourth plinth and who do you vote for and why. The winner was to go up for eighteen months and then the whole process would begin again.

Ken Livingstone said he couldn't pick a winner so two were selected to go there consecutively. The first was a twelve-foot high marble statue of the pregnant disabled Alison Lapper and after that the pigeon-hating Mayor will have to see every day the Hotel for the Birds which is really just sheets of coloured perspex designed by a German artist Thomas Schutte. Marc Quinn modelled the woman statue on a friend of his, Alison Lapper, when she was eight and a half months into her pregnancy. She was born with no arms and shortened legs.

The sculptor said of his work: "Most public sculpture, especially in the Trafalgar Square and Whitehall areas, is triumphant male statuary. Nelson's column is the epitome of a phallic male monument and I felt the square needed some feminism." Sandy Nairne, Director of the National Portrait Gallery and chairman of the commissioning group said: "We live in an age that doesn't have a consensus about history. In the 21st century I don't believe you can put up a statue to somebody permanently."

A poll for the *London Standard* newspaper carried out at the time found that seventy per cent of the people interviewed preferred an empty plinth to any of the six designs. Every other year artists from around the world will be invited to develop work especially for this fourth plinth. The statue of Alison Lapper opened just before the 200th Celebrations of Nelson's famous victory over the French and excited considerable praise and considerable criticism with some saying Nelson looking down from his column would wish he was blinded in both eyes. Those campaigning to raise money for a statue of Reagan – the Conservative Way Forward group – still want to honour the former American President for the work he did to win the Cold War and have still to find a suitable site, liking the idea of Trafalgar Square. Given the uncertainty of statuary in London's most famous square perhaps it wasn't surprising in July 2006 to find that when Nelson's Column was actually measured it was found to be 16ft shorter, at 169ft 5in than had been generally believed for the previous 163 years.

Plans to erect a statue of Nelson Mandela in Trafalgar Square also descended into a bitter row that could cost the taxpayer a huge sum. A consortium including Richard Attenborough and Mayor Ken Livingstone want to erect a 9ft bronze statue of the South African statesman on the north terrace of Trafalgar Square. But Westminster City Council refused planning permission saying it would destroy an open space and damage views. It wants it built outside South Africa House a few yards away but the Mayor put his foot down and put aside £100,000 to appeal the decision. A public enquiry decided in favour of the Council, a view supported by Deputy Prime Minister John Prescott.

Prescott vetoes Mandela statue

Statue to Mandela sparks costly feud

A row erupted last year in Derby between councillors and residents over a plan to return a statue of a wild boar to the city's restored Arboretum Park. The council leader backed objections from Muslims who regard pigs as offensive and unclean but his deputy disagreed pointing out the statue had been there since 1840.

Religious anger over boar statue

The cult of Joseph Stalin, one of the worst tyrants in world history, is enjoying a revival across Russia with proposals to erect new monuments to the monster. The Kremlin has approved proposals to remember Stalin for his 'outstanding war leadership.' Yalta in the Ukraine was where Stalin, Churchill and Roosevelt met after the War in 1945 to decide how to carve up Europe. Sculptor Zurab Tstereteli has produced a wonderful statue of the three leaders seated at the Yalta Palace where it was intended to be put. However with a change in the Ukranian leadership in 2004 and protests from relatives of Stalin's surviving victims it was moved to Volgograd (ex-Stalingrad). These problems however have not stopped a number of small towns and villages quietly erecting memorials to the tyrant although officials in Moscow say there will be none in the capital.

Our leaders cause trouble too. Remember the marble statue of Margaret Thatcher that was decapitated by a vandal whilst on display in a London art gallery? Well, a new statue of the Iron Lady was commissioned – by a different sculptor and in a different pose and destined for the Members' Lobby in Westminster Parliament where, hopefully, there aren't so many vandals. Peter Stringfellow of London nightclub fame is a great fan of Mrs Thatcher and is behind a move to have The Iron Lady permanently on that empty plinth in Trafalgar Square. However, remembering the Poll Tax rows, there is little likelihood of a similar campaign to remember Mrs T. in Scotland.

Bassingbourn in South Cambridgeshire has a statue of fossilised dinosaur dung on the village green to commemorate the fact they were mined for fertiliser in the 19th century.

Statues are often used as a tourist attraction. One of the strangest is at Mabalact airfield in the Philippines from where the first Japanese kamikaze pilots took off during the Second World War. Although over a million people died under the wartime occupation by Japan, tourists from that country now form a major source of income to a country bedevilled by poverty. The sculpture of a kamikaze pilot was paid for and cast in Japan and is proving popular with visitors from the Land of the Rising Sun if not with locals who say it glorifies war. The panel describes Lt. Yukio Seki, leader of the first kamikaze raid in October 1944, as The World's First Official Human Bomb.

Philippines kamikaze statue lures the tourists

A Polish teenager faced five years in prison in Wadowice after he knocked over a statue of John Paul II in the home town of the late pope whilst under the influence of drugs.

Pole, 18, faces jail over pope statue

One of the world's most repressive and eccentric dictators with a bizarre taste in statues died at the end of 2006. Saparmurat Niyazov had ruled the former Soviet republic of Turkmenistan as head of state since 1985, a record for that region. He was buried in a gold-domed mosque he had built for himself at a cost of £50million paid for by the country's huge gas reserves. Among his stranger deeds was to erect a giant gold statue on top of the capital Ashgabat's biggest building and have it on a revolving plinth so that it would always face the sun. He ruled with an iron fist banning facial hair, make-up for women, cinema, ballet and the opera as alien to Turkmen culture.

Another memory of wartime has caused tensions in Spain. On 17 March 2005 the last statue of General Franco in Madrid was removed on the back of a truck. This bronze equestrian statue, built in 1975, was known as 'El Caudillo' and had been a target for protestors with rude slogans, red paint etc. for years. After Franco's death in 1975 those of the Left had argued for its removal but its actual removal caused quite a storm of protest and debate between those who wish to remove any trace of the dictator's legacy and those who say you can't rewrite history. Officials in Santa Cruz, capital of Tenerife and the starting point for the Spanish Civil War, are fighting to preserve a statue of the dictator there. It is an extremely elaborate affair with Franco holding a sword with both hands whilst riding on the back of an angel. The Socialist government want the statue down – the city authorities have said they will put it straight back up again if that happens. Franco was in Tenerife before starting the coup that led to the war. The Socialists are in opposition in Tenerife and have to wait to win power locally although some older people still remember Franco with affection and the rows will rumble on.

A 62 ft statue of Lenin is going back to Berlin to remind visitors of the city's Communist past.

The huge monument once stood in Lenin Square – now United Nations Square in East Berlin – but in 1990 was cut into one hundred and twenty-five pieces and buried in woods on the edge of the city. But souvenir hunters found the secret grave and began chiselling off bits so the decision was taken to resurrect it – a big task since the head alone weighs over three and a half tons.

In a main square in Lusaka, Zambia in 1978 a statue was erected of Black Africans breaking their chains to show their freedom from slavery. Soon some cynical expatriate students wrote on it "These bloody blacks will break anything." An armed guard with four soldiers at each corner was immediately placed on the statue.

One of the biggest statues anywhere – the 100ft bronze Colossus of Rhodes which was destroyed by an earthquake in 224BC is to rise again. One of the seven wonders of the ancient world, the original was built between 304 and 292BC and the face reputedly modelled on Alexander the Great. The surviving fragments of the destroyed giant were sold off. But now a new statue is planned, to go not in the port of Rhodes but in the island's Faliraki resort. What the drunken British holidaymakers will make of it there is anybody's guess but according to legend the Delphic oracle warned islanders not to rebuild the Colossus after it was destroyed. But that hasn't put off the Mayor of Faliraki who says the new statue will be a miracle of the 21st century. It will certainly be a miracle if the hordes of drunken British holidaymakers who flock to Faliraki every year don't find a way to deface the statue in some way. Big rows have developed in Greece. For years Greek designers have dreamt of rebuilding the statue but permission was never forthcoming to restore the statue to its original location. The Archaeological Museum in Rhodes supports neither the statue nor the site calling the proposal to put it in Falikari a 'gross distortion of history.' But it might never happen, a budget of £35 million is required for the project which will take four years to complete. The British-based Greek artist in charge of the project, Nikos Kotziamanis, plans to cast each section of the Colossus in London's docklands before shipping them to Rhodes for re-assembly.

In June 2006 a religiously motivated attack on statues in a Cairo museum raised further fears that Islamic fundamentalists would strike further in Egypt. The Grand Mufti of Cairo, Ali Gomaa, had issued a fatwa banning all decorative statues of living beings and a veiled woman screaming 'infidels' had damaged statues, not of living people, but of other works.

After months of debate between Muslims and Croats in the divided city of Mostar, scene of some of the worst fighting of the Bosnian civil war, they have decided whose statue will adorn a new peace memorial. You will be surprised. They chose Bruce Lee, the martial arts legend. You would imagine a more peaceful figure could have been chosen but after the decision the estimated cost of the life-size bronze statue was quickly provided by private donors. A poll of residents showed he was chosen by both sides as a 'symbol of solidarity' and beat The Pope and Mahatma Gandhi in the contest. The decision is still causing controversy. Lee was born in San Francisco but his family returned to Hong Kong when he was still a baby. He was a star of many martial arts films but died of a brain haemorrhage in 1973 at the age of thirty-two unaware he would became a cult figure internationally. The city authorities say they chose Lee because he was not associated with any political party and gives off a good feeling. They expect it to become a major tourist attraction to their rebuilt city.

Captain Cook is still causing trouble Down Under.

It isn't just in Britain that it isn't always plain sailing. A statue in Sydney, Australia of Captain Cook with an inscription recalling him as the man who discovered Australia has been described as insulting to Aborigines who were there first. The statue was erected in 1879 and supporters say it needs to be seen in its historical context but suggestions were made last year for a new statue to commemorate an Aborigine leader.

As well as being removed statues are often moved – Queen Victoria has been to more parts of Aberdeen than many of its visitors – and they are moved for all sorts of reasons. A huge marble bust of Lord Horatio Nelson was removed from storage and returned to its original home at Windsor Castle in early 2005 to mark the 200th anniversary of his great victory at Trafalgar in 1805. The head is nearly 3ft high, weighs three quarters of a ton and was commissioned by William IV, who was a naval officer and greatly admired Nelson whom he served with in the West Indies. It is sculpted by Sir Francis Chantrey, the most renowned sculptor of portrait busts in the country.

But there can be money in statuary. At the end of 2005 a 22inch bronze maquette (model) for the sculpture of Winston Churchill in London's Parliament Square by Ivor Roberts-Jones fetched £114,000 from a private buyer at Christie's auction.

Some memorials certainly take time – in April 2005 an appeal went out for donations for a memorial to be built at National Memorial Arboretum in Staffs to men who lost their lives on duty or as an act of terrorism since World War Two – sixty years after the War ended and the first such memorial of its kind. Work started on the Armed Forces Memorial, a 140ft diameter circle of stone by architect Liam O'Connor, on 24 July 2006 with unveiling planned for October 2007. Already worth seeing there is emotive Shot at Dawn statue of blindfolded Pte. Herbert Burden shot at age seventeen for desertion.

The small Serbian village of Zitiste thirty-seven miles north of Belgrade is planning to erect a massive statue of film boxer Rocky Balboa because it is fed up with making the news only when it is flooded. The idea came from village resident Bojan Marceta who saw the film and thought a statue of the fighter Sylvester Stallone made famous in several films would be "a symbol of the ability to bounce back every time you are knocked down." The village suffers regular heavy flooding and landslides and has become something of a disaster zone in recent years. They have asked for help from the US city of Philadelphia where a monument to Rocky already exists.

Arguments over statues go on around the world. A life-sized bronze of Scotland's Dr David Livingstone has stood overlooking Victoria Falls for over half a century. But after years of neglect by the Zimbabwe government (who are the current owners) the Zambian government across the river Zambezi say they want it. The statue has been seen by millions of tourists over the years and is an impressive reproduction of the great Victorian explorer. But as Zimbabwe has descended into chaos those tourists have started going to the Zambia side. Now Zambia want the statue to go to the town of Livingstone where they say it rightly belongs and where the great man is still revered. It was from the Zambian side of the river after all that he became the first European to sight the falls known as 'the smoke that thunders.' Locals say the statue was originally on their side of the river anyway but was moved during the 1950s. The bronze was done in 1932 by Sir William Reid Dick and 2005, the 150th anniversary of Livingstone's sighting of the Falls, saw renewed efforts by the Zambian authorities getting nowhere.

Arguments over David Livingstone continue as Zimbabwe slides into further distress.

It's often said the British prefer their dogs to people and as a nation of animal-lovers we have been sometimes been quicker to remember our animals than our war heroes. In November 2004 the Princess Royal unveiled the Animals in War Memorial at Brook Gate, Park Lane in London. This monument honours all the animals who have served in wartime. It is all embracing, honouring all animals, from the eight million horses that died in the Great War to the glow worms by whose light soldiers read their maps in World War One. Dogs and horses are the best known but in fact over two hundred thousand messenger pigeons served Britain in the World War Two saving countless lives.

Oscar Wilde in an unusual pose for a statue – lying down and painted vivid colours – in a Dublin park.

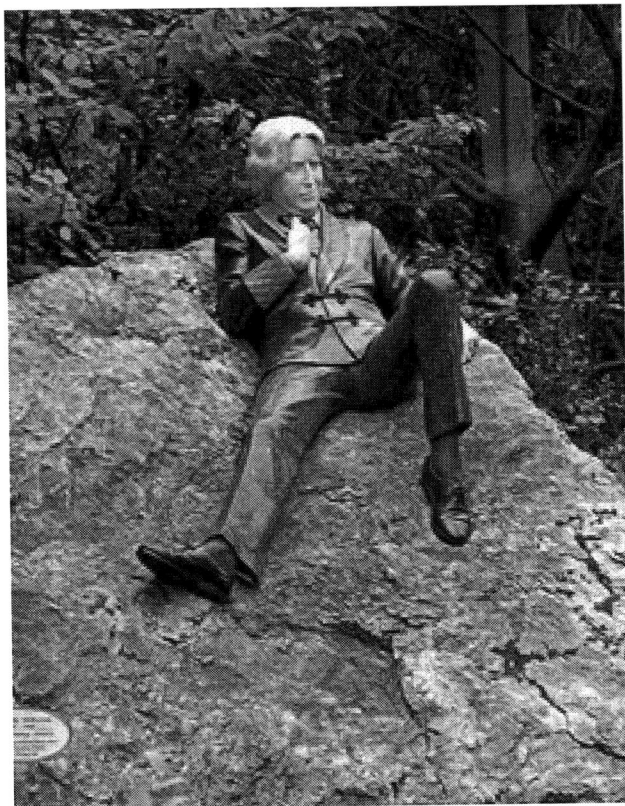

Ireland has a wonderful respect or perhaps you can call it disrespect for its colourful characters from the past. In Dublin's Merrion Park Square is a statue of Oscar Wilde, in bright colours and lying on a rock. Locals call it The Fag on the Slag. The city honours diverse characters such as author Patrick Kavanagh (on the canal in Dublin sitting quietly on a bench with arms folded) and pop musician Phil Lynott (in Harry Street off Grafton Street). Nearby, Molly Malone is known as The Tart with the Cart and another statue, The Floozie in the Jacuzzi, had to be moved from O'Connell Street to a safer location because of what was being done to her on Saturday nights...

Some of the most famous statues in the world were destroyed by the Taliban in Afghanistan in 2001 evoking an international outcry. The towering Bamiyan Buddhas were over 1,600 years old and stood on the old Silk Road linking Central Asia and Europe. The two Buddhas standing at 175ft and 115ft high – were of great cultural significance but the Taliban leaders considered them anti-Muslim and used dynamite to reduce them to rubble. An elaborate laser show hoping to recreate the images is due to open in June 2007.

A tiny 2,500 year old Greek sculpture looted by German or Italian soldiers during the Second World War was returned in May 2005 to the Island of Samos after a London dealer discovered its history. The piece, a bronze statuette of a young boy, only four-and-a-half inches high was made in the 6th century BC and the Greek Government welcomed its return.

Politicians can be a problem when it comes to statues. Just listen to this comment from Colin Rigby, Conservative group leader on Blackburn Council when plans for a statue to the town's former MP were mooted: "Barbara Castle has had a road named after her already – that's more than enough. An inscribed urinal might be more appropriate."

Sometimes events move on. Most people asked what they associate with Nottingham are likely to reply Robin Hood. He has probably done more for the city than anyone else, with his statue a popular landmark, but in 2005 the town wanted a new image and to do away with the old logo which was a Robin Hood figure with the slogan 'Our Style is Legendary'. Unfortunately the new symbol for Nottingham met with a distinctly cool response. It was a large purple, lopsided giant N with the word Nottinghamshire below.

Appendices

Appendix I

Everyone has their own view of who are the greatest Scots of all time. There is certainly a Top Ten of those remembered at home with full statues – they are (in no particular order) Robert Burns, William Wallace, Robert the Bruce, James Watt, Thomas Carlyle, Rob Roy Macgregor, John Knox, Sir Walter Scott, David Livingstone – and Queen Victoria although you would have to say she is only a honorary Scot. Here is the author's attempt at a Top 100.

(S) Denotes a full figure statue in his or her native land.

Top 50 Greatest Scots

1 Robert Adam (architect)
2 Robert Burns (poet) (s)
3 J.M. Barrie (writer) (s)
4 Alexander Graham Bell (inventor)
5 Robert the Bruce (monarch) (s)
6 John Logie Baird (inventor)
7 John Buchan (writer)
8 Thomas Carlyle (philosopher) (s)
9 Sean Connery (actor)
10 Billy Connolly (comedian)
11 Andrew Carnegie (philanthropist) (s)
12 Sir Arthur Conan Doyle (writer) (s)
13 John Boyd Dunlop (inventor)
14 Kenneth Grahame (writer)
15 Sir Alexander Fleming (inventor)
16 Earl Haig (soldier) (s)
17 David Hume (philosopher) (s)
18 James Keir Hardie (politician)
19 Lord Kelvin (industrialist) (s)
20 King James VI (monarch) (s)
21 John Knox (minister) (s)
22 Sir Harry Lauder (entertainer)
23 Eric Liddell (missionary) (s)
24 Dr. David Livingstone (explorer) (s)
25 Mary Queen of Scots (monarch) (s)
26 The Queen Mother (monarch)

27 James Ramsay Macdonald (politician)

28 Charles Rennie Mackintosh (designer)

29 John Muir (conservationist) (s)

30. John McAdam (engineer)

31 Flora Macdonald (heroine) (s)

32 Rob Roy MacGregor (outlaw) (s)

33 Macbeth (monarch)

34 Tom Morris (golfer) (s)

35 Lord Reith (businessman)

36 St. Mungo (saint) (s)

37 Sir James Young Simpson (inventor) (s)

38 Thomas Telford (engineer) (s)

39 Sir Robert Watson-Watt (inventor)

40 Sir Henry Raeburn (painter)

41 Sir Walter Scott (writer) (s)

42 Alexander Selkirk (sailor) (s)

43 Marie Stopes (family planning)

44 Mary Slessor (missionary)

45 Dame Muriel Spark (writer)

46 Adam Smith (economist)

47 Prince Charles Edward Stuart (would be monarch) (s)

48 Robert Louis Stevenson (writer) (s)

49 James Watt (engineer) (s)

50 William Wallace (fighter) (s)

Second Top 50 Greatest Scots

1   Sir William Arrol (engineer)

2   James Miranda Barry (medicine)

3   Jim Baxter (footballer) (s)

4   James Braid (golfer) (s)

5   John Boyd Orr (nutritionist)

6   John Brown (ghillie) (s)

7   Lord Byron (poet) (s)

8   James Boswell (writer)

9   William Deacon Brodie (burglar)

10 James Chalmers (inventor)

11 William Chambers (publisher) (s)

12 Jim Clark (racing driver) (s)

13 Admiral Thomas Cochrane (s)

14 Kenny Dalglish (footballer)

15 Donald Dewar (politician) (s)

16 John Elder (industrialist) (s)

Appendix 1

17 Robert Fergusson (poet) (s)

18 Will Fyfe (entertainer)

19 William Ewart Gladstone (politician) (s)

20 James Graham, Marquis of Montrose (s)

21 Dr Thomas Guthrie (cleric)(s)

22 Thomas Glover (Samurai)

23 Highland Mary (lover) (s)

24 James Hogg (poet) (s)

25 James Hutton (geologist)

26 Elsie Maud Inglis (medicine)

27 Field Marshall Keith (soldier) (s)

28 William Kidd (pirate)

29 Lord Joseph Lister (medicine) (s)

30 William McGonagall (poet)

31 Hugh Miller (geologist) (s)

32 Hugh McDiarmidd (poet)

33 Chic Murray (entertainer)

34 Sir Hector McDonald (soldier)

35 Bill McLaren (rugby)

36 James Clerk Maxwell (mathematician)

37 Alastair Maclean (writer)

38 Kirkpatrick MacMillan (inventor)

39 Charles Macintosh (inventor)

40 John Napier (mathematician)

41 Robert Napier (shipbuilder)

42 Mungo Park (explorer) (s)

43 Allan Ramsay (painter)

44 Allan Ramsay (poet) (s)

45 Donald Ross (golf course designer)

46 Jackie Stewart (racing driver)

47 Jock Stein (football manager)

48 Johannes Duns Scotus (philosopher) (s)

49 Jimmy Shand (musician) (s)

50 Sir James Young Simpson (medicine)(s)

Appendix II

**National Monuments Record
of Scotland**
John Sinclair House
16 Bernard Terrace
Edinburgh EH8 9NX.
Tel: 0131 662 1456

Historic Scotland
Longmore House
Salisbury Place
Edinburgh EH9 1SH.
Tel: 0131 668 8600

**Scottish National Portrait
Gallery**
1 Queen Street
Edinburgh EH2 1JD.
Tel: 0131 624 6200

National Library of Scotland
George IV Bridge
Edinburgh EH1 1EW
Tel: 0131 226 4531

**Royal Museum and Museum
of Scotland**
Chambers Street
Edinburgh EH1 1JF.
Tel: 0131 225 7534
(switchboard) or
0131 247 4219 (information)

National Trust for Scotland
28 Charlotte Square
Edinburgh EH2 4ET
Tel: 0131 243 9339

Edinburgh Room
Central Library
George IV Bridge
Edinburgh EH1 1EG
Tel: 0131 242 8030

**The Royal Incorporation of
Architects in Scotland
Bookshop**
15 Rutland Square
Edinburgh EH1 2BE
Tel: 0131 229 7545

**The Royal Incorporation of
Architects in Scotland
Bookshop**
Scott Street
Glasgow G3 6NU
Tel: 0141 332 9414

Powderhall Bronze
21 Graham Street
Edinburgh EH6 5QN
Tel: 0131 555 3013

Beltane Studios Ltd
2 Soonhope Holdings
Peebles EH45 8BH.
Tel: 01721 724888

Black Isle Bronze Ltd
42 Balmakeith Business Park
Nairn IV12 5QR 8BH.
Tel: 01667 455172

The Gerald Laing Art
Foundation
Kinkell Castle
Dingwall IV7 8AT,
Tel 01349 861485

Public Monuments and
Sculpture Association
72 Lissenden Gardens
London NW5 1PR.
Tel: 0207 485 0566
website – www.pmsa.org.uk

Save Outdoor Sculpture
Heritage Preservation
1012 14th Street
NW Suite 1200
Washington DC 20005
USA.

Appendix III

Major Scottish Milestones

1265	Duns Scotus born
1297	Wallace defeats English at Stirling
1305	Wallace executed
1306	Coronation of Robert the Bruce, King of Scots
1314	Victory at Bannockburn
1320	Declaration of Arbroath
1329	Death of Robert the Bruce
1513	Battle of Flodden
1542	Mary Queen of Scots born
1587	Mary Queen of Scots executed
1603	Union of the two Crowns – James VI of Scotland becomes James I of England
1649	Charles I executed
1650	Montrose executed
1707	Act of Union passed
1715	Jacobite Rising
1720	Bonnie Prince Charlie born
1723	Adam Smith born
1759	Robert Burns born
1745	Jacobite Rising
1746	Culloden
1771	Sir Walter Scott born
1795	Thomas Carlyle born
1796	Death of Robert Burns
1822	King George IV visits Edinburgh
1846	Scott Monument in Edinburgh unveiled
1850	Robert Louis Stevenson born
1855	Balmoral Castle built

1890	Completion of Forth Road Bridge
1900	Queen Elizabeth The Queen Mother born
1901	Death of Queen Victoria
1934	SNP Founded
1947	First Edinburgh International Festival
1950	Removal of Stone of Scone from Westminster Abbey
1952	Queen Elizabeth I of Scotland & II of England Coronation
1955	Scottish Television starts broadcasting
1976	First Devolution Bill
1996	Return of Stone of Scone from London to Scotland
1999	Scotland has a new Parliament
2000	Death of Scotland's First Minister Donald Dewar.
2004	Scotland has a new Parliament building

Bibliography

RIAS Illustrated Architectural Guides

Already Published

Aberdeen
Ayrshire and Arran
Argyll & the Islands
Banff & Buchan
Clackmannan & the Ochils
Dumfries & Galloway
Gordon
Borders & Berwick
District of Moray
Midlothian
West Lothian
North Clyde Estuary
Stirling
Orkney
Shetland
South Clyde Estuary
Ross & Cromarty
Kingdom of Fife
Perth & Kinross
Caithness
Deeside & the Mearns
Dundee
The Monklands
Sutherland
Edinburgh
Central Glasgow
Contemporary Glasgow
Falkirk & District

In preparation (text ready)
Western Seaboard
Greater Glasgow

To come
Angus
Inverness, Nairn, Badenoch and Strahspey
Lanarkshire
Cumbernauld, Kilsyth & the Campsies
East Lothian

Famous Scots by Raymond Lamont-Brown (1992 Chambers).

Monuments and Statues of Edinburgh by Michael T.R.B. Turnbull (1989).

Edinburgh Statues by E.T. Uldall (1988) held at Central Library in Edinburgh.

Public Sculpture of Glasgow by Ray McKenzie (Liverpool University Press & PMSA 1999).

The Architecture of Glasgow by Andor Gomme and David Walker (Publisher Lund Humphries with J. Smith 1987).

100 Famous Scots by Lily Seafield (Lomond Publishers) 2000.

The Scottish 100 – Portrait of History's Most Influential Scots by Duncan A. Bruce (Carroll & Graf 2000).

Chambers Scottish Biographical Dictionary, Editor Rosemary Gowing (Chambers 1992).

Collins Encyclopaedia of Scotland edited by John Keay and Julia Keay (Collins 2000).

Scottish Firsts by Elspeth Wills (Mainstream 2002).

Scottish Inventors by Alistair Fyfe (Harper Collins 1999).

Virtue & Vision, Sculpture and Scotland 1540–1990 by Fiona Pearson (Publisher National Galleries of Scotland 1991).

Dictionary of British Sculptors 1660–1851 by Robert Gunnis (Odhams 1953).

A Dictionary of British Sculptors from the 13th Century to the 20th Century by Col. Maurice H. Grant (Rockcliff 1953).

British Sculptors of the Twentieth Century by Alan Windsor (Ashgate 2003).

Scotland's Story in Her Monuments by David Graham-Campbell (Robert Hale 1982).

Buildings of Scotland Series

Lothian By Colin McWilliam (Penguin 1978). Revision by John Gifford in progress as original volume published before research was complete.

Edinburgh by John Gifford, Colin McWilliam, David Walker (Penguin 1984).

Fife by John Gifford (Penguin 1988).

Glasgow by Elizabeth Williamson, Malcolm Higgs, Anne Riches (Penguin 1990).

Highland by John Gifford (Penguin 1992).

Dumfries & Galloway by John Gifford after Colin McWilliam (Penguin1996).

Argyll & Bute by Frank Arneil Walker (Penguin 2000).

Stirling & Central Scotland by John Gifford & Frank Arneil Walker (Yale University Trust 2002).

Borders by John Dunbar and Catherine H. Croft (2006);

Forthcoming

Tayside (2 volumes) by John Gifford (probably 2007).

Grampian by Ian Shepherd (possibly 2007).

Renfrewshire, Ayrshire and Lanarkshire by Anne Riches (probably 2008).

Index